STEPMONSTER

STEPMONSTER

A New Look at Why Real Stepmothers Think, Feel, and Act the Way We Do

Wednesday Martin, Ph.D.

ISBN 13: 9781517071387

CONTENTS

INTRODUCTION

My marriage was meant to be. It was also doomed to fail. You see, I chose a man with children. Experts estimate that more than half of all adult women in the United States will do the same in their lifetimes and that up to 70 percent of those partnerships will fail. Factor in all the odds and on the day I said "I do," I might as well have picked out a divorce lawyer as well. The greatest predictor of divorce is the presence of children from a previous marriage. In fact, divorce rates are 50 percent higher in remarriages with children than in those without. Even more alarming for my marriage, according to the statistics that I was blessedly unaware of until after I committed myself for life, was the fact that my husband had not one but two teenage daughters and was living with one of them when we got engaged. (Unbeknownst to me, some experts recommend delaying marriage to a partner whose child is between the ages of ten and sixteen, so great are the risks of conflict for the couple and the household during that particular period of a child's development.) The final high-risk factor: I was a childless woman marrying a man with children. (Some research suggests that women with their own children fare better in a marriage to a man with children, although they face a whole different set of emotional and practical challenges.) The chances of our union surviving were arguably in the realm of the hypothetical.

And I had no idea. Not because everything was fine — from the very first moment, things hadn't been fine, exactly — but because I had my head placed firmly in the sand. I wanted this thing to work. I wanted a wedding and a happy ending, and I was going to ignore everything and anything I had to in order to make it happen. When a coworker, a stepson himself, advised that I should run from my boyfriend as fast as I could owing to a less-than-ideal co-parenting situation with his ex-wife, I attributed it to sour grapes. When a friend saw a picture of my stepdaughter-to-be (looking every inch the rebellious preteen she was) and commented, "Uh-oh," I pretended not to hear. And whenever I came across books or articles about stepmothering, I rolled my eyes, if I noticed them at all. They were full of gloom and bland advice — from where I stood in those early, "everything's great" days — and stuff about other people. None of that was going to happen to me. I was nice; I was fun; I was young(ish). Step-hell was for stepmonsters, and I wasn't going there. Until I was.

We were going to find a wedding dress.

It was our first weekend alone together in two months. My fiancé and I — who had decided to elope and had told everyone, including his kids — were about to set off in search of something modern and fashion-forward (no princessy flounces and lace for me). And then his daughter, who was not scheduled to be with us that weekend, said she'd like to be, after all. My fiancé told her she could without asking me about it. I said the wrong and wicked thing. I admitted, insisted in fact, that I wanted a quiet weekend without his girls. I wanted us to pick out my wedding dress alone, together. My fiancé went silent, obviously unhappy. I went silent, feeling misunderstood, guilty, and then resentful. Was I being unreasonable? I didn't know anymore. When it came to marrying a man with children, I was discovering I couldn't find my footing or trust my judgment much of the time.

It wasn't that I didn't like them, I insisted defensively to my future husband on that day and many others. I *did*. I looked forward especially to spending time with my older stepdaughter-to-be, the one who didn't live with us, because I wanted to have the opportunity to get to know her in the way I was getting to know her little sister. But in those early days, I found the girls equal parts "adorable and fun to be around" and "exhausting and demanding." Sometimes, even though I didn't want to admit it, I even found them "bratty and difficult." Let me add that this was not their fault, not by a long shot. Getting used to me couldn't have been easy for them. And to make matters worse, I was coming to understand that for the entire six years of my fiancé's separation, divorce, and subsequent single life, he had made sure that weekends were a whirlwind of activities planned with the girls' wants in mind. They were pretty much in charge of all the decisions — where to have lunch, which DVDs to rent, how many glitter pens and henna tattoos and pairs of shoes to buy, when to go to bed. In my future husband's words, "They've come to expect that they can show up whenever they feel like it and that my life is all about them whenever they do."

It was only natural that, during the deepening of my relationship with him and my acquaintanceship with his girls, he and I would not always see eye to eye regarding the fact that I needed a little more time away from them than he did. But it felt like a failure to argue so much — Does the TV have to be *that* loud? Shouldn't she do her homework? Can't they put their own dishes in the dishwasher? Where was his sense of privacy and of romance, anyway? — and I could sense it pulling us apart. We were in the outer circle of step-hell, though I didn't realize it yet.

I wrote this book about women with stepchildren, for women with stepchildren, because being a woman with stepchildren is not easy. E. Mavis Hetherington, Ph.D., psychologist and author of the landmark, three-decade Virginia Longitudinal Study of 1,400 families that divorced and remarried, notes that whereas children frequently come to appreciate having a stepfather — particularly if he brings in income, provides companionship to Mom, and proves to be a friend to the child — "the situation with stepmothers is more difficult and stepchild resentment is more intense." And this state of affairs is more or less unavoidable. As Hetherington writes, "Even those [women] who would like to be less involved [in running the family] rarely have the chance. They are often expected to be nurturers to already difficult and suspicious children [and] to impose some kind of order on the household, which is angrily and bitterly resented by many stepchildren." Hetherington found "a real demonizing of the stepmother" in situations where the husband did not support his wife's efforts to parent and discipline, and where the husband's ex treated her as a rival and was highly involved in the children's lives and their father's household. Reporting with some surprise that so many of her subjects described their stepmothers as "evil, malevolent, wicked, or monsters" and gave them nicknames like "Dog Face" and "The Dragon," Hetherington concludes, "Stepfathers rarely encountered this level of vitriol." Of course, there are plenty of kids who give their stepfathers a hard time; some ultimately break off relations with Mom's second (or third) spouse altogether. But the stepmonster, it seems, is a uniquely *female* hybrid. She is easy to hate; she is pervasive in the culture (including our collective unconscious); and we are petrified of becoming her. Often we turn ourselves inside out to avoid it or berate ourselves for having feelings that strike us as "stepmonsterish." It is no shock, then, that several studies find that stepmothers have the most problematic role in the "family" and experience significant adjustment difficulties.

Yet stepfamily life, remarriage with children — whatever you want to call it — has been largely viewed through the prism of its repercussions and emotional effects on the children. Books on the subject tell women how their stepchildren feel, what their stepchildren need and want, and how they can help their stepchildren adjust to and accept their father's remarriage. This is tremendously helpful — it can only improve matters to know where his kids are coming from and to have confirmation that it is all more or less normal. But where, we are likely to wonder at some point, is the stuff about stepmothers and how we feel? That is more difficult to find. And friends, however well-intentioned and sympathetic, aren't always a lot of help either. None of mine had stepkids, for example, and so, like the how-tos I finally picked up when the going got rough, they tended to advise things that felt maddeningly child-centric and unreasonable — even impossible. How, for example, could

I possibly be expected to always think about the kids when they weren't mine and their mere presence sometimes seemed enough to tear my relationship apart? How could I not take their behavior personally when they apparently reveled in the discord they caused, from passing along their mother's pointed remarks to dramatically disliking my cooking to hanging up when I answered the phone? How could I become a better stepparent when his girls wouldn't look me in the eye? What got lost in these child-centric exhortations and lists about how to be a better stepmother, it seemed, was any acknowledgment that the experiences and emotions of the woman with stepchildren mattered just as much as anyone else's.

Exploring the issue of how children can threaten and stress a marriage, rather than how a remarriage may affect a child, is a reframing many are likely to find unsettling. As a society, we feel for the children and identify with them, and all for good reason. Children are in fact powerless when it comes to their parents' decision to divorce and remarry. In this most fundamental and urgent matter, they have very little say and a great deal to lose. Once a parent has remarried, however, it's a different world. Remarriage experts Kay Pasley, Ed.D., and Marilyn Ihinger-Tallman, Ph.D., note that stepchildren have incredible power to break the remarriage up. They may intentionally create divisiveness between spouses and siblings and set parent against stepparent. They also may pass along unkind messages or invite interference from members of the other household, creating conflict and tremendous resentment. Stepfamily researchers such as James Bray, Ph.D., of Baylor University emphasize that in stepfamilies, children all too often set the emotional tone for the entire household, while Bray, Hetherington, and Francesca Adler-Baeder, Ph.D., of the National Stepfamily Resource Center, all concur that preadolescent and adolescent children are often the initiators of conflict with stepparents.

Acknowledging the simple fact that stepchildren can and do affect a remarriage, sometimes for the worse — that they are, if you will, actors as well as acted upon — can help us better understand what we might call "stepmother reality," the specific, shared experiences of women with stepchildren. This reality has been largely ignored by feminists, sociologists, and even some of the very authors who write about stepmothers and stepmothering. Why might this be? I believe that we tend to sweep the stepmother's difficulties under the rug because they strike us as unseemly. Her pain, struggles, and failures set us on edge, make us want to turn away, because they smack of guilt. A stepmother's suffering is, more than anything else, an indictment — of her. An admission not so much that she is falling short as that she is flawed. Thinking we understand it, we decide there is nothing more to learn — "Anna's stepmother is awful!" "If the stepmom is nice, everything will be fine; if there are problems, it's because she's not trying hard enough" — and so we are left comprehending very little. Disliking stepmothers is easy; suspecting them is more or less automatic. Caring about stepmothers, expressing concern about what they're going through, considering their reality at any length — all this requires a leap of faith.

Even by women with stepchildren themselves. I set out to better understand women having a hard time with stepmothering because the research amply demonstrates that most stepmothers will have a difficult time, certainly in the earliest phases of stepfamily formation and perhaps intermittently for decades. Only a very few women with stepchildren insist that stepmothering has never been difficult for them. For this minority, stepmothering is simply gratifying.

Research indicates that these women aren't just rare; they're also lucky. Stepmothering is easy and joyful for the few for whom all the determining factors for success — supportive husbands and cooperative exes who are not permissive parents; children free of loyalty conflicts who happen to be at just the right stage of development to accept a stepparent — are felicitously there. But the planets are unlikely to line up just so for the majority of us. So many of the women I interviewed did in fact seem worn-out from their efforts to "do the right thing" and put the kids first. So many were emotionally exhausted from years of biting their tongues and biding their time in a position that could feel thankless, with the tacit understanding that their own feelings mattered less. Most broadly, my aim in this book is to counter that tendency and to put the woman with stepchildren back at the center of her own life. *Stepmonster* explores who she is and what she does. It asks what she wants and needs, and why. I have tried to approach the topic — one so often sanitized and sugarcoated — with candor and compassion for stepmothers. In a larger sense, I hope to reframe our culture's discussion about stepmothering so that it is finally and truly about the woman married to a man with children and not just the idealized version of her — well-intentioned, patient, fun! — we seem to be increasingly expecting her to be. The less perfect and more human parts of us must be considered, too, if we are to understand who we are and what stepmothering is: the mean thoughts that scare even us; the big, impolite feelings about our stepchildren and our husbands and our role. At times, the issues and emotions that surface in this most overdetermined role can lead us to act in ways we have never acted before — jealous, angry, "vindictive," like the classic stepmonster — and do things we never suspected we were capable of. (I could write an entire chapter on wicked stepmother behavior, starting with the time I got fed up with asking my stepdaughter to clean her room. I could make a million excuses — it was a stressful time, just days after 9/11 and two months after the birth of my son — but the long and short of it is that while she was out, I put all the things she had left on the floor in garbage bags and hurled them toward the front door.) It is time to consider these unattractive, taboo aspects of the stepmothering experience dispassionately, rather than simply denying them or insisting that we rush to rid ourselves of them in order to make ourselves better stepmothers, to improve ourselves in the service of others.

As any seasoned stepmother knows, our own feelings and experiences are just one factor in the equation. What of the feelings that stepmothers inspire in others? Whether they are our husbands, our stepchildren, our own children, friends, acquaintances at a party, or strangers on the street, the convictions of others will inevitably bear on us. These convictions are often passionate and unshakable: "My stepmother is a witch, plain and simple," a surprising number of adults told me. Yet such entrenched beliefs only beg further questions: How old were you when your stepmother came into your life? What kind of adolescent were you? What part might you have played — and might you still be playing — in engineering the current, less-than-perfect relationship the two of you have?

For the past thirty years, we have turned to psychologists for help with stepfamily matters. But stepmothering problems are more than purely emotional or psychological, as the best psychotherapists are well aware. Anthropology, sociology, evolutionary biology, and feminist literary and cultural theory might help us just as much in our quest to understand why having stepchildren can be so difficult. Understanding the history of stepmothering might also help us see that, quite often, the problems we encounter feel bigger than us because they are. In some cases, our stepmothering dilemmas have actually preceded us by thousands of years, and there is likely tremendous relief in this knowledge. Ancient Roman women were sometimes tortured on suspicion of having poisoned their stepsons. Court documents indicate that husbands and wives in the American colonies frequently came to blows over disciplining stepchildren. Suddenly, modern life in a remarriage with kids doesn't feel so novel or anomalous. And figures that others might find deflating, such as the ones I enumerated at the beginning of this introduction, assure us that we are neither alone nor unusual.

We seldom hear that many of the fundamental stepmothering struggles are nobody's fault, and so nobody's particular burden to "fix." But this is what I heard from a number of experts, who told me that economic, social, psychological, and even biological factors have been pitting women and their stepchildren against each other for centuries. And so it should come as no surprise that remarried families usually take many years to jell in spite of our best hopes and efforts. Stepfamily developmental expert Patricia Papernow, Ed.D., estimates that most stepfamilies take anywhere from four to twelve years to come together. In some cases, they never do, and much of the time, no one can be singled out for blame. In the words of anthropologist and evolutionary biologist Steven Josephson, Ph.D., who shared with me a favorite pedagogical analogy among human behavioral ecologists, "Relatedness matters, period. Imagine telling people in the hospital to give birth, 'Just pick any old baby out of the nursery on your way out. They're all the same.' We would consider that bizarre — criminal actually. *Because relatedness matters profoundly.*" In general, our bonds to our biological and adopted children are different — stronger — than those to our stepchildren. Bulwarking psychological insights with evolutionary theory this way might help us put our feelings of frustration in perspective and help us understand that what we are up against is not quite so bewildering, incomprehensible, or unique.

It is time, then, for a radical reconsideration of what we might realistically expect women with stepchildren to feel, think, and accomplish. For example, we cannot always make our husbands' children love or even like us. Sometimes the feeling may be mutual, and it is time to strip away the veil of distorting sentiment about "female nature" and "the inherent openness of children toward all good women" that have thus far compelled and confounded us on this topic. Will we feel shut out, angry, or jealous? Sometimes. Although parts of the wicked stepmother legacy are outrageous, gender-biased distortions, others are, I have come to believe, inescapable, true, and even edifying. University of Oklahoma anthropologist and family expert Kermyt Anderson, Ph.D., explains: "In some cases — like allocation of resources and access to the husband/father — the conflicts of interest between stepkids and stepmothers are ancient, fundamental and very real." Canadian evolutionary psychologist Martin Daly, Ph.D., who has written extensively about stepfamilies, concurs. "Let's face it," he told me, "in many ways stepchildren and stepmothers *are* rivals." And some-times we act like it. Is that so surprising, or so tragic? Is it not, perhaps, even normal?

My stepdaughter joined us for our wedding dress excursion. Initially enthused, she eventually became annoyed and impatient, and so did I. After all, picking a wedding dress, even one for an elopement, is a labor-intensive process. At one point, her father bought her something, probably to assuage her sense of being excluded, and she lamented, "She gets a beautiful, expensive dress, and all I get is a cheap belt? *How come?*"

Maybe because I'm the one getting married? I thought to reply tartly. I didn't, of course. I knew it wasn't my place, and so I waited for her father to say something. And as usual, I waited in vain. I might have been every stepmother just then as it sank in, between dress number four and dress number five, that, dress it up however I wanted to, the simple truth was that the girls sometimes acted entitled and jealous when I was around, and their father, perhaps because he felt guilty for giving them something to act entitled and jealous about, did nothing to put a stop to it. I hated all three of them in that ugly, revelatory moment and wondered whether I should even be getting married. And then came a powerful wave of disbelief and self-loathing. I was becoming what I believed I would never be: a stepmonster! *Me.* How was this possible? That day was full of drama, resentment, and hostility, much of it engineered — albeit unwittingly — by me. I have made hundreds more mistakes since that day when I fought with my husband, made my stepdaughter feel unwelcome, and was myself pushed aside on an excursion that should have been all about me. No one was precisely in the wrong there; everyone was, in some sense, wronged. It's like that sometimes in a remarriage with children.

But improbably enough, my story does have a happy ending. Nine years later, my husband and I are still going strong. I am typical in that, with the passage of time and the birth of my sons, my life and my heart have been rearranged. Focusing on my marriage, which seemed more consolidated and secure with each passing day, I was able to relax my unrealistic expectations of my stepdaughters, tone down my hopes, and better see and appreciate them for who they are. For their part, my stepdaughters, interesting young women now, are more focused on their own lives and goals than on the drama of where they fit in with us. They are accomplished people and, quite often, lovely company. Many of my subjects and much of the literature describes similar shifts of feelings after the first five years or so of a remarriage with children.

Yet as a great deal of research now indicates, and for a number of reasons explored in the pages that follow, some children and adult children simply never come around to their stepmothers. And in spite of what we read and what we suspect and what we're often told, the drama, difficulty, or simple indifference that is likely to enfold us when we marry a man with kids is not necessarily an indictment or a referendum on our value as people, wives, or step-mothers. This realization can be life altering. I hope that we will learn to stop giving our stepchildren the power to make us "good" by liking us. It only confuses them and sets us all up for a fall. The women with stepchildren who make it with their personalities and self-respect intact, I have learned, are very good at negotiating with their own hopes and adjusting their expectations, and they have learned to simply ignore the opinions of the uninformed. Of course, the need for approval — especially in matters regarding children — runs deep in women, and it is no easy thing to buck. Maybe that's why, once we have gotten to the place of caring a little less about how others view us, once we have decided, on some level, to focus our hopes in directions other than winning his kids over no matter what it takes and put our energies elsewhere, we sometimes refer to ourselves, with knowing smirks, as "stepmonsters." "I hear you're interviewing women for a book called *Stepmonster.* I definitely am one!" a doctor, mother, and stepmother e-mailed me, and I knew immediately she was not. Over and over, I was struck by the way my subjects looked to themselves for answers about why stepfamily life was often so difficult, rather than focusing on the entire system they were only one part of.

This is not a book about how I learned my lesson or won my stepkids over or became a better person by marrying a man with children. My reality, like that of the women with stepchildren I interviewed, is not nearly so neat or cut-and-dried. This is not a book about how to change yourself or how to act in order to be a better stepmother. I have learned that there is no one recipe for success, no single "right way." Rather, my goal has been to synthesize and distill some of the less readily available studies and insights from experts in a number of disparate fields. This work, generally published in academic and professional journals, might not be easily accessible to the very women who would benefit from it most. I also have sought to suggest a few alternative lenses through which to view stepmothers and stepmothering, and I have drawn on my background in literary and cultural analysis in an attempt to understand the elusive, frightening, and fascinating character who is the stepmother, as well as the force field of social relations, emotions, and cultural associations from which she emerges.

For this project, I interviewed eighteen women with stepchildren, twelve adult stepchildren (six men and six women), and several men with children who had divorced and remarried. I also had more informal conversations with at least a dozen other people. I used the snowball method of recruitment — first interviewing friends and acquaintances married to men with children, who then told me about friends or acquaintances of theirs who also were stepmothers. This is a strategy social scientists frequently use with populations that are wary of "outsiders," an apt description of stepmothers who are having difficulties. Two of my interview subjects were both stepdaughters and stepmothers, bringing a valuable "double vision" to the table. Instead of trying to recruit a representative sample, I spoke to women with stepchildren of all ages and to adult stepchildren in order to bring real voices into the book and hear basic issues framed in human terms. I filled in the gaps by turning to the comprehensive longitudinal studies on stepfamilies conducted by psychologists and social scientists and to interviews with experts on the experiences of women with stepchildren.

All the women I interviewed were asked to answer the same questions. Interestingly, all but one of them wanted to talk longer than the one and a half hours that I had told them the interview would take, and all but one gave expansive and detailed answers to my questions. Many women were anxious to remain anonymous, as they felt that what they were sharing was "controversial," "not pretty," and "brutally honest in a way that might make me look bad." Several told me that this was "like therapy" for them. To protect the privacy of the many women who were so forthcoming and helpful to me, I have changed their names and identifying details.

My interview subjects were largely upper-middle-class white women living in the Tri-State Area (New York, New Jersey, and Connecticut). However, many were originally from other parts of the country, lending some regional diversity. I also interviewed subjects currently living in California, Hawaii, and the Caribbean. Because I have a number of friends who work in the mental health field — as psychologists, psychoanalysts, psychiatrists, and psychiatric nurses — and because a number of them are stepmothers or stepchildren, my interview pool included a fair number of people from these professions. This slant may be helpful because it demonstrates that even the experts struggle with stepfamily realities.

In the end, it was difficult for me to interview the lower-income and minority women who expressed an interest in being part of this project because they had less control of their work schedules, fewer child-care options, and less free time. I ended up speaking to experts and reading research on the stepmother experiences of Latina, African American, and lower-income women. The research of Francesca Adler-Baeder, Susan Stewart, and Margaret Crosbie-Burnett, among others, helped fill this unfortunate but typical gap in my work. Lesbians in partnership with divorced mothers are another under-researched group whose numbers are growing. "Under the radar" might best characterize this family form, but in my informal recruiting, I spoke to several such women. I found that they shared many of the essential stepmother issues outlined in the chapters that follow, with an added dose of role ambiguity and lack of social and institutional acknowledgment and support, making things even more difficult for them. Until more work is done with all these women, our understanding of stepmothering is contingent, and our ability to help women with stepchildren is compromised.

I found a wedding dress that day. It was my husband's idea, really. He said, "Let's go over here and look a little more." I was ready to rush out, feeling defeated and guilty and resentful that his daughter was obviously not enjoying herself, was in fact miserable with our excursion, and so "ruining" what I had hoped would be my special day. But he insisted, and there it was. "It won't fit," the saleswoman tut-tutted, but she was wrong. It was divine, and I loved it. I still wear my knee-length, riotously patterned, colorful Pucci wedding dress occasionally. Every time I put it on, it feels fresh, irreverent, and appropriate all at once. And I remember the day I got married, how perfect it was — the blazing heat, the blue sky, the red rocks in the desert — not just the bickering, the feelings of betrayal, and my unhappy epiphany about how hard it was all going to be. Against the odds, things have worked out better than fine for my husband and me, and for millions of other women as well. I hope that *Stepmonster* might help readers feel that if someone as impatient and imperfect as I am can survive the most statistically harrowing of all step-situations, there is plenty of hope to go around.

PART I
THE STEPMOTHERING SCRIPT

CHAPTER ONE
A WALL OF ONE'S OWN

Becoming a Stepmother

MY VERY FIRST ACT as a stepmother was to build a wall. Literally. Things had already become serious, and my boyfriend of less than a year and I were talking, not for the first time, of merging our possessions and lives. Why don't you just move in? he asked.

I was crazy about my boyfriend — he was kind and accomplished, sexy, smart, and reliable. Everything about him — his love of cooking, his deadpan sarcasm, his trustworthiness, his nerdy micro-knowledge of New York City history — was endearing. But there were complications. Two of them. They were almost fifteen and eleven. The younger one, who had tousled blond hair and a depth beyond her years, lived with him; the older one, who had a guarded, beautiful smile, lived with her mother. I knew the fact that I was not the first serious girlfriend after their father's divorce might make things a little easier. But I had heard what being a stepmother was like. I had read the stories and seen the movies and listened to the gossip about friends' stepmothers. Surely, I wouldn't be like *that,* I thought. But my happiness was already weighted with caution.

Why *didn't* I just move in? It was complicated, the idea and the reality of him and me and his daughter under one roof, in ways I both could and couldn't put my finger on. It was also largely unspoken. "It's a lot to think about that you have two daughters," I said quietly and carefully as we sat on the couch and I mulled over his suggestion. His younger daughter was upstairs, and I didn't want her to hear us. Editing myself was already becoming a habit.

"Don't worry," my boyfriend replied, hugging me. "It'll be fine."

It'll be fine. I stiffened against the cushion behind me. His optimistic nonchalance, his non-answer to my non-question — it felt like an evasion — added to the anxiety that had been slowly taking over a corner of my mind. Maybe because we didn't talk about it, this whole issue — his relationship with the girls, and mine with him and his with me, and mine with them — slowly got twisted up in and mapped onto his house. The house had made me wary from the beginning. The first time I saw it, he showed me two beautifully decorated rooms on the second floor, explaining that he had moved there so that each of his daughters could have her own bedroom. "I want them to know that they can always come live here with me," he told me solemnly. The house, I found myself thinking from then on, was less a place where people lived and slept and ate, and more a stage set — hushed, meticulous, waiting for life to happen in it. Or was it a shrine to the past, a cordoned-off memorial to a happier time when he lived with his children in a less complicated way? I wasn't sure.

And then there was his bedroom. It didn't have a door. Or a wall to put the door in. It was just an open, loftlike space at the top of the stairs on the third floor. There was no privacy whatsoever — anyone on the first or second floor could hear everything going on up there. "Are you *serious?*" my girlfriends demanded, incredulous, when I described it. Every time I was there, I found this absence of a boundary, the permeable nature of the house, uncomfortable. All these months into our relationship, all these weekends and days and nights with his daughters later, the architecture of the house still made me feel vulnerable and exposed.

It didn't help that I literally could not get my bearings there. It was five or six times bigger than the apartment I'd been living in, and I was constantly losing things — my keys, my agenda, my purse. I seemed to spend half my time walking around in circles, frantically retracing my steps and trying to find what I'd misplaced.

One evening after my boyfriend had left on his weekly six-hour trip to drop off one daughter and pick up the other, I searched for a can opener for almost an hour. I was, I felt, the outsider in many ways. I bumped my shins, tripped on carpets, struggled with locks. In the house — the beautiful, quiet space that led virtually anyone who visited to remark, "Oh, it's so peaceful!" — I was virtually never relaxed. And so on that winter morning, as we chatted about my moving in, I considered the future and announced, "Not until you get a door." After a moment I added, "And something to put a door *in*. Please?"

Like a lot of women who become stepmothers, I was trying to block out the stress, trying to make a peaceful place. Because stepfamily life is chaotic, confusing, and exhausting, especially in the beginning. One woman I know likened it to being thrown into the ocean during a storm. "Everybody screams, 'Swim!' and walks away from you," she said with a laugh. Another woman compared stepmothering to "setting up housekeeping on an ice floe." The analogies of trying not to drown and slipping on a constantly moving, inhospitable surface are apt. The pressures on women who partner with men who have children — to blend, to love, to come together, to fix it, to take the high road, to put his kids first, to have a sense of humor in the face of repeated rebuffs — are overwhelming. Perhaps the most intense pressure of all is to win his kids over. Our husbands love them. We hope we will love them. We hope they will love us. But everybody knows that nobody wants a stepmother.

Nobody wants a stepmother. A less frequently acknowledged but equally potent truth — and one that is without doubt more unsettling to those who stand outside it — is that *nobody wants to be a stepmother either.* Just as our stepchildren do not choose us, we do not choose them. They are incidental and, if we are lucky, also supplemental, a kind of add-on to the man we love. We may tell ourselves that we will love them, that we will be patient with them, that we will befriend them, that we will not have much to do with them (if they are grown), that we will let things take their own course. Regardless of what we hope for, the relationship with our stepchildren always starts from this mutual lack of choosing. They are as unessential to us as we are to them, accidental even. It is not exactly an auspicious beginning for a story. The story does not always end badly, of course. But for the majority of women, the ones who find stepmothering difficult, it may be helpful — even a tremendous relief — to get the unhappy truths about that difficulty on the table. "We wasted so much time blaming each other, feeling like failures," a woman married to a man with children told me. "If only someone had said, 'Just about everybody with step-kids goes through this, you know.'"

A litany of how and why it is difficult may send the woman considering marriage to a man with kids running — or at least give her serious pause. But for those of us already in such partnerships, the details that seem so discouraging, even depressing, to others may sound almost like an affirmation. "Aha," we think, "so this is just how stepfamilies *are*!" And for those of us who don't have friends who are stepmothers, and the sanity-saving reality check they can provide, knowing that we're not alone in the difficulty can help us through the day. Meanwhile, an exploration of precisely why it can feel so tough, sometimes for years on end, might help us take the struggle with his kids less personally, increasing the chances that something can be salvaged, or built, something like a friendship, or perhaps just a friendly enough, good enough, polite yet distant mutual caring.

Although it's a disappointment, it's no real surprise that when wives of men with children and those children come together, regardless of our good intentions, we are on a collision course of sorts. "These children have become so close to their parents," Patricia Papernow, a leading stepfamily expert, explains. "The challenge then is to transfer the seat of decision making and intimacy from the parent-child dyad to the couple dyad. And that can be a lot of work." The lack of rules and privacy in my husband's house preme, the weekends devoted to searching out stores the girls wanted to shop in, movies they wanted to see, and restaurants they wanted to have dinner in, were all par for the course for postdivorce dads.

They were also routines that were hard to reconcile with romance. Just by coming into the previously child-centric picture, the step-mother-to-be changes things, and she is bound to be resented heart-ily for the palpable shift in priorities and the overall family culture as it segues (if all goes well) into the healthy configuration Papernow describes, in which the bond between husband and wife (or part-ners) becomes central. My younger stepdaughter could have been speaking for stepkids everywhere when she told me recently, "When I was eleven and you showed up, I didn't want Dad to be with any-body. I didn't think he should have a girlfriend!" The sense that you are taking something away, detracting from the amiable situation that Dad and kids have finally worked out after already adjusting to a divorce, is there no matter how kind you are.

"I had my dad all to myself and then you came along, and I felt like I was losing him," my stepdaughter explained simply. "It was like you stole him away." You want romance; they want all the atten-tion. Nobody's in the wrong here, but it can be remarkably difficult to strike a balance. "When the stepmother-to-be joins in the weekly Friday pizza and pajama night ritual that Dad and the kids have, she sits down next to her boyfriend in front of the TV. And his little girl comes and plops right down between them, shoving her to the side," Papernow told me, explaining that this "battle of who's an insider and who's an outsider" is a typical dynamic from the earliest stages of coming together (if you can call it that).

From the perspective of the woman with stepchildren, being shoved to the side eight or ten or a hundred times is hard to ignore. And her understanding of what the kids are going through becomes tinged with resentment the longer her partner pretends that none of this is happening. By ignoring problems with his kids' behavior and adjustment — a disease to which every father who divorces and re-partners seems prone — he leaves the woman in an unenviable position, with a few equally unappealing options: she can fend for herself, feeling unsupported; tell the man something about his child that he may hear as criticism; or go silent. "I did a lot of quiet fuming, to tell you the truth," Kelly, a teacher who married a man with a ten-year-old daughter, told me. "It just seemed too petty to bring up the things she did that felt hurtful or rude. So I swallowed it." Staying quiet eventually made Kelly feel angry, hurt, and alone. This dynamic, addressed in chapter 6, can be lethal for a partnership.

A woman seriously involved with a man with kids is bound, sooner or later, to begin lobbying, subtly or not so subtly, for changes around the house. Even though she is asking for things that make sense — divorced dads are notoriously permissive — there will almost certainly be fireworks. Like millions of other stepmothers, I fell into this trap with hardly a push. Once my fiancé and I were engaged and I was spending all my time with him and his daughter, I came up against the fact that there were no discernible rules about bedtime, homework, TV, or computer use. That didn't bother my fiancé, but my needs regarding privacy, order, and especially sleep were different. I began to push, gently and then not so gently, for structure. I didn't try to enforce new rules myself — I knew that would not go over well — but instead asked my fiancé to. He was unaccustomed to asking his daughter to do things that did not suit her, however, which put us constantly at cross-purposes and reinforced my sense that she was indulged because he couldn't draw the line. In my mind, I was only trying to make the household run more like her mother's and help us all get a decent night's sleep.

But as reasonable as these attempts at change seemed to me, they caused huge upheaval — between her and me, between him and me. "No TV until your homework's done, remember?" I would urge him to remind her on my way out for the evening, inciting a tantrum. The TV would go off, but the second I was out the door, I would discover later, my fiancé would let her turn it back on. I told him that yes, she *should* have to go to school the next morning, but he would tell her that if she wanted, she could stay home. On and on it went. I felt undermined and grimly determined, some days, to "win," though I wasn't exactly sure what winning meant. We argued and pushed and negotiated — with each other, with her — constantly. There were clashes and preteen tantrums and tears; the house roiled with drama. Contractors being contractors, the wall was still just a concept for much of our coming-together period, and that only made matters worse.

"Please tell her to go to bed," I would say some nights, frayed and impatient from listening to the TV blaring downstairs, unable to close the door that didn't exist in a wall that had yet to be built.

"Oh, just relax," he would reply, implying that I was overreacting. And the fight was on.

Stepmothers become the bad guys in the family system quickly. In pointing out problems, we *become* the problem. We come to seem shrill, rigid, and intolerant almost overnight. Compared to laissez-faire dads, we are party poopers par excellence. We fight with our partners about how the kids behave, feel resented by kids who resent us (and perhaps resent them in return), and are quickly villainized by everyone in the household, including ourselves. Seeing ourselves transformed this way — turned into stereotypical stepmonsters when we have the best intentions — can take a tremendous toll on our self-esteem. "I felt like an awful person," at least a dozen women with stepchildren told me in describing the early months and years of step-motherhood.

As for the kids, there are new household rules, new household members, changes in the usual routines — all of which seem custom designed to incite confusion, insecurity, and hostility in a child. Feeling threatened by the changes, the kids will surely respond by making it clear that *you* are the outsider, the interloper, and *they* are the ones who belong here with Daddy. After all, experts point out, it's so much easier for his children to be angry at expendable, unnecessary Stepmom, to blame her for changes, than to confront beloved Dad or process the fact that they're mad at him, too. This intense polarization of the household (discussed at length in chapter 6) can create a sense that Dad is somehow a passive and torn victim caught in the middle as his wife and child battle it out. In fact, by not making it clear to his kids that Stepmom is here to stay and working with her to form a coalition, Dad may actually be orchestrating much of the household tension in these initial stages of stepfamily formation. (This is discussed at length in chapter 5.) Other dads/husbands may unconsciously enjoy being in the middle, since it means being the object of everyone's attention and desire. One woman told me that when she got home from work every evening and walked over to greet and kiss her fiancé, his ten-year-old daughter would rush past her to sit on his lap. *Don't even think about it,* the girl's actions said. The woman's fiancé never said a word, contributing to her sense that she was "making a big deal out of nothing," which in turn made her enormously resentful. "There was just this big, unspoken tension I couldn't even mention," this woman explained.

Transparent as it is, this possessiveness and territorialism about Daddy — especially if the couple never finds a way to acknowledge and defuse it — can be wearing for a woman trying to adjust to life with a new partner and his kids. It is likely to be particularly difficult if she has no children of her own to counterbalance the sense that they are the family and she is the party crasher. These feelings are only exacerbated by the typical scenario in which a childless woman moves in with a man with kids from a previous union and winds up finding herself on unfamiliar ground in all kinds of ways.

Even if a woman doesn't make the mistakes I did — even if she has the smarts or the self-control to hold back, to go with the flow, to surrender to the way things are in the household for a while before coming up with a reasonable, strategic plan to change things slowly — she is likely to be resented in the first tumultuous years of becoming a stepmother. This is not only because she's a convenient screen for the kids' anger at Dad for changing the order of things. Prominent stepfamily researchers Marilyn Coleman, Ed.D., and Lawrence Ganong, Ph.D., of the University of Missouri are among the many who note that when a stepparent, particularly a stepmother, comes on the scene, children begin to feel intense conflicts of loyalty. "Liking the stepparent raises their anxiety and makes them feel guilty about being disloyal to their [mother]," Coleman and Ganong explain. These tortured feelings intensify if Mom communicates to her kids, directly or indirectly, that Dad's remarriage (and hence Stepmom) is making her miserable. If stepmoms think they can overcome this conundrum simply by liking their stepkids and being likable themselves, and by giving the kids time to come around, they are wrong. Experts such as Coleman and Ganong have found that the nicer, the more appealing, and the more attractive a child finds a stepmother, the worse these feelings of divided loyalty will be, and the more intensely the stepmother will be rejected. Counterintuitively, then, our niceness often backfires. "The more I try, the more he retreats," Laynie sighed, while describing her relationship with her nine-year-old stepson, Teddy. "And when he has a good time with me, he feels guilty." It is hard, thankless work to reach out to a child in a loyalty bind.

Thirty-eight-year-old Brenda described her initial hunch about how her relationship with her husband's son would unfold: "My friends' kids like me. I'm a young, approachable, and fun person. I do things a kid might consider cool, like hang-gliding. And I don't want to replace [my stepson's] mom; I just want to be his friend. So he'll like me, and I'll like him." But after ten years together, her stepson has yet to warm up to her, and Brenda is getting tired of the rebuffs, which she largely attributes to "him thinking it's not fair to his mom to like me and him just hating all adults in charge right now. I don't really try to have a relationship with him anymore." Brenda's case is especially hard because she is now dealing with a teenager. Those of us who come into our stepkids' lives when they are preadolescents or adolescents will, experts such as psychologist E. Mavis Hetherington tell us, have the hardest time of all, but not necessarily because of anything we do. The developmental imperative of the adolescent, researchers who study stepfamilies explain, is to separate, while the stepmother and her partner are likely feeling the imperative to blend. So when a family is forming at just this moment in the child's life, it gives new meaning to the concept of being at cross-purposes (see chapter 3). "Kids are at great pains to show they have no use for a parent at this point in their lives," Manhattan psychoanalyst Stephanie Newman, Ph.D., told me. "They're rejecting and impossible even to the people they love most. Can you imagine how they're going to treat a *stepparent?*" Brenda can. "I've never had anybody be so rude to me in my life," she said flatly.

Even if the stepkids aren't teens, yet another factor puts stepmothers and stepchildren or stepchildren-to-be at odds. The thing that gives a woman with stepchildren such great happiness — her partnership — is the death knell of the kids' fantasy that Mom and Dad will get back together. There is a reason, the experts tell us, that kids love movies such as Disney's *The Parent Trap,* in which resourceful twin girls drive their stepmother-to-be out of the picture, effecting a mother-father reunion. Such fantasies of reconciliation are not just the stuff of fiction; they are profoundly real, if unconscious, often even into the adult years. British psychotherapist Sarah Corrie, Ph.D., who treats adults with stepparents, reports that even well into middle age, her patients are sometimes devastated to belatedly confront the reality that Dad and Mom will not be getting back together. Stepmom is the proof that the dream is over, and often it is held against her. If Dad is a widower, Stepmom is living proof that he is moving on, and this, too, can create tremendous sadness or resentment in both children and full-grown adults.

And what about us? It certainly can be disorienting to realize that the most important development of your life, a relationship that you perhaps feel you cannot live without, is shattering another person's dream. "When we told my husband's two girls that we were getting married, they started crying hysterically," forty-year-old Cindy told me. "Then came weeks of acting out. They were nine and thirteen. I had put in a lot of effort with them and had lots of good times, but I had also put up with a lot of rudeness and anger. And I remember thinking, *Can't it be easy just once?*"

The big day itself is likely to be fraught, to put it mildly. I heard a number of stories about grown children crying through the entire wedding ceremony and children old enough to know better throwing tantrums at just the wrong moment. Before becoming a stepmother myself, I had never considered how disconcerting and hurtful that sobbing and acting out, or even a simple lack of enthusiasm, could be for a woman who was supposed to be at the center of something beautiful, and who may have been looking forward to this day for decades.

Simple and Complex Stepfamilies

Women and men with children from a previous relationship consolidate their lives in different ways, but none of them are easy. A "simple stepfamily" (quite a misnomer) is one in which a childless woman marries a man with children; he is often older than she is. She generally moves in with him, and custody arrangements being what they are, she is more likely to be a part-time (or "nonresidential") than a full-time (or "residential") stepmother to his kids. If it sounds "simple," it isn't. Research confirms that, counterintuitively, part-time step-mothering is the most difficult arrangement of all. First, part-time status leads to confusion about your role. Are you a weekend mother figure? An every-other-holiday friend? Balancing being a friend and being an adult who gets respect can be difficult indeed, but doing so at infrequent or unpredictable intervals is more difficult still. "We just never got into a groove, because they weren't around much. Now that they're young adults, it's even harder to figure out how to be with them when they're around," one woman told me about her stepsons.

Uncertainty about how to act dogs nearly every stepmother, but particularly the nonresidential ones. Experts even have a special term for their confusion about how they should be with their stepkids: "role ambiguity." Think of yourself as another parent. Think of yourself as a friend. Think of yourself more like an aunt. The advice goes on and on. It's no wonder stepmothers don't know how to act or who to be.

These part-time arrangements also leave women with very little time to build a relationship with his kids. Being together for intense, weekends-only increments ratchets up the pressure — *I only have two days!* — and the exhaustion. "We just ran around trying to keep them happy and entertained all the time, because that is what my fiancé got them used to," forty-five-year-old Hope told me about the first year of her relationship with her husband and his seven-year-old twins. "I have always really cared about his kids. But it got exhausting with our weekends always revolving around them." All of what experts call our "affinity-seeking behaviors" — that is, our attempts to get our stepkids to like us, attempts we are likely to have all the more energy for and optimism about when we don't have kids of our own — can be draining indeed. "In my practice, I've seen stepmothers jump through all kinds of hoops to get on the good side of their stepkids," Stephanie Newman observed. "Overextending yourself this way is depleting and can lead you to really resent them when they reject you in all the ways that are pretty normal." Trying to discipline stepchildren too early can be disastrous, yet being walked on doesn't feel good either. Women whose stepchildren are there only part-time are more often expected to "just let it go — they're only there once in a while." This often means that these women are expected to swallow their feelings, while the stepkids' snippy remarks or hostility go unchecked for years.

Overall, simple stepfamily partnerships are often characterized by imbalances of power. According to Jamie Kelem Keshet, Ed.D., a step-mother, author, and psychotherapist in private practice in Newton, Massachusetts,

> *The husband who is older is often more successful than his wife. He often expects her to move into his home because he owns it, it is bigger than her apartment and/or his children are already accustomed to spending time there. Several wives in this position expressed the sense that their husbands merely wanted them to fill an empty place in their lives, rather than to build a new life together from the ground up. The women felt they were blocked when they requested changes in the family home or lifestyle.*

Like the women who spoke with Keshet, I began, eventually, to chafe at the way I perceived I had been shunted into my husband's life on his terms. I had donated my furniture, sold my car, and moved in with him and his daughter, turning my entire life upside down, I felt, while he hadn't altered so much as a throw pillow. Compounding the problem was the fact that my husband lived near his extended family, while I lived far from mine. And so at big family dinners or on stays at the family vacation compound, the kindness of my in-laws notwithstanding (and they *were* kind), I sometimes felt like a barnacle that had affixed itself to a coral reef: tacked on, overwhelmed. Often I had the sensation that the old me had been swallowed up, disappearing without a trace. Going out with my friends was a wonderful counterbalance. They were my version of family, and among them I felt myself in familiar, friendly territory again.

The house was another matter. It had become a hostile environment. In an attempt to help me feel more at home, my husband had agreed to a little redecorating, something many couples in such a position undertake, it turns out, as a way to try to reset the balance. But these changes — representing, as they did, far more profound ones — did not go over well with his girls. "This looks totally *weird*," my husband's daughter pronounced acidly when she saw how we had altered the living room. "And I like my mom's curtains better."

"I hate this room. I hate your bedspread, and I hate your lamp," her sister told me when she walked into our bedroom. "That's okay," I responded flatly, by now worn down their hostility. "It's not your room." I wanted to add, *Feel free to stay out.*

Unfortunately, our sense that we are extraneous, unnecessary, and excluded and that our stepchildren seem to want to drive us away or split us from our partners may dog us for years. Patricia Papernow coined the term "intimate outsider" to explain the paradoxical nature of our position, the sense of simultaneous exclusion, estrangement, and enmeshment with "them" that stepmothers invariably describe. Most insidiously, our outsider status can leech away our sense of ourselves as good, loving, and lovable people, rendering the most self-confident among us insecure, off-kilter, occasionally even bitter. The outsider role is the special burden of women who come to their husbands without children of their own.

But women with children of their own who marry men with kids also face many of the same pitfalls I did, plus a few others. They confront the daunting task of trying to bring two family cultures together and of dealing with the inevitable conflicts that will arise as man and wife and kids and kids try to reconcile many different rituals (What time is dinner? Is the seder long or short? What day does the Christmas tree go up?); expectations ("Why do I have to share a room?" "Do we have to go to Florida for vacation just because that's what Stepdad and his kids always do?"); and philosophies ("You're strict with us, but Stepdad's kids never get in trouble!" "We have to do chores, but his kids don't."). Not to mention the agonizing turf wars over deciding who will live where, and the wear and tear on the couple as different kids change their minds and their residency again and again (as research indicates is typical in remarriages with children).

More than just logistical matters, there are emotional ones as well. Many mothers who married men with kids told me they felt that their husbands' kids, having fewer rules, were a bad influence on, or even hostile toward, their own kids. Sally told me that her husband's kids were "very angry and very defiant, and they weren't careful with toys and things. My kids were mild and got steamrolled sometimes. It made me feel guilty!" The upside of this type of merger, then, is also its downside. In having kids, the woman feels part of what Jamie Kelem Keshet calls her own "mini-family," rather than simply feeling excluded from his mini-family. This can give her a sense of belonging, but it can also create pressure to protect her kids, and it can factionalize the household as each parent sticks up for his or her own kids in disputes (see chapter 6).

Fortunately, there is some good news here. The man with kids who divorces and remarries "is very likely to be doing it for the right reasons this time, and to want to get it right," Mary Ann Feldstein, Ed.D., a Manhattan psychotherapist who has worked with couples with stepchildren, told me. Many of my interview subjects felt lucky to have husbands who had learned the value of communication and the need to work at a marriage, a quality they said they didn't see as often in first-married men. As one man told me, "The first time was a disaster. Then I got this second chance. Why do it again if I wasn't going to commit to it and make it the most important thing in my life?" The numbers bear him out. Although the divorce rate for remarriages with children is dramatically higher than that for remarriages without children in the first three years, such marriages, having passed the three-year mark, are actually more likely to survive than first marriages. In fact, after about five years, researchers have found, a remarriage with children is more likely to succeed than any other type of marriage. The extraordinary effort of coping with the ordinary struggles of stepfamily life, it seems, cements couples who do not succumb to the pressures early on. Passing through this crucible is more than worth it, my subjects who managed to come out on the other side told me over and over. "Marriage is hard, but marriage with stepchildren is so much harder," a stepmother in her late sixties told me over lunch one day. She went on to describe her own experience as "hell that makes you happier and stronger after the fact. My husband and I are so much closer for all the drama his kids brought to the picture and all the arguing we did."

WHAT KIND OF STEPMOTHER ARE YOU?

There is not a single way to be a stepmother. Nor, it turns out, is there a "right" one. Some women embrace the role, throwing their entire beings into forging a relationship with their husbands' kids; other women, like Laynie, think of stepmothering as a "not-me experience, something I want to get right out of a sense of duty to my husband and his son, but it's not central to who I am." And often, a woman's experience of stepmothering, and of herself as a stepmother, will change over the years. "Things were easy when they were little, but now they're on the verge of becoming stormy preteens. So I'm trying to strike a balance between being kind of a mommy and a reliable friend," Ella told me.

The simple fact that there are many ways to be a stepmother may seem pretty extraordinary to those of us who have had it drummed into our heads that there is one "best" way to do it. Soon after I married, I told a friend over the phone that "my daughter" was with us for the weekend, feeling that my use of the term "stepdaughter" might strike her as unfriendly. My friend was completely flummoxed — had I suddenly had a child? — and my older stepdaughter and I both cringed the moment I said it: she, I imagine, at my presumption, and I at my hypocrisy. That model of stepmothering — the one where the line between mother and stepmother blurs — was not for us. My younger stepdaughter, however, sometimes refers to her father and me as "my parents," other times we are "my dad and my stepmom" or just "Dad and Wednesday." Different kids, different days, different stages, different roles. Nothing about being a stepmother is written in stone.

One-size-fits-all expectations of what's "right" only increase the tensions in a stepfamily, fueling feelings of inadequacy and resentment with every perceived failure to do things "correctly" or make the family just like a "real" (first) family. As it turns out, there are actually several ways to be in a marriage to a man with children. Some presage better outcomes. Some are not so much stepmothering styles as reactions to specific circumstances and experiences. But in general, researchers seem to have discovered that who we are, who his kids are, and who the other players in the remarriage scenario are all help determine whether and how we will act as stepmothers. For this reason, we can't simply "choose" a stepmothering style from a menu, any more than we can choose our own eye color. But getting a sense of what kind of stepmother we feel like — anywhere at all along the spectrum that extends from "not a stepmother at all" to "just like another mom" — is a good way to get oriented when we're feeling lost or overwhelmed. A few studies provide a loose stepmothering "map."

When psychologists Ann Orchard, Psy.D., and Kenneth Solberg, Ph.D., asked 265 women how they would characterize the relationship with their stepchildren, 25 percent chose "respectful/polite." Almost the same number described it as "friendly/caring," and just slightly fewer characterized the relationship as "distant." The answers were not mutually exclusive; many women chose more than one description, or even all three, to sum up how they felt. Their answers to the next question, "How would you describe your role?" showed just how creative we can be in the absence of clear guidelines about being a stepmother. Thirty-three percent thought of their role as "another parent/mother-like." Another 31 percent described their role as "a friend/supportive adult," while half that number felt that their role was "Dad's wife/support to Dad." Sadly, 13 percent thought of their role as "outsider," while 10 percent chose the truly alienated-sounding descriptor "household organizer." Like other researchers, Orchard and Solberg found that the "friendship style" of stepmothering — characterized more, it seems, by noninterference and the absence of conflict or getting involved in parenting than by an actual reciprocal friendliness — was the "most functional" model. A stepmom named Belinda told me of her relationship with her husband's now young-adult daughters, "I wanted an aunt type of role. Supportive, a plus to have in your life, someone you could turn to. Not the disciplinarian."

Another study, of thirty-two Israeli couples by University of Washington researcher Pauline Erera-Weatherley, Ph.D., found four step-mothering styles: the super-good stepmom; the detached stepmom; the uncertain stepmom; and the friend. The super-good stepmoms were reacting to a stereotype. Petrified by the specter of the wicked stepmother, they bent over backward to prove themselves kind, were rebuffed nonetheless, and tended to feel unappreciated by their stepchildren, husbands, and in-laws. It is not hard to imagine these women deciding that their efforts weren't worth it, then withdrawing, angry and defeated, from their "families" and marriages. This was exactly the direction I saw upbeat, sunny Kendra moving in when I interviewed her. She had thrown herself entirely into the task of mothering the teenage stepdaughter who lived with her and her husband, but after years of rejection, she told me, she was ready to throw in the towel. "I don't think anybody realizes how hard I've tried," she said. "In fact, I don't think they even notice."

Erera-Weatherley found that the detached stepmothers were minimally involved in their stepchildren's lives. This style tended to be something of a default mode, one the women adopted after feeling rebuffed and rejected in their friendly or parental overtures toward their stepchildren. "I'm just done with this," one long-term stepmother told me, "done with trying and not getting any warmth back. So I'm not putting myself out so much anymore." Several other stepmothers echoed this sentiment (as discussed in chapters 4 and 10).

Meanwhile, stepmothers with the uncertain style expressed doubt, uncertainty, distress, and confusion in Erera-Weatherley's study. Many of them, like me, had had no experience of parenting before becoming a stepparent. One woman said, "I feel like I'm alone. I don't know exactly what I am supposed to do. Should I react [to my stepchild doing something provocative]? Should I not react?" These women felt very apprehensive about criticizing, confronting and quarreling with their stepchildren. It is not hard to see how their stepkids would eventually become very empowered and, as stepfamily expert James Bray puts it, end up calling the shots on the emotional trajectory of stepfamily life.

The last style, friend, was pointedly "nonparental," yet characterized by conveying a sense of caring and being available. With the adoption of this style, Erera-Weatherley noted, women seemed to accept their stepchildren without necessarily expecting themselves to love the kids or to be loved in return: "We developed friendly contact. He hugs me . . . [but] there is no real love between us. I don't act like a natural mother, but I take care of [my stepchild]. I care about him, and I try to help my husband in his relationship with his son."

Although the "friend" seems to be the most rewarding and successful stepmothering style, a woman cannot simply choose it in an effort to improve stepfamily relations. For while the stepmother's own personality and attitudes about parenting and stepparenting play a role in determining which style she adopts, the expectations and behaviors of the stepchild, the father, and the mother are usually more important in determining how things will go and which of the roles the stepmom will play. For example, I spoke with a stepmother named Dana. The mother of Dana's stepdaughter, Tania, moved across the country when the girl was nine, tacitly ceding all mothering duties to Dana. Not long after, Tania's father and Dana broke up, with Dana retaining custody of the girl. Not surprisingly, Dana describes herself as Tania's "mommy," a sentiment Tania reciprocates. Another stepmom, Gabby, found herself cast into the role of villain by her husband's ex-wife, who communicated both implicitly and explicitly to her children that to befriend Gabby would be to betray her. Gabby's good intentions and efforts were hobbled by other circumstances, agendas over which she had no control.

Stepmothering does not happen in a vacuum, but rather within a force field of other relationships. A stepmother's own preferences and efforts are only one piece of a larger puzzle of determining factors, probably the least important of all. Knowing this, perhaps we will begin to give ourselves permission to feel less responsible for outcomes with his children.

Several months after I moved in with my fiancé, the wall finally went up. His daughters seemed displeased. The younger one sulked and stormed away from me more often. She wanted badly to provoke me, it seemed, and too often I obliged her. I had largely abandoned my project to win her over. There seemed to be very little payoff, and the more hostile she was toward me, the less inclined I was to continue to try. We lived under the same roof but in different worlds, in a kind of perpetual standoff. I had sunk to her level, and on my worst days, I resented her and my fiancé terribly for it. But part of me was concerned about her. We had had good times together, and occasionally still did, and it saddened me to see that the transitions in the household were so rough on her.

I often found myself wondering, *Why does it all have to be so difficult? Why does she dislike me? What am I doing wrong?* Then, like a lot of women who marry men with kids and ask these questions, I heard the voices:

What did you expect? Just deal with it.

They're part of the package. Suck it up.

You're not the important one here; she is. Stop being so selfish.

My own response to this stepmothering reality — the stress, the competition, the judgments, the ambivalence, the ambiguity, the being rebuffed — was to bunker down, erect a fort, dig a moat of sorts. I built a wall. The truth is that this many years into it, I am not, and do not aspire to be, a stepmother who says, "Just show up. Stay as long as you want. This is your home!" I have drawn lines and set boundaries that have nothing to do with the way I was sure I would be. This bewilders me, since I have come to really like my stepdaughters and am the person everyone told:

His daughters are going to love you.

You won't have any wicked stepmother nonsense to deal with. You're not like that.

Those girls are so lucky. I wish you were my stepmom!

You'll be the nicest, funnest stepmom in the world.

I built a wall. It sounds predictable when I write it. Wicked. But building walls was, for me, unavoidable, inevitable, a question of survival. I was a new stepmother. And in spite of everything we have been taught about stepmothers, everything we are sure we know about them, I felt powerless, vulnerable, and very afraid. I was frightened of my own feelings, of my ambivalence, and of the ugliness that these new, intense relationships brought out in me. I built a wall — a lot of them, in fact — because I needed a place to hide, a place to remember who I really was, to figure out what I was becoming. A new stepmother, any sort of stepmother, it seems to me, needs a wall of her own, and a place to be.

CHAPTER TWO

"SHE'S SUCH A WITCH!"

Fairy Tale History and the Stepmothering Script

W HO ARE WE? Where did we come from?
One day we are real, normal people, living alongside everyone else in the regular world, in normal time. Then we marry a man
with children, and somehow we become something utterly different from what we had believed ourselves to be. When we become a
stepmother — even if defining ourselves by this role is the farthest
thing from our minds, even if we have kids of our own and are
loving mothers, even if his kids are grown — there is a certain ines-
capability to the transformation. Like some perverse untelling of
Cinderella's magical makeover via the Fairy Godmother's wand, and
in spite of the fact that step-mothering and stepfamilies are more
common than ever before, we are likely to find ourselves wrenched
from whatever identity we inhabited and forced into another way of
being seen entirely. *Just my dad's wife. Tries too hard. Doesn't really make
an effort. Favors her own children. Doesn't let me near Dad. A gold digger.
Cold. Jealous. Selfish. Unmaternal.* "She's having a hard time with his
kids," someone whispers to someone else. The implication is clear:
*If she were nice to those children, they'd warm right up to her. If there's a
problem, the problem is her.*

"Oh, you don't want to talk to me. I'm a wicked stepmother. I'm
horrible," an intelligent and appealing woman named Brenda, the
mother of a two-year-old and a three-year-old and the stepmother
of a teen, told me when I approached her about my book. She said
it wryly, but it obviously pained and angered her that she was seen

by her stepchildren, and presumably by others, as something she hoped she was not. Her irony, I realized, was a way of pushing back against what she felt had been forced upon her. In that instant, I recognized and understood her absolutely, because I, too, had been transformed — from someone who was considered something of a heroine by a number of teenage girls I knew to someone two girls in particular sometimes seemed to consider the enemy. My step-daughters were the agents of this transformation; they had effected it with their wariness and dislike. The knowledge that their feelings toward me were due to my role and not to myself was little consola-tion, especially since the girls themselves seemed to draw no such distinction. I felt that they resented and blamed *me* much of the time — not my role, but me the person — and I sometimes found this unexpected state of affairs unbearable. Like Brenda, I was often overcome by an urge to set the record straight about who I really was. How dare they turn me into something — a stepmonster — I was not.

Talking to women married to men with children, even the ones with the strongest self-concepts, the most gratifying marriages, the highest professional achievements, the most loving children of their own — in other words, the ones least likely to internalize the criti-cisms and unflattering opinions of others — I realized that, inevita-bly, the negative ways we are seen threaten to seep into, to inflect, to determine even, the way we see ourselves. Researchers have amply documented that becoming a stepmother has an impact on a wom-an's self-esteem, and not for the better. We are likely, when faced with the difficulties of stepfamily life — rejecting stepchildren, unsupportive husbands, friends and too frequently even therapists who don't get what we're going through — to feel like failures and to internalize notions about stepmothers being cruel, uncaring, insensitive, and ignorant about children. No matter who we are, after we marry a man with children, we cannot fail to notice that we are suddenly less likely to be given the benefit of the doubt, to be presumed innocent, kind, loving, and maternal. Quite the contrary, as so many women told me, we feel that our actions, especially those that involve our stepchildren but even those that do not, are suddenly scrutinized, suspect:

Now that I'm having trouble with my husband's kids, my friends say stuff like, "Have you tried just being really nice to them?" It's hurtful, because the suggestion is that they're acting up because I'm nasty. Being "nice" doesn't fix things. Please, it's so much more complicated than that!

My stepson says rude things about my husband and refuses to come for his scheduled time with us. But it's not because his mom is saying awful things about us, or because my husband has never once drawn the line with him. It's because of me. That's the feeling I get from all my in-laws. The other day, my mother-in-law said, "He never acted like this before." I knew what she meant — she meant "before you came along." Sometimes it really gets me down and makes me want to stop trying.

My husband can get furious and exasperated with his daughters. He can tell them off or rant to me in private about how rude and ungrateful they are sometimes. But if I so much as roll my eyes about something they've done or said, he acts like I've stabbed them.

Wake Forest University sociologist Linda Nielsen, Ph.D., points out that, when it comes to assessing people in particular roles, assumptions can be destiny. "We generally tend to be on the lookout for and to remember those characteristics that we have been taught to believe are representative of given groups," she explains. "Whether we're talking about a stepmother or a used car dealer, we generally seek out evidence, invent facts, and remember the incidents that support whatever beliefs we had about each group to begin with."

Stepmothering so often feels like a setup because it is, and so is the scrutiny that comes with it. Psychologist Anne C. Jones, Ph.D., likens the stepmother's situation to "living under a social magnifying glass" and notes that it is stressful and wearying to be continually evaluated and judged, as stepmothers are bound to be. The breadth and comprehensiveness of the list of "stepmother sins" enumerated by stepchildren is astounding. I have heard adult stepchildren fault their stepmothers for not trying hard enough, for trying too hard, for being too remote, and for being overeager. In my experience, when people speak of stepmothers from whom they are alienated, they invariably say the same thing: "She's nice to everyone but me" or "Everybody likes her, but I know what she's really like." How likely is it, we have to ask ourselves once we are stepmothers, that all these women are really so awful, and only to their stepchildren, and "for no reason"?

Who are stepmothers? Real people, of course. Quite often, we are women in tough situations, trying to do our best with stepchildren who resent us and partners who, though well-meaning, are likely to minimize the problems we face and perhaps even undermine our efforts. But we are something else as well, something more. Being a stepmother means being part person and part icon, living on the disorienting edge of what is imaginary and what is real. We may do the grocery shopping, but we are also potent and frightening signifiers from history and myth. In our gossip, movies, myths, and collective cultural history, the stepmother emerges in various guises — gold digger, death dealer, witch, bitch — over and over again. In the late 1800s, folklorists identified nearly 350 versions of the Cinderella story alone, tales that hailed from countries as varied and far-flung as France, China, India, and Japan. The wicked stepmother, it seems, like the incest taboo and the fear of snakes, is a cultural universal, easily recognized and justifiably loathed.

Like the character of the wicked stepmother and the stories she drives, stepmother history tends to recur, repeating itself in endless loops. The titanic battle between Jackie and Christina Onassis for Ari's affection, attention, and assets — "I don't dislike her. I despise her," Christina famously told reporters of her stepmother — echoed in the ugly hostilities between Heather Mills and her stepdaughter

Stella McCartney, who was frankly and publicly hostile about her father Paul McCartney's remarriage and is rumored to have played an active role in its demise. Stories of stepmonsters cross genres and crop up generation after generation. In his recent memoir, *Oh the Glory of It All,* Sean Wilsey paints a portrait of a stepmother who shamelessly favored her own two boys, lavishing them with everything they could desire while forcing her stepson (Cinderella?) to sleep in an unheated attic. The Wicked Queen in Disney's *Snow White,* with her glistening, skintight black outfit, wasp waist, and red lips, echoes Racine's Phèdre — an older, lustful seductress who would murder the stepson she desires — who in turn parallels Wilsey's real-life stepmother, Dede, watching him watch her in the mirror as she stands, smiling provocatively, in stockings, a garter belt, and little else.

The stepmother lives outside of time, at the interstice of fact and fiction, of myth and history, rendering them nearly indistinguishable. No story illustrates this point more succinctly, demonstrates our culture's preoccupation with stepmothers and stepmothering more vividly, or dramatizes the way we inhabit a space between fantasy and reality more explicitly than Edna Mumbulo's.

WHERE THERE'S SMOKE, THERE'S FIRE: "THE TORCH KILLER OF 1930"

Who was Edna Mumbulo? Did she kill her eleven-year-old stepdaughter by setting her ablaze one March morning in 1930, or didn't she? Once notorious, she has receded from our collective memory, her alleged crime lying fossilized in layers of nearly impenetrable cultural sediment. Criminologist and historian Joseph Laythe of Edinboro University of Pennsylvania has painstakingly excavated Edna Mumbulo from her obscurity. His 2002 article, "The Wicked Stepmother? The Edna Mumbulo Case of 1930," brings Edna back to life, filling in the outlines of her ordeal and linking the willingness of her contemporaries to believe that she had committed murder to centuries-old preoccupations and paradigms regarding mothers, mothering, and stepmothers.

Before Edna was an alleged killer and a stepmother, Laythe amply documents, she was an ordinary person. However, she had some unsavory secrets that would emerge years after the fact, lending very particular weight to the accusations against her. According to Laythe, sixteen-year-old Edna DeShunk of Pittsburgh gave birth to twins out of wedlock in 1902, while living with her parents, and soon sent them off to live with her sister. Edna married her children's father, but he died less than a year later, and Edna found herself in need of work. Eventually, after resettling with her increasingly infirm father in upstate New York, she found employment as a dressmaker in the New Berlin silk mill, where Ralph Mumbulo also worked. Shortly after Edna began a relationship with the married Mumbulo, his wife, Edith, died suddenly. Upon her mother's death, Ralph's eight-year-old daughter, Hilda, came into an estate of about $6,000.

It seems that Ralph and Edna quickly settled into a domestic routine, with Edna taking over all wifely and motherly responsibilities, as well as continuing to work in the mill. But with the onset of the Great Depression, the silk mill shut down. And so, having left Edna's father with one of her siblings, Edna and Ralph worked their way, with young Hilda in tow, to Erie, Pennsylvania, where they rented what was by all accounts a cramped and dreary apartment in a tenement building. Ralph found work at a forge; Edna continued to toil as a dressmaker. They led a hardscrabble life, but neighbors reportedly found the family — for all presumed they were husband, wife, and child — endearing and trusted Edna so implicitly that they did not hesitate to leave their children in her care. No one even considered that Edna might not be Hilda's mother. She used the extra money she earned babysitting to support the household, including treating Hilda to movies and ice cream.

No doubt there were strains. The three lived more or less on top of one another in the extremely small apartment. It must have been a suffocating and stressful way to live, and Edna, who so many years before had fostered her own children out to someone in better circumstances, now found herself caring for an eleven-year-old stepchild. According to Laythe, Edna resented that Ralph spent money on Hilda freely, while the health of her father steadily declined, his need for expensive medical care growing more pressing.

Was this resentment the backdrop against which tragedy unfolded, perhaps even a motive for murder? Or was it merely an irrelevant detail of everyday life that only seems significant after the fact? Either way, on the morning of March 21, 1930, shortly after Ralph left for work, the apartment went up in flames. This is the moment when Edna was transformed from a person into a character, a prototype, a sinister cliché. Her story now swerved into conjecture, fantasy, and a kind of perfect indeterminacy. All that is certain is that minutes after 7 A.M., Hilda, her garments ablaze, was found in a corner of her room. By 11 A.M., she was dead.

Ralph was not at her bedside when she died and did not accompany her body to the morgue. Allegedly, he was at the Erie Insurance Company, attempting to file a claim on his daughter's estate. Relatives and friends would recall that at Hilda's funeral in New Berlin, Edna was oddly unemotional; she did not shed a single tear. Meanwhile, neighbors were gossiping. Edna, one of them was sure, had demanded "Where's my fur coat?" over and over as her daughter lay groaning on a cot, covered in fatal burns. Another neighbor claimed that she had seen Ralph pawing through a drawer looking for documents when he should have been with his dying daughter. This same woman noted that when Edna had run past her on the staircase, she had refused to answer a question about how the fire had started, shouting only, "Get out of my way or I'll sock ya' in the jaw!"

Tipped off by Hilda and Ralph's suspicious neighbors, authorities reviewed the case file and discovered that Edna had told two different stories about what had happened. In one, she said that Hilda had probably tried to light the gas stove. In another, she claimed to have been cleaning a dress with gasoline when the pan holding the gasoline had ignited. Attempting to throw it out a window, she had dropped it on Hilda by accident. The child had gone up in flames.

Unable to locate Edna and Ralph for further questioning, Erie officials began a search, and soon the Erie public was fully in the thrall of the "manhunt." In fact, Edna and Ralph had gone to New York to be married. Just three days after becoming man and wife, they were arrested while staying with relatives. The two were held in the Norwich, New York, county jail for five days after a judge refused their petition for release, calling them a "flight risk." Edna strenuously protested her innocence through hours of questioning without a lawyer of her own present. During this time, according to historical accounts, Edna was often tearful. Sometimes she paced her cell; other times she seemed on the verge of collapse. According to officials, she was often stoic, motionless, and somber. After she was given medication to sleep at night, Edna allegedly began to beg for opiates throughout the day. Soon newspaper stories were portraying her as a craven drug user. Edna's infamy, quite separate from Ralph's, had begun.

Erie had been filling up with journalists in anticipation of Edna and Ralph's trial, and when their train pulled into the station, they were besieged by dozens of photographers and reporters. From this moment on, Edna was no longer referred to in news stories as a "mother." Reports now described her as a "stepmother" instead. Laythe notes that whereas many of Edna's contemporaries had initially dismissed the story, finding it implausible that a mother would kill her own child, the stepmother wrinkle suggested more sinister possibilities. In screeching headlines, Edna was the "Wicked Stepmother" and "Erie's Own Torch Killer."

The trial itself was a spectacle. From the day it began, the prosecution's strategy was simple and straightforward: the lawyers portrayed Edna as vicious, "poor," and "jealous," suggesting that she had wanted Ralph, the money they had earned, and Hilda's inheritance all for herself. She was, in their descriptions, a textbook wicked stepmother — callous, unmaternal, rapacious. Defense lawyers countered that the evidence against Edna was purely circumstantial. Where was the proof? They called an expert witness who testified that yes, it was in fact possible to start a fire with friction in gas, and though Edna's hands were not burned or scarred, that was likely because she had carried the gasoline-filled pan in her apron, which was singed in a pattern consistent with events as Edna had described them. Why, another expert witness for the defense asked, would someone intent on murder use only half the bottle of gas, as Edna had? "Murderers are not concerned with conserving the implement or medium through which the crime was committed," he pointed out. Another expert witness said that it was "perfectly natural for a woman in the condition [Edna] was found in to make conflicting statements as to what happened at the time of the fire."

A few days into the trial, events took a melodramatic turn. A young woman, crying hysterically, walked into the courtroom and embraced an apparently shocked Edna. It was Edna's daughter. They hadn't seen each other in years, and now they clung to each other and sobbed. When Edna herself was questioned, her mantra was "I treated her as if she were my own," as she recounted, over and over, what had happened the day Hilda died. If she had another chance, she insisted, she would give her life for Hilda's. But observers were more interested in what Edna was doing — or not doing — than in what she was saying. Laythe notes that according to newspaper reports, while her eyes welled with tears, none fell. Edna never sobbed; her voice did not break or even quaver. Unlike during the emotional courtroom reunion with her biological daughter days earlier, and just as at Hilda's funeral, when Edna told the story of her stepdaughter's death, she was subdued, dry-eyed, and relatively composed. Jurors deliberated for more than twenty-four hours. Finally, a lone dissenting juror was persuaded to change his vote. Edna Mumbulo was found guilty.

At the Muncy Institute for Women in Muncy, Pennsylvania, Edna served eight years of her ten-to-twenty-year sentence, exhibiting model behavior. In 1938, the judge who had presided over Edna's trial recommended that she be granted a pardon, saying he had always had doubts about her guilt. Edna rejoined Ralph (who had never been charged), and they moved to Rochester, New York. Edna Mumbulo, "the Torch Killer of 1930," died in the Erie County Geriatric Center, forgotten, in 1990.

Did Edna Mumbulo do it? We will never know. And we might view the unknowability of her crime as the story's single most important detail, the place to start. Why, we might ask, were people so sure that Edna had committed a crime when there was no proving it? How could she be convicted on the basis of circumstantial evidence alone? And how could people hold such fanatical convictions about something that could not possibly be proved?

In Edna's case, it seems, the stepmother role added an element of "knowability" to an indeterminate scenario. Suspicions of her and a kind of frenzied interest in her being "the Torch Killer" coincided with the moment she was referred to as a "stepmother" rather than a "mother" in the press. In fact, given the number of people who initially dismissed the story as impossible — "Mothers don't kill their own children!" — it is arguable that Edna would not have been prosecuted at all had she not been portrayed as a stepmother in the first place. Once the protective halo of motherhood was wrenched away, Edna was caught up in the nets of a larger cultural story, the story of stepmothers and stepchildren, as well as our culture's ur-story of the wicked stepmother. Edna's guilt, hazy and conjectural and circumstantial as it was, crystallized into a recognizable form, became legible and meaningful, Laythe suggests, because the jurors and the public "organized the known facts into a wicked stepmother framework."

To better understand precisely what kind of thinking, feeling, and unconscious associations were likely influencing the jurors who convicted Edna and the public that condemned her, a detour of sorts is in order — a detour through dark forests, darker hearts, and the gingerbread houses of plotting cannibals and their innocent victims.

FAIRY TALES AND EDNA'S FATE

Ralph Mumbulo, initially accused of murder as well, was never prosecuted, let alone convicted. Of course, he had not been home during the blaze. But the charge of accessory to murder (those visits to the insurance company had aroused much suspicion) were quickly dropped as well. In fact, once Edna had been publicly accused, there was a refusal to acknowledge, to even consider, the possibility of Ralph's complicity. Why was this so? What made Ralph seem so innocent, so suddenly? As a biological parent, Ralph was in fundamental ways above suspicion. But Ralph was arguably exonerated by something even more powerful than blood ties. In many ways, the public's refusal to go after him, its unspoken agreement to forgive him or at least overlook his complicity, had its roots in centuries-old fairy tales, specifically the Grimm brothers' versions of tales such as *Snow White, Hansel and Gretel,* and *The Juniper Tree,* as well as their historical antecedents in ancient Greece and Rome. In fact, the story of Edna, Ralph, and Hilda resembles and repeats the central structural and thematic aspects of these previous texts about destructive stepmothers, duped fathers, and innocent victims in a number of uncanny, fundamental ways. While the fairy tales may have frightened and thrilled us when we were young, we are likely less familiar with their earlier, rawer versions, the ones that were ultimately altered for children's ears. It is worth noting that fairy tales such as these were told and retold during historical periods when mortality rates were staggeringly high. Growing up was far from certain; women commonly died in childbirth, and entire families succumbed to disease, harvest failures, and starvation. The gruesome violence of the earlier versions of these tales, with their devouring mothers, murderous stepmothers, and indifferent fathers, may have been less cautionary tales or fantastical departures from reality than embroidered meditations on the terrifying risks of everyday life and the inability of parents to protect their children from perils of all sorts.

THE REAL *SNOW WHITE:* NARCISSISM AND CANNIBALISM, PASSIVITY AND INNOCENCE

The Grimms' post-1810 version of *Snow White* gets started by committing a murder of its own. It transforms an earlier tale of a girl with an evil *mother* into the story of a girl with a *dead* mother and an evil *step*mother (more of such transformations later). We are all familiar with what kick-starts the narrative. The mirror informs the Wicked Queen that Snow White is the fairest in the land, ushering in a theme that will preoccupy us for hundreds of years: the stepmother's narcissism, which stands in stark contrast to our cultural ideal of maternal selflessness. The queen flies into a rage, demanding that a huntsman take the child into the woods, kill her, and return with her lungs and liver as proof of the deed. But the sympathetic huntsman lets Snow White run off, returning with a wild boar's organs instead. The queen has these boiled in brine and proceeds to eat them, presumably in an attempt to eclipse Snow White not only by having her killed but by ingesting her essence and her beauty as well. Meanwhile, Snow White has stumbled onto the home of seven dwarves, who invite her to stay with them in exchange for housekeeping and cooking. Where, we wonder at this point and others, is Snow White's father? He is simply a gap in the narrative; his absence is the crack through which all menace seeps into the story.

Alas, Snow White's new home is no safe haven. Shortly, the mirror informs the queen that Snow White is still alive, and she springs into action, transforming herself into a crone who attempts to kill the naive and trusting girl first with a lace collar, then with a poisoned comb, and finally with an efficacious poisoned apple. The dwarves, who have warned Snow White repeatedly, return home to find her dead and place her in a crystal coffin on a mountainside. There she remains until a prince discovers her and begs the dwarves to allow him to bring her home to gaze at and "cherish as my beloved." Snow White's victimization is inextricable here from her immobility and passivity: being still, as a hallmark of being acted upon as opposed to acting, is part and parcel of her goodness. During the descent from the mountain, the apple is freed from Snow White's throat. She awakens; she and the prince fall in love. The Wicked Queen comes to their wedding, never suspecting that the celebration to which she has been invited is for her stepdaughter. There she is forced (the story does not specify by whom) to put on a pair of iron slippers heated over a fire and dance in them until she drops dead. Envious and narcissistic like Edna, who reportedly screamed for her fur coat while her stepdaughter lay singed on a cot, the queen is ultimately subjected to social humiliation, her sinister core revealed for all the world to see. In her degrading and spectacular death, the evil schemer is vanquished, less by a passive, innocent Snow White (who never "does" a thing) than by the force of her very own malevolence toward the girl.

HANSEL AND GRETEL AND THE JUNIPER TREE: SCHEMES, TEARS, AND GRUESOME FEASTS

If Snow White's narcissistic stepmother envied the younger girl's beauty, other Grimm stepmothers are characterized by envy that is even more fundamental and destructive. They begrudge their husbands' children the food they eat, the space they take up, even the air they breathe. Repeating many *Snow White* themes, *Hansel and Gretel* and *The Juniper Tree* reframe the stepmother's narcissism as materialism and greed, a kind of primal "hunger" that renders her a murderous cannibal, utterly unable to put her stepchildren first.

Hansel and Gretel is set in a time of famine, an all-too-literal reference to the time in which it was written, and once again the story begins with a biological mother who has, by the 1840 version, been transformed into a stepmother. One night, when there is nothing left in the cupboard, she tells her husband that they must get rid of the children, two additional mouths to feed. Initially resistant, her husband eventually agrees. Hansel and Gretel, overhearing the plot from their bedroom next door, where they lie awake with hunger, are petrified. Gretel sobs, but Hansel plans. Running outside, he fills his pockets with pebbles. The next day, their stepmother announces that the family is going into the forest to chop wood. Hansel drops his stones as they walk through the woods. Later, the children find themselves abandoned in the forest. Gretel wails inconsolably when she realizes they have been left there to die. But Hansel has marked their way home. Waiting until the moon comes up, they follow the pebbles back to their cottage. Their father is overjoyed to see them. In deceptive doublespeak — the language of scheming and plotting — their stepmother insists that she, too, is happy: "Why did you wicked children stay in the woods so long? We thought you would never return!"

Predictably, the stepmother renews her campaign to banish the children shortly after their return. Overhearing her whispers, Hansel tries to go outside to collect pebbles once again, but he discovers that his stepmother, ever the plotter, has locked the door. The next morning, she gives each of the children a heel of bread as they set off to "chop more wood" deep in the forest. Hansel tears his bread into crumbs, dropping these along the trail. This time when the husband and wife sneak off, however, the children discover that the birds have eaten their markers. Again Gretel sobs and sobs. Bereft and nearly starving, they wander the woods for three days, until they come upon a magical candy house. A witch, pretending to be kind like their deceptive stepmother, lures them inside with a mouthwatering meal and clean beds. But she soon reveals her wickedness, locking Hansel in a woodshed, forcing Gretel to work for her, and cackling about her plan to fatten the young boy up to eat him. Again Gretel wails, while the clever Hansel holds out a stick instead of his finger whenever the nearsighted witch tries to determine how fat he is, effectively undoing her plot. In the end, Gretel pushes the witch into the oven and frees Hansel. The children return to their delighted and relieved father, whose wife has died, cementing her association with the baked witch. Entirely invisible in *Snow White,* the father of Hansel and Gretel is innocent despite his complicity.

The cannibalistic witch and the stepmother, separated yet linked in *Hansel and Gretel,* are sutured together seamlessly in *The Juniper Tree,* one of the wildest, most violent, and most graphic of the surviving Grimm tales. Based on a late-eighteenth-century tale by Philipp Otto Runge, the version of the story published by the Grimm brothers in 1857 begins with a childless couple praying for a baby. Soon the wife senses she is pregnant and is overjoyed. She gorges herself on juniper berries, however, and falls ill, telling her husband, "If I die, bury me beneath the juniper tree." She recovers and gives birth to their child, a son, only to die of happiness when she sees him for the first time. Later, the man remarries and has a second child, a girl, with his new wife. This woman "feels nothing but love" when she looks at her daughter, Marlene, but is filled with hatred whenever she sees her stepson.

One day, she offers the boy an apple from a heavy wooden chest. As he bends down to retrieve the fruit, she slams the top of the chest onto his neck, decapitating him. Although she acts out of passion, this murderous stepmother is a schemer, just like the wicked stepmothers in *Snow White* and *Hansel and Gretel.* Cleverly, she ties the boy's head back onto his neck with a handkerchief and puts the apple in his hand. "Slap your brother if he will not speak to you when you ask him for the apple," she instructs her daughter, and when the girl does, the boy's head falls off. Marlene, horrified, sobs hysterically, reminding us of Gretel. In response, her mother — ostensibly loving, maternal, and protective — tells her, "Don't tell a soul about the dreadful thing you've done!" Then, in a moment of mythical horror, she proceeds to chop the boy up and cook him in a stew. Marlene continues to wail inconsolably. It is as if her cries are a musical score to the unfolding plot, so often are they mentioned.

When her husband returns, the woman tells him that his son is off visiting relatives and serves him the gruesome stew. Marlene cries and cries as she gathers the bones of her half brother in a silk handkerchief. These she places under the juniper tree, to magical effect. In a flash of light, a bird emerges from the top of the tree, and Marlene's heart is filled with joy. The bird sings a song to her before she returns home:

My mother she slew me
My father he ate me
My sister, Marlene
Gathered my bones,
Tied them in silk
For the juniper tree
Tweet tweet, what a fine bird am I!

The bird then sings the same song to various villagers, who reward it with three — again that number — different objects: a gold chain, a pair of children's shoes, and a millstone. Flying to the family's home, the bird sings until the boy's father emerges from the house, then drops a gold chain on his neck. When the boy's half sister emerges, the bird drops the pair of shoes for her. Hearing them exclaim about the beautiful and generous bird, the stepmother goes outside herself. The bird drops the third object, the millstone, on her head, killing her. At the instant of her death, the bird is transformed back into the boy, and the family, reconfigured and set right, goes inside the house together and eats. Like Hansel, the clever bird, this time magically aided by his dead mother, schemes against his plotting stepmother, subverting her and bringing himself back from death to life. And as in *Hansel and Gretel,* the bird-boy of *The Juniper Tree* is ultimately transformed from an active schemer back into a passive innocent who rejoins his family.

How can this happen, given that the father has allowed himself to be deceived by the evil stepmother here and, even worse, as in *Hansel and Gretel,* has colluded in her plotting? How are fathers absolved of their crimes? One possibility is that in the logic of the fairy tale world, the vanquished, all-bad stepmother erases the father's complicity, rendering him all-good. Bruno Bettelheim, in *The Uses of Enchantment,* famously noted that such "splitting off" in fairy tales allows children to process their own ambivalence about their complicated relationships with real-life parents, who may seem both "good" and "bad" and who elicit tremendously powerful feelings of both love and hate in their offspring.

THROUGH THE LENS OF FAIRY TALES: EDNA AS DRY-EYED SCHEMER

Precisely this type of splitting — first of mothers from fathers, then of stepmothers from mothers, of the all-bad from the all-good — likely played a central role in ensuring that Edna Mumbulo, and not her husband, would pay the price for the crime that was supposedly committed. The story begins, in classic fairy-tale style, with a dead, generous (the $6,000 inheritance) mother and a beautiful child. Edna, like the wicked stepmother of the Grimm brothers' tales, is presumed to be full of destructive envy, greed, and narcissism, a primal hunger that leads her to put her own appetites above the needs of all others, even the most vulnerable. Like the cannibalistic wife driven by a primitive logic (because the child has consumed what is rightfully hers, she will literally consume the child), Edna wants for herself what she believes she should not have to share — in this case, her own wages and those of her husband, as well as the inheritance. Unlike the passive, innocent girls in the fairy tales (Gretel and Marlene), whose copious tears testify to their goodness and their victimization, Edna is conspicuously dry-eyed. In not crying, she becomes, in the logic of the fairy tale to whose laws she is subjected, an anti-victim, a perpetrator even.

The number three, so important in all the fairy tales, is at work in calamitous ways in Edna's story as well. The very fact that she has lived in and been part of a triad — a "family" of three, which was not one — was presumably fatal for Hilda. Like the stepmother in *The Juniper Tree*, Edna loves her own child best and, in spite of her protests to the contrary, presumably feels "nothing but hatred" when she sees Hilda. Indeed, we are suspicious when we read that Edna's first husband and Ralph's first wife both died unexpectedly. Presumably, jurors would have been aware of these facts and were bound to have wondered whether this might be not her first but her third killing. And as in *Snow White* and *The Juniper Tree,* Edna's guilt is established in a spectacular and humiliating public forum. Inside the home, the murderous plot is hatched and executed, the grisly feast is consumed, but outside, in the purifying light of day, in the public realm, it is exposed for all to see, and the child is avenged. Edna's story seems custom-made to satisfy our desire for formulaic stories of scheming, murderous stepmothers, and sensational retribution.

Perhaps most important of all, like the evil stepmothers of fairy tales, Edna is presumed to be a plotter and a deceptive schemer, a woman who does things. In this way, she stands in contrast to the passive child/victim, who is acted upon and against, as well as to the complicit but essentially innocent father, who is cajoled or deceived into going along with an evil plan. In this way, Edna, like every other wicked stepmother, is indispensable to and inextricable from the very pleasures of the narrative itself. Without her — her evil, her plotting, and most of all her power, which leads directly to her crimes and guilt — there would be no motion forward, no action, and literally no story. Harvard folklorist Maria Tatar could be writing about Edna when she describes the Disney version of Snow White's stepmother as "a figure of gripping narrative energy . . . [whose] disruptive, disturbing, and divisive presence . . . allowed the film to take such powerful hold in our culture." Motoring the engine of the plot that excited and petrified the public, Edna may very well have been convicted precisely because of the centuries-old, ingrained association between thrilling plots, innocent child victims, and scheming, *guilty* stepmothers.

ANCIENT STEPMOTHERS, ANCIENT BIASES

Jurors in the Mumbulo case may have unwittingly convicted her in part based on cultural logic that reaches back as far as the origins of the Western literary tradition. For the fairy tales underpinning the public reaction to Edna's story were themselves indebted to even older texts and beliefs. Classicist Patricia Watson points out

40

that the *saeva noverca,* or "evil stepmother," is a stock character in ancient Roman myths and literature. In particular, she notes, the stepmother who poisons her stepson to gain his inheritance or who attempts to seduce him seems to have been a Roman obsession. Hesiod, in *Works and Days,* observes that there are good and bad days, or mother days and stepmother days. Other uses of the word *noverca* in Latin suggest the linking of stepmothers with peril, deception, and treachery. For example, in military jargon, *noverca* was used to describe a place that was too risky for soldiers to make camp, such as a site where they could be easily seen by the enemy.

According to Watson, the ancient Greeks also associated stepmothers with danger. Plato advised that widowers with children should be forbidden to remarry, and Euripides, in *Alcestis,* has the eponymous protagonist plead with her husband not to remarry after her death: "And do not remarry and impose on these children a stepmother, who, being a woman more ill-intentioned than me through jealousy will lay hands on your children and mine. Please do not do this, I entreat you. For a stepmother comes as an enemy to the children of a former union and is no more gentle than a viper."

A stepmother's capacity for evil was presumed to persist even after her death. In the Garland of Philip, a poet writes, "A boy was [honoring] the grave pillar of his stepmother, a small stone, / thinking that in changing life for death she had changed her / character. / But the pillar fell and killed the boy as he was bending over the grave. / O stepsons, avoid even the grave of a stepmother!" Similarly, Seneca referred to the story of a stepmother convicted of poisoning her stepson. Under torture, she named her own daughter as an accomplice. Seneca described the woman as *"nefaria mulier, filiae quoque noverca, ne mori quidem potuit nisi ut occideret":* "an abominable woman, a stepmother even to her daughter, she could not even die without killing."

Centuries later, Edna was a kind of palimpsest, an amalgam of these centuries of representations and preoccupations. For Edna, fire, rather than poison, was the fatal element in her witch's arsenal.

And she stood to gain not just her husband and his undivided love, attention, and income, but, like the *saeva noverca,* her stepchild's inheritance as well. Finally, her contemporaries likely suspected that killing simply satisfied some deep and undeniable malice in Edna, a perverse "evil for its own sake," like that of the woman under torture who indicted her own daughter, or the dead woman who killed her stepson with her grave pillar.

Edna's story continues, in many ways, to be our own. Although she was "real," she was also perceived through the lens of the mythical, and painted, in strokes both bold and meticulous, with colors from a palette that had been determined centuries before and thousands of miles away. Like the wicked stepmothers of Seneca's declamations and Plato's social criticism, Edna teeters between the fantastical and the real, the historical and the histrionic. Like the cannibals, narcissists, and murderesses of the Grimm brothers, she grips and repels us, and so she must be to blame. *Guilty.* Weaving together the mythical and the mundane, Edna remains maddeningly out of reach. Once we give up our conviction that we already know who she is, surrender the hope that we can ever figure out what she has actually done, she slips beyond our comprehension.

New Fairy Tales, Old Cultural Logic: Hildur

Once upon a time, we thought that stepmothers were bad. But non-stepmothers, and a few stepmothers as well, might be tempted to insist that things are better now. Aren't they? After all, statistically speaking, stepfamilies and stepmothers are the new normal. Doesn't that mean that representations of them are bound to be more balanced, more realistic? With this enormous demographic shift under way, isn't the wicked stepmother cliché going the way of gingham aprons and homemade apple pie? In short, no.

As many of us know from firsthand experience, the wicked stepmother myth lives on, continuing to inflect our experiences of being — and having — a stepmother. And the emergence of a new normal brings with it a new cliché as well. The flip side of the stepmonster myth — its updated, thoroughly "modernized" other face — is the equally unrealistic stereotype of what I have often thought of as the stepmartyr/stepmom. Often this pop stepmother is a younger, "cooler," more bionic counterpart to boring, reliable old Mom, a friend to her stepkids instead of the foe of lore, someone originally outrageous and selfish who comes around to understanding that giving it all up for her stepkids is the best thing that could ever happen to her. (The movie *Stepmom*, starring Julia Roberts, and Sally Bjornsen's *The Single Girl's Guide to Marrying a Man, His Kids, and His Ex-Wife* both trace this trajectory.) Enthusiastic and earnest, these new, retooled stepmoms of popular culture never look back. More than anything, they want to do right by and be loved by their stepkids.

Certainly, it is laudable that the media now show us images of a kinder, gentler stepmother. And without a doubt, there are stepmothers who manage — mostly due to felicitous circumstances — to become best girlfriends or good pals with their stepchildren. This cannot be anything but healthy and rewarding for everyone involved. But stepfamily expert Elizabeth Church, Ph.D., asserts that many of these ostensibly new assumptions about stepmothers — such as "You should always put the kids first, even if they're not yours and regardless of whether they mistreat you" — actually reverberate with a very old myth. In the centuries-old Hildur story of Iceland, she notes, a woman agrees to marry a king, but only on the condition that she be allowed to live alone with his daughter, Ingebjorg, for three years first. During this time, she cares for the girl, endeavoring to remove three wicked spells that Ingebjorg's dead mother has put on her. Church points out that contemporary children's stories such as *The Good Stepmother* and the Mary-Kate and Ashley Olsen movie *It Takes Two* have similar themes: a child selects the stepmother for his or her father; the stepmother puts her stepchild first, considering this bond more important than the bond with her husband; and the stepmother acts as a kind of servant to her stepchild. If the Grimm brothers' fairy tales allow children to indulge in the fantasy that their stepmother is all bad and their father is all good, a plethora of contemporary versions of the Hildur story allow them to believe that "Daddy and Stepmom don't really care about each other; *I* am the center of things."

In the Hildur myth and its contemporary descendants, the stepchild is fantastically empowered. "Instead of Cinderella serving her stepmother, we have the good stepmother dancing attendance on her stepchildren," Church notes. It is as if the Hildur myth itself were doing penance for the generations of wicked stepmothers that came before it. And untenable as it is, many women do in fact try to be Hildur to their stepchildren, bending over backward in order to seem nice and be loved and to avoid, at all costs, the fearful possibility of being, or being perceived as being, wicked. In interview after interview, women reiterated these sentiments:

> *I'm scared to tell my stepkids to pick up after themselves. They might think I'm a witch.*

> *I don't mind yelling at my daughter if she's being a pill. Now and again, I let her have it. My stepson? Never. I do everything not to offend him or upset him.*

> *It's terrible, but I kind of tiptoe around [my grown stepchildren] out of fear. Even when I don't like something they do or say, I don't have the nerve to be direct with them like I am with other people. It's been years, and I still bite my tongue around them.*

The stepmonster label, as Church points out, is a tremendously effective gag. Many of us submit to it every day. Hildur is the manifestation of our tendency to overcompensate out of fear.

While our cultural vocabulary about stepmothers and stepmothering may have expanded, it is no more realistic or forgiving of our real needs, feelings, and selves. Between the myth of total self-abnegation and instant love on the one hand and the myth of total, narcissistic evil on the other, we are presented with two impossibly, completely irreconcilable versions of Stepmother to choose from. We can chart the "progress" of stepmothers from destructive and all-powerful to utterly servile and abject, with largely no reality or resting place in between. We would have to have mythical powers, it sometimes seems, to make stepmothering work.

Part II
Remarriage Realities

Chapter Three
"You're Not My Mother!"

And Five Other Universal Step-Dilemmas

Y*ou're* NOT MY MOTHER. You're not my *mother. You're not my mother.*
It is the stepchild's most potent incantation — a warding-off,
a provocation, a taunt. *Go away. Leave me alone. I don't have to listen
to you.* It is a warning, a punishment, a threat. *You're just an intruder,
an afterthought. You're not real.* It is often conjured as the ultimate
insult — a slap in the face, cold water thrown on the ember of the
"blended family" fire you are presumably set on nurturing and fan-
ning, against the odds, into a flame. *You're not my mother.* Whatever
precedes it, whatever comes after, it becomes the heart of the matter, obliterating all else in the sentence, the argument, the relationship. It is where everything starts and ends. It is a fact.

Talk to women with stepchildren, read the studies by psychologists, interview the experts, and the truth about stepfamilies quickly
comes into focus: stepfamilies are different from first families. The
notion that stepmothers and stepchildren should be able to coexist
with one another, share with one another, love or even (sometimes)
like one another without ambivalence — the kind of ambivalence
that sometimes seems as if it will split us in two — is beyond wistfully
sentimental. It is, the research demonstrates, wrong. A number of
studies have revealed what may strike women with stepchildren as
a stunningly obvious but virtually unspoken fact: stepfamilies are
not as bonded or cohesive as nuclear families. The ties do not bind
in the same way we presume they should and more frequently do

in a traditional family; stepparent-stepchild relationships are not as emotionally close as parent-child relationships. In fact, they are frequently characterized by heightened conflict, much of it stemming from feelings of loss and loyalty binds that lead stepchildren to reject and resent us. Other problems include what stepfamily expert Patricia Papernow calls "stepfamily architecture" — the reality that someone, namely the stepparent, is the outsider in the family structure. Whether we live with our stepchildren or not, whether we have children of our own or came to his family as a single woman, we may fight the fact of stepfamily difference for years, feeling that we should be able to make us all closer than we are. Yet only 20 percent of adult children feel close to their stepmothers, according to a landmark longitudinal study by clinical psychologist and stepfamily expert E. Mavis Hetherington. Similarly, in her comprehensive study of 173 adults whose parents had divorced, psychologist Constance Ahrons, Ph.D., learned that whereas fewer than one in three children with divorced and remarried parents think of their stepmothers as a parent, more than half regard their stepfathers as a parent. Fifty percent of those whose moms remarried were happy about it, but less than 30 percent were pleased when Dad remarried. Inserting real human feelings and responses into these dry facts, imagining the lives and experiences behind them, drives the point home: although stepfamily life is not easy for anyone, being a stepmother is the most difficult role of all.

For thirty-four-year-old Ella, a social worker, the challenges are both internal and external. She and her husband have three kids together, and he has two from a previous relationship, all under age ten. "His kids live across town. When they forget something here and my husband wants to drive right over there and deliver it to them after they've been here for the weekend, right when my kids want to wrestle with him, I say, 'Hold on. They can come get it tomorrow. Or we can drop it off at school for them.' I want to make sure everyone gets their fair time together as a family." Ella also wishes she could have a professional photographer do a family portrait of her husband, herself, and their three kids. "The problem is that it feels mean toward his kids," she told me. "We can't do that. Or can we? I mean, we *are* a family separate from them, too. Right?" How "blended" are we, we ask ourselves, and how blended should we aspire to be? How close?

A few basic dilemmas create conflict for women with stepchildren. The five discussed in this chapter are by no means an exhaustive consideration. But based on conversations with stepmothers and experts, they are nearly universal. Just knowing about these "step-dilemmas" and seeing them spelled out in black and white may demystify them and help us feel less lost, less isolated, and less at fault when step issues threaten to overwhelm us.

STEP-DILEMMA 1: THE MYTH OF THE BLENDED FAMILY

"Ugh. It's just so exactly *not* what we are," a quiet and articulate thirty-eight-year-old woman named Annie, whose father remarried after her mother died a decades ago, nearly shouted at one point during my interview with her, trying to help me get it. "Blended my *arse*," another woman said with a laugh, summing up the general consensus among stepmothers I spoke with: the blended family — both the term and the idea — is a big lie. Virtually everyone I interviewed for this project told me that he or she disliked the term "blended family," which the media loves. For many of us, "blended family" may feel particularly disingenuous when we have children of our own — either with our husbands or from a previous marriage — and our stepchildren live elsewhere. For others, it feels like a negation, paving over all the very real bumps and difficulties and differences of stepfamily life, implying that they are soothed and smoothed — or should be, or even *can* be. In general, saying "our blended family," pretending to aspire to it, gives short shrift to what is perhaps the most impressive accomplishment of stepfamilies: that we manage to survive in spite of so much dissonance and distinctness, so many lumps. Stepfamily life is not smooth.

The National Stepfamily Resource Center, or NSRC (formerly the Stepfamily Association of America), a consortium of stepfamily experts and a clearinghouse of helpful information for stepfamilies, actually urges therapists and other professionals in the field to avoid the term "blended family" precisely because it engineers such unrealistic expectations and elicits feelings of failure and guilt. Francesca Adler-Baeder, coordinator of the NSRC, explained to me the ways in which the term is out of touch with the reality of stepfamily life. "It paints the picture of the stepfamily as one cohesive entity," she said. "But what does that mean for the child who has two households? That he or she has to choose? Moreover, research shows us that while cohesion is comparatively low in the stepfamily, the stepfamily can be functioning very well. People connect to each other in different ways in stepfamilies, with different levels of attachment. Making blending the standard can make us feel we've failed when really stepfamilies are just different."

Patricia Papernow, who does not use the term "blended family" in her practice or her writing, had this to say: "When stepfamilies 'blend,' somebody is getting creamed. Either the 'family' is using the old parent-child model and the stepparent gets creamed, or the adult couple has set up a whole slew of new expectations and rules and the kids are getting creamed, asked to move too fast." The bottom line, Paper-now said, is that early cohesion or blending is an indication that issues have been swept under the rug. They're still there, however, and inevitably, she insisted, "they come back to bite you."

But many of us, including those of us who live its impossibility every day — or on holidays and alternate weekends — keep expecting that we *can* blend. Why? It is understandable, perhaps, that our husbands want to maintain the fantasy of a perfect family frappé — it would absolve them of a lot of guilty feelings if our lives were in fact an effortless, ambrosial smoothie, with love all around. Therapists are in the business of holding out hope and helping us feel better, or helping us live with our feelings. Perhaps that is why so many of them refer to their work as "blended family practice." Books for stepparents want us to feel encouraged, too, and optimistic. Sometimes, to that admirable end, they use this unfortunate, unrealistic term, perpetuating an unfortunate, unrealistic myth. But what about us, stepmothers, who should and do know better? Why do *we* continue to circle back to the blended family, embracing not just the term but the underlying notion that everything could be perfect, that it *should* be perfect, even though this idea often makes us feel frustrated, cynical, hurt, or somehow bad, like failures? Gabby, a vivacious woman in her fifties with three grown stepchildren, has struggled with the idea of the blended family plenty. She told me, "I have it in my head that I am going to get all his kids here for the Jewish holidays again. It happened once, and it was nice. Then when we invited them the next year, my stepdaughter said to my husband, 'It's been done already,' and my stepson asked him, 'Why do we have to do *that* again?' I was so hurt, I started to cry. I felt so dissed. I would still love to have them here with us for the holidays. I don't know why!" And she began to cry.

Perhaps the blended family endures because, like Gabby, we want it, because we need it. It is frightening, after all, to think that so many of us are taking a risk that so very easily might not break our way. When I asked Gabby why it is so important to her to have her stepkids around when they obviously don't want to be, and why she keeps trying, she thought for a moment, then said, "My husband's not young. We had [our daughter] Suki late in his life, and I'm not getting any younger either. I want Suki to have someone other than us, someone to help her and love her and make her feel like something bigger than just the three of us. And I want them to be there to help her when we're old and need to be taken care of, too. I just don't want her to be so alone, burdened with us, all by herself." Gabby started by discussing something very specific — her husband is older — but in the end, she circled back to the simple idea of family and togetherness, of not being alone, of something that endures. This, it seems, is what she really wants, and she will keep trying, regardless of the toll that pursuing this phantasm of idealized togetherness takes on her self-esteem and her happiness.

Every family culture is different, of course, as varied as the people in it. So it goes with our expectations and hopes. Unlike Gabby, some women with stepchildren may actually be relieved when his children opt out of a holiday invitation or a weekend visit, knowing there will be another chance and looking forward to a little privacy. But many of us find that we can't give up on the dream of the blended family entirely. It continues to aggravate and reassure us in equal measure, promising something we are perhaps too cynical to believe entirely yet too optimistic to renounce.

STEP-DILEMMA 2: THE MYTH OF THE MATERNAL STEPMOTHER

The blended family myth depends on and derives its potency from another myth, a notion just as widely embraced, just as dearly cherished, and just as fantastical — namely, that all women should love all children all the time. It is an unrelenting and pitiless expectation and makes no exceptions — not for the stepmothers of adults who have busy lives and careers and partnerships of their own; not for women who marry men with reckless, angry young sons hell-bent on alienating them or jealous, resentful daughters who wish they'd disappear. Somehow, it seems, we have gone from praising and valuing women who would sacrifice anything for their own children to expecting that women should sacrifice equally for the children who are *not* their own. Indeed, most books for stepmothers position the fact that we are not our stepchildren's mothers as a limitation, a sad, hard truth that we must work to resign ourselves to and accept. Often we hear advice like this from friends, therapists, and the media: "Don't start thinking of them as 'your' children, and don't ever refer to them that way in conversation." Or this: "They already *have* a mother. Remember that." But in general our culture refuses to acknowledge the flip side of the assertion that we are not their mothers, the ugly, unsentimental truth of stepmothering, a truth at once liberating and brutal: We are *not* their mothers. We did not give birth to them, and in many cases we did not come into their lives while they were babies or even toddlers. Our stepchildren do not feel like our children. And so logically, inevitably, many of us do not — cannot — feel maternal toward them. While we did indeed choose a man with children, it would be disingenuous (for most of us) to pretend that we chose the children. We chose him, and they came on the side. "You knew what you were getting into," unsympathetic listeners might say when we complain about our difficulties with his kids. "What did you expect?"

Stepmothering is a country apart, yet it is not so utterly foreign. For example, many of those who judge us most harshly for what we "chose" may also be in relationships that they "chose" but are less than perfect and sometimes conflictual — relationships with mothers-in-law come immediately to mind. Imagine saying, "You knew what you were taking on when you married a man with a mother. What did you expect?" Or perhaps our beloved husband can't stand our beloved sister. In spite of these other models of imperfect relationships and tensions that often characterize a marriage, the notion that a relationship between a stepmother and a child is conflictual or even less than perfect sets people on edge, because these dice are loaded; a woman who doesn't like kids — even those not her own — every second is "unnatural."

And so it is with great confusion and guilt that we find that our feelings for our stepchildren are sometimes markedly unmaternal. One stepmother told me, angry and ashamed, that the smell of her stepdaughter (not an unpleasant smell, just a particular one) and the girl's physical clumsiness nearly turned her stomach sometimes. "Some days I can't bear it," she confided urgently, convinced, it seemed, that this was a black mark on her soul. Other stepmothers are nearly driven mad by the mess their stepchildren make — at once an all-too-concrete reality and a symbol of everything they cannot easily put up with or overlook. Stepmothers tend to seize on these details, these grating particularities, as if they explained everything. In a sense, they do; they sum up our inability to tolerate the way a mother would and express, in convoluted form, our inability to forgive ourselves for it. It must be the tic, the habit, the smell of the child, the jumble of dirty laundry she leaves on the living room floor that we find so unappealing; it couldn't be the child herself. That would make us terrible, and we hope, we need to believe, that we are not.

One woman told me how enthusiastically she looked forward to weekends without her stepson around, clearly feeling guilty about it. Shaking her head, she noted, "I think I must be missing that chip: the mommy chip." She fails to see, it seems to me, that this explanation explains nothing at all. She won't know if she's lacking a mommy chip — maternal drive, maternal sentiment, whatever it is that she means — based on her responses to her *step*child. Mommy chips, if they can be said to exist, are for *mommies*. This truth is so obvious that we continue to look past it, to search for something more complex, more indirect, more tortured, to account for our ambivalence toward our stepchildren. They don't love us like they love their mothers, and it is supposed to be a dagger in our hearts. We don't say it, but how many times have we thought, *Don't worry: I don't want to be your mother.*

STEP-DILEMMA 3: DIFFICULT DEVELOPMENTAL STAGES

Mothers know that kids go through phases when they are more and less lovable. They witness their feelings for their children ebb and flow, subside and surge again, day after day. Mothers are used to feeling stymied, frustrated, pushed too far. They often vent to one another: "Why didn't anybody tell me my son would be even more impossible at four than he was at two? I can't stand him!" Or, "Let's send all the teenage girls to an island. They deserve each other." But when we become stepmothers, having these thoughts — let alone articulating them — feels terribly taboo. "If I told you what I really think and feel on the bad days," one women with a teenage stepson said to me, laughing, "you'd have to call child protective services." The mother's valve for letting off steam is not nearly as available to stepmothers. Perhaps this in part explains something experts have pointed out: that stepmothers — even when they are seasoned mothers as well — tend to experience difficulty with a stepchild as ongoing, unremitting, and overwhelming. For example, stepfamily therapist Jamie Kelem Keshet noticed that her patients who were stepmothers might see their partners' children "as having enduring opinions and attitudes rather than expressing the feeling of the moment." If a step-child shouts, "I don't feel like talking to you — get away from me!" a stepmother will likely not just retreat. She may very well take the outburst as a statement of fact and avoid the child for days, afraid of further rejection and understandably angry, yes, but also taking the child at his or her word. Keshet calls these "literal and long-lasting interpretations of children's statements" and notes that they can drive a wedge between spouses as well as stepparent and child.

The tough times with his kids may feel especially insurmount-able when a bond between stepmother and stepchild is not com-pletely or incontrovertibly forged, when we can't remember the time when this teenager was cute and sweet and cuddly. The good news is that these difficult interactions may in fact be just what our grandmothers used to call them, "a phase." Research and firsthand experience suggest that the "terrible twos," age four, and especially adolescence are difficult times for a woman to enter a stepchild's life. At any of these stages, the stepchild, in the throes of attempting to individuate, rejecting adults and authority figures left and right, is at his or her most alienating.

The tantrums of the terrible twos are tough on everyone, but a stepmother is probably more prone than others to feeling person-ally rejected or implicated by a toddler's frustrations. She is likely to wonder whether she is provoking the child or creating stress just by being around. Still, two-year-olds become three-year-olds, with winning ways and charms. And as they become articulate, relatively masterful four-year-olds, their frustrations and tantrums may largely abate. Yet during this phase of development, they may become mouthy, truculent, and painfully direct. "I don't like you!" can be hard to hear from an otherwise adorable preschooler whose father you're dating or married to. In addition, four is the age of attach-ment to the opposite-sex parent. Boys become romantically and sexually interested in their mothers and, fearing the father's retri-bution, may shirk from him. He becomes, in their eyes, the ultimate rival. The same holds true for girls, who grow so attached to their fathers that they may say, as my older stepdaughter reportedly did at age four, "It's my turn to be married to you now!" Being the object of such possessiveness is likely to amuse and flatter a parent, and the same-sex parent can likely ride out this phase of being the bad guy with a laugh. It's not quite so easy for a stepparent. As thirty-four-year-old Lauri told me, "Everybody thought it was so cute when my four-and-a-half-year-old stepdaughter would literally walk up to my husband and me and pry our hands apart so she could hold his hand. I had to remind myself that she was only little!"

New York City psychoanalyst Nicholas Samstag, Ph.D., told me that stepmothers in general "may be especially prone to anxiety about their legitimacy." A stepmother may think, *I don't really deserve to be holding his hand or spending time with him at all; his little girl does.* As Samstag pointed out, this "would make the stepmother feel particularly vulnerable, even threatened by such a normal attachment." Although four-year-olds may be alienatingly possessive, rigid, and assertive, they are generally interested in interacting and forming emotional bonds, and these situations may resolve themselves within a year or two or even a few months. The woman who marries a man with toddlers or preschoolers has, statistics tell us, the best shot of all. The (admittedly exhausting) privilege of experiencing our husbands' children as cute, endearing tykes or preschoolers provides a larger context for the predictably awful 'tween and teen years, as well as the often surprisingly tumultuous young adult years, making them more bearable.

Those of us who come into the picture during adolescence, however, are most likely in for turmoil on a scale we could not have imagined. I considered myself something of an expert on teenage girls (I worked in advertising and had a special interest in the teen-girl demographic; later, as cofounder of a market research agency, I went on to study teenage girls in depth), but I often found my stepdaughters' behavior alienating, even appalling.

In fact, they reminded me of myself when I was in junior high — disorientingly labile ("I love you! I hate you!"), gossipy, and manipulative. Putting up with typical teen traits such as self-centeredness and selfishness is hard enough when the kids are your own. When they're *not* your own, it can be, and usually is, excruciating. As forty-year-old Dora told me,

I don't know how we survived my eighteen-year-old stepdaughter's visits in the first year of our marriage. There was always some crying fit, some drama, some bullshit, so that she could have all the attention and make me look like the bad guy. She'd say to her dad, "You're so different now; you're so strict ever since you married Dora. You changed so much!" and then start crying. This always happened when she had asked for something — money, a later curfew, a pair of expensive shoes — and [we] had said no. I used to see red when she tried to blame me like that!

This story has it all — attempts to split the couple, emotional outbursts that cast a pall over the entire day or holiday, and typical teen-girl self-centeredness and melodrama. Putting such pressure on a fragile new marriage can, not surprisingly, be a make-or-break proposition. In fact, it is difficult to imagine a strain greater than living with a teenage girl who is not one's own, and much research confirms this. Although teenage stepsons may be less overtly communicative and jealous, they are not necessarily any easier to deal with. Researchers suggest that boys are more likely to direct aggression, defiance, and rage at others. In addition, it seems that a divorced mother is, in Wake Forest University sociologist Linda Nielsen's words, "more likely to say derogatory or hateful things about the father to her son than to her daughter. This is especially harmful as boys who hold negative opinions of their fathers tend to hold negative opinions of themselves." Such self-esteem issues inevitably lead to acting out around Dad and Stepmom, as well as a host of other problems.

Adolescence and its attendant turmoil is an American cottage industry. There are literally thousands of books on the topic, endless talk shows dedicated to it, article after article in parenting magazines. This is one of the most dangerous things about remarriage with an adolescent stepchild: his or her tendency to decenter us from our own lives, to draw our focus and our energy away from ourselves and our partnerships, to drain us. Teenagers are utterly consumed with the huge task of forging and integrating their identities, a job that requires virtually all their attention. Moreover, sociologists have pointed out that adolescence lasts longer and longer in postindustrial societies such as ours. Even into their early thirties, then, stepchildren may tend, in the words of many a stepmother, to "suck all the oxygen out of the room" when they're around.

Experts suggest a number of strategies for remarriages when there is a teen in residence, any of which might make this volatile and exhausting time seem more survivable. E. Mavis Hetherington recommends timing the remarriage "before a child's tenth birthday and after his or her sixteenth." Miss those sweet spots at your peril, she counsels; otherwise you will find your marriage "on a collision course with a teen's developmental agenda" to reject and individuate. For many of us, however, that advice may be impractical or just too self-abnegating to embrace. Adults have a right to their relationships on their terms, and bad timing vis-à-vis teens and remarriage is something many of us have survived. In these cases, lowered expectations and a mantra such as "This is normal" can take you far. It always helps to accept that your "family" will likely resemble a "dorm roommate" situation rather than an episode of *The Brady Bunch.*

Most important, advises Albany, New York, clinical psychologist Lauren Ayers, Ph.D., who specializes in the treatment of adolescents, pay attention to your own adult life. For example, don't expect yourself to put in a sixteen-hour day with a teenager, even though the teen seems to require it. Limit your emotional investment in a teen. Separate your emotions from his or hers, and do not make your happiness contingent on the teen's being in a good mood. Your life matters as much as the teen's, Ayers emphasizes, knowing our tendency to give in to the pull of the endlessly needy, volatile, and demanding adolescent. In this regard, a stepmother can set an example for her husband, helping to free him from "shackled-to-my-tortured-teen syndrome." The other side of the detachment, and even the occasional dislike we may feel toward our stepchildren when they are in one of their less endearing developmental phases, is that it allows us to model a healthy balance between caring and letting go. My younger stepdaughter, for example, knew whom to turn to when she wanted to go to boarding school and asked me to help her sell the idea to her parents. I sensed that such an option would allow her to opt out of the charged issue of whether to live with Mom or Dad. Without parental sentimentality or guilt clouding my view, I also could see that we *all* might do better with a little physical distance. As it turned out, my stepdaughter morphed into an independent young adult at boarding school, and my marriage got a break from potentially corrosive teen-girl drama at close range. I am convinced that she and I are closer for it.

Patricia Papernow has some additional advice for surviving remarriage with teenage stepchildren. In my interview with her, she outlined her recommendations. First, keep activities with teens one-on-one (dad and child, or stepmom and stepchild), since whole-group activities are bound to activate a teen's urge to opt out or act out and to underscore insider/outsider dynamics as well. Minimize "all of us together" activities in spite of your urge to be the Waltons. Second, keep activities "shoulder to shoulder" rather than "eyeball to eyeball." Puzzles, movies, and baking projects allow you to be with your teenage stepchild yet have a focus other than relating directly to each other. Finally, remember that time apart as a couple is all the more imperative for the woman with teenage stepchildren and her partner — and just retreating to your bedroom at night doesn't count. A weekly date night can give the couple much-needed rejuvenation and relief.

Unfortunately, sometimes such practical steps might be too little too late. As E. Mavis Hetherington reminds us, teens of divorce are more than twice as likely to have serious social and emotional disorders. If difficulty with a teenage stepchild in residence is unremitting, a return to Mom or another living arrangement is an option that may merit consideration. Do not dismiss such alternatives out of hand as proof of failure or wickedness. Marriages require protection from the strain and drain that adolescents often create.

When stepmothers no longer live with their teenage or young-adult stepchildren, or when the stepkids move on figuratively (into young adulthood, college, work, and relationships of their own), a huge burden is lifted, and relations tend to improve. Their messes and hostility are less galling when we must endure them for only a day or two at a time. Rejecting behavior abates when a kid's focus shifts away from you to romance or choosing a college major. We may even find that we unexpectedly become a stepchild's valued confidante. "I guess I could be helpful because I wasn't a parent," Gabby explained as she told me about her stepson seeking her out for advice about safe sex. We alone, perhaps, have the capacity to care for this child without feeling quite as panicked or drawn in by the stomach-churning curves of his life's course.

STEP-DILEMMA 4: COMPETITION

Competition often seems to be at the center of the stepmother-stepchild relationship, informing everything about it. Competition over money, over access to the partner/father, over his time. Competition over influence, over who wields more power — stepmothers, whose arsenal is the present, in all its undeniable relevance and immediacy; or stepchildren, who have at their disposal something equally potent, the nostalgic, seductive sway of the past, with all its sweet details and sentiment and plangency. Competition is the elephant in the room, the big ugly boulder in the road that everyone is supposed to ignore. But ignoring unpalatable realities does not make them go away. Angie, age forty-three and married to a man with two adult children, told me this classic story about stepfamily dynamics.

> They used to all go skiing all the time before I came on the scene. But I can't ski, and I hate the cold. Still, every year they start saying, "Let's go on a ski trip! We used to have so much fun!" It hurts and bothers me that they keep asking, knowing that I can't do it. Last winter, I told my husband they should just go on a weekend ski trip, and I'd stay at home. It seemed like a good compromise to me. They did — and instead of enjoying the peace and quiet, I felt left out

and was pissed when they returned and the kids went on and on about how great it was.

Angie's story expresses what so many of us have felt. Our step-children are always there. Taking up time and space and energy. Demanding. Wanting. Calling. Asking. Being. Excluding us. Life is a pie, and because of them, there is less for us. Once we have to share in this way, it brings out the worst in us; the most infantile, regressed parts of our brains, it seems, are activated. And some-times we lash out. But more often, like Angie, we withdraw, become sullen, lick our wounds in private. We might even nurture those wounds, encourage them to grow, with all the energy and convic-tion of the anger we don't express. Even when we have kids of our own — which is supposed to transform us and make it all better — we may still feel pushed to the margins when his kids appear. And, in fact, his kids may have just this in mind. The challenge of step-family life, the experts concur, is to create a scenario in which no one feels like an outsider.

Angie is an expert scuba diver. Perhaps for their next vacation, they could all go somewhere scuba-friendly, where she could teach her stepkids what she knows rather than being the excluded out-sider on another of their ski excursions. Such simple changes can quickly alter unhealthy dynamics that seem set in stone. These strat-egies can mean the difference between a life that feels unbearable whenever your stepchildren are around and remains tense even when they are not, and a marriage that feels good and right all the time, even if it gets a little bumpy when his kids show up.

Other forms of competition, such as those over money and access to Dad, may be more difficult to resolve. The challenge here may be to simply take the steps we can, then put our energies elsewhere.

Competition over Money

There is nothing like money to bring the fractures and conflicts in a remarried family to the surface — or to create new ones. "If it weren't for them, there would be more for us," a woman with step-children seethes, depositing her paycheck and writing a check for child support. "There goes the inheritance," a stepchild cracks when her father tells her that he's going to marry a younger woman. We all know the clichés, but why is it so hard to shake the stereotypes — of the entitled step-brat or the rapacious stepmonster — even when we, stepmothers and stepchildren alike, want to be gracious and fair rather than grasping?

Perhaps, most obviously, the answer is because money is real, and it is finite. There is only so much of it to go around. It does no good to deny that the stakes may be very high indeed for everyone involved when a stepmother comes onto the scene. Just how threatening this change will feel depends on a number of things, among them the type of remarriage and the financial situations, temperaments, and anxieties of the individual players.

When a childless woman with wealth or a job marries a man with children, for example, there may be issues between husband and wife about whether and how much she will contribute financially to his children's lives. But overall there will be a relatively low incidence of conflict between her and his kids over money. When both partners bring kids to the remarriage picture, there is likely a feeling of symmetry and even less of a tendency to fixate on or argue about finances and fairness. Many couples in this situation seem to settle on a "mostly merged" financial strategy (for example, while they keep college savings apart, they may contribute equally to all other expenses — utilities, mortgage, food, spending money for all the kids, etc.).

By contrast, when a woman without wealth or a job marries a man with children or a newly married woman quits her job, statistics show a higher likelihood of conflict of all sorts. This configuration seems to bring out all our impulses to draw lines and create sides: My husband and me versus *them*, the intruders. Our dad and us, the *real* relationship, versus *her*, the interloper. Money is such a real thing, its value so literal, that we may forget that it is also a symbol — and as such the likely site for acting out a number of our unacknowledged, unconscious desires: to even things out, settle the score, prove our importance or primacy, even express our feelings of victimization. *Those kids are a black hole! We're never going to be able to retire because of them! I guess we can kiss grad school goodbye — Stepmonster's redecorating!*

Phil Michaels, a trust and estates lawyer who also teaches at New York Law School, has pointed out that, in addition to the fact that money is at once very real and very symbolic, there is a third reason it can cause friction between women and their adult stepchildren. "A generation ago, inheritance was an unexpected but welcome windfall," he told me. Today, adults frequently count on an inheritance and literally budget it into their lives. "So if their father remarries, buys a new place, redecorates it, goes on expensive vacations with his wife . . . his kids [may feel], *Hey, there goes college for* my *kids.*"

This enormous cultural shift in expectations toward a feeling of entitlement to a parent's assets, which has crept up on us between generations, can create frustration, mistrust, and fear on both sides. More than one woman told me that her adult stepchildren had lobbied their father to pressure her into signing a prenuptial agreement before the wedding, in order to protect what they felt was "rightfully" theirs. It goes without saying that such presumption and overstepping of boundaries, if it goes unchecked by Dad, can create hard feelings and uneasiness for years to come. As Julie, a fifty-nine-year-old woman with a grown stepson, told me, "I have nightmares about [my stepson] dragging me into court if my husband dies first. It's not like there's a ton of money. It's just that . . . I suspect that me getting *anything* at all is going to [upset him]. He seems to feel [things] *should* stay the same for him . . . even though his father remarried."

Like Julie, many women with stepchildren find themselves wishing for a solution that acknowledges that they have sacrificed and given much in a marriage, without shortchanging his kids in the process. This desire for balance tends to feel especially urgent if we have children of our own. Remarried couples with children may find that it's worth the money and time to talk to a trust and estates lawyer. "The trend is away from just divvying everything up evenly between all the kids of the two marriages, or between all the kids and the wife," Michaels told me. "Couples will come in and say, '[His] kids are older and everything's paid for. They'll need less than our daughter, who's only two, if one or both of us dies tomorrow." There are many paradigms for fairness, from splitting it up so that everyone gets the same amount to couples who vow to die broke.

Michaels offered one general and very simple observation: "Too many people — kids, wives, and husbands — believe that the material legacy is the one and only true communication, the ultimate proof." This reflects what so many family therapists have also observed: when a man with children remarries, *everyone*, not just the stepmother, may be required to make adjustments that are difficult, even painful, to their concept of what they "deserve." In their book *Step Wars*, Grace Gabe, M.D., and Jean Lipman-Blumen, Ph.D., note that most adult children presume that their parents have an arrangement whereby one will be provided for if predeceased by the other. That is, they know that they won't inherit Dad's money if Mom is still alive. They may not presume the same about a parent and a stepparent. If a stepmom's husband is clear about his intention up front — "I plan to provide for Susan after my death, just as I'm sure you plan to provide for your spouse" — there may be blowback early on but less ambiguity and fewer hard feelings (not to mention a decreased likelihood of litigation) down the road. Regardless of his children's expectations, every couple must come up with their own concept of what is fair. They may find that they return to and refine the idea as the years go by and his children get older and have kids of their own. Just acknowledging that there can be conflicts and hard feelings over finances, that money is as symbolic as it is real, can be a relief.

Competition over Access to the Husband/Father

Like money, husbands are a finite resource. There is only one of him, and he has only so much time and energy. Your stepchildren want it, and so do you. The solution seems obvious — the expectation is that stepmoms should be gracious and back off — but this battle can be profound, excruciating, epic. It is not just a matter of little kids wanting Dad all to themselves. I have been surprised to meet people in their forties and fifties — accomplished and apparently well-adjusted grownups — who clearly resent that their fathers have remarried and have less time for them now, or that they have remarried at all. Patricia Papernow shared an anecdote about a patient in his fifties, himself divorced and remarried, who was furious at his eighty-five-year-old father and stepmother for taking a romantic trip to Europe for their first Christmas together. "This older man had been a widower for many years and he finally found happiness," she told me. "It's not so surprising that his wife didn't want to spend the holiday with all six of his kids and all *their* children — that could be very overwhelming." Nevertheless, Papernow's patient fumed that his father was "abandoning the family." Papernow said that seeing a fiftysomething man act this way was "a great illustration of how powerful" — and I might add how unreasonable — "our fantasies that stepfamilies are supposed to be just like first families are."

Margaret, a psychiatric nurse who has what she calls a "nice relationship" with her stepmother, tried to explain how, even though she was delighted that her father remarried, she also had a kind of mental block about it. "Part of you accepts it," she said. "My stepmother is very loving, and she takes wonderful care of him. But there's another really primitive part of your brain that sees Dad and says, 'Okay, there's Dad, so where's Mom?' I know Mommy and Daddy aren't . . . together anymore, but I still sometimes feel it, or expect it, like a phantom limb."

In order to set this wrong right, to rebalance the perceived asymmetry, stepchildren without Margaret's level of awareness may dwell on the past when they see their fathers. For the stepmother, this can feel a lot like having a door slammed in your face. At one point, my stepdaughters seemed unable to resist telling long, detailed anecdotes about trips the three of them had gone on together, adventures they had shared, and fun times with his ex-girlfriends in the time B.S.M. (before stepmother). Usually, they recounted these fond times when we were in the car and I couldn't escape. They might have been innocent longings for times past, but just as likely they were unconscious (even conscious) pricks directed at my admittedly thin new-stepmother skin.

After all, girls especially tend to compete with their stepmothers for their fathers' affection. And the competition doesn't necessarily end when they get a boyfriend or even when they get married. Many girls whose parents divorce never stop needing to be the center of their fathers' lives. All too often, they get their way, because Daddy, either plagued by guilt or gratified by the attention, allows it. (See chapter 5 for a detailed discussion.)

"Maybe Dad should get a boat, and he and the baby and I can go on it and you can stay at home, since you don't like boats," my stepdaughter suggested in her singsongy "I know I'm being provocative" voice one summer afternoon when she was sixteen. I might have responded, "But your dad likes to spend time with me" or "Maybe you feel excluded, and that's why you're talking about excluding me." Instead, I rolled my eyes and said nothing, quipping later to my husband, "Daddy, maybe you can leave your wife and marry me and live on a boat with me, and we'll have our very own baby!" My husband has a decent sense of humor, and from then on, we cracked plenty of jokes about the girls' apparent desire to get rid of me, jokes that reframed their attempts to drive a wedge between us as normal and funny. My husband and I had managed to find a language (the wisecrack) that both acknowledged an ugly truth of stepfamily life and put it in perspective. As far as I can tell, these issues do not ever go away, not entirely, in a remarriage with children. Attempts to put Stepmom on the outside are likely to persist as long as his kids feel insecure about where they stand. However, at the risk of sounding reductive, as soon as you and your partner both feel the centrality of your relationship, your indivisibility as a couple, the attempts at exclusion are a lot less upsetting.

STEP-DILEMMA 5: MISINFORMATION FROM THE STEPMOTHERING INDUSTRY

Books for stepmothers tend to perpetuate certain myths. The myth of the blended family and the myth of the maternal stepmother are the most glaring examples. These books' relentlessly upbeat tone can make stepmothers feel as though our own occasional negativity and impatience regarding his kids are freakish. Other books on stepmothering are so lighthearted, so insistent that we see the humor in our situation and in our responses to it, that reading them feels suspiciously like being told that our concerns don't matter and that we just need to lighten up. But the real problem with many books for stepmothers is not what they imply, but what they actually say:

Remember that his kids will always come first.

Leave the disciplining to him.

You will regret it forever if you lose your temper or say something nasty to your stepchildren, so whatever you do, don't.

With patience and love, they will come around.

The fact that these directives have become a virtual mantra, the unassailable golden rules of stepmothering does not mean that they are right. For example, a number of stepfamily experts concur that in a remarriage with children, giving the couple relationship priority is crucial (see chapter 6). It may jar us to learn that our concept that "the kids are the most important thing" is misguided, even destructive to our partnerships. The ideas that you should be second and should accept it, that his kids came first chronologically and so are first in his heart, and that his believing and acting on these ideas makes him a good person are powerful, deeply ingrained beliefs. But all of them can be fatal for the remarriage with children. They are even bad for the children, giving them an uncomfortable amount of power and focusing an undue amount of attention and pressure on them.

Andrew Gotzis, M.D., a New York City psychiatrist and therapist who works with couples, echoed the advice of a number of marriage counselors when he told me, "In a remarriage with children, the hierarchy of the family needs to be established quickly and clearly. The kids need to know that the husband and wife come first and that they are a unified team." Otherwise, Dr. Gotzis cautioned, the kids can split the couple apart and create tension in the marriage indefinitely. To remarried couples with children, the scenario of kids turning to Dad when Stepmom has said no, or vice versa, in an attempt to split the team is all too familiar. A woman with stepchildren may exhaust herself with her attempts to resolve such situations. For this reason, sociologist Linda Nielsen notes that a woman with stepchildren will have more success when she adopts the attitude "My main goal and my main focus is to build an intimate, fulfilling relationship with my husband and to take better care of my own needs, not to bond with or win the approval of my stepchildren." Nielsen notes that a shift like this cannot happen in a vacuum; the woman's partner needs to be on the same page with her. If the marriage is to work, Nielsen insists, "her husband has to be committed to creating a [partnership] around which his children revolve rather than a marriage that revolves around his children. Especially when his children dislike their stepmother, the father has to make it clear that the kids will not be handed the power or given the precedence over his marriage."

"Things didn't improve until I let my daughter know that, even though I loved her, my ultimate loyalty was to my wife," one man who had survived a rocky early remarriage with children observed. We can only imagine the resultant fireworks in that household. But the outcome was a stronger marriage. This in turn gave his daughter proof that marriages can last. It also replaced what could have become profound confusion about her unchecked power in the family with a sense of secure belonging.

As for the advice "Leave the disciplining to him," whoever said it never went to a home while the stepkids were visiting and their father was out. Certainly, no one is saying to step right in and start issuing orders to your stepkids in your first days and weeks together — and few of us are likely to do that, fearing that we will be perceived as wicked. But what works in theory — you should hold back more or less indefinitely so that you don't seem like the villain, backing up your husband rather than doing things yourself — doesn't always work in practice. What happens when a stepchild does something that crosses the line but hubby isn't around? Are you to sit on your hands and bite your tongue rather than issue a firm "That's not okay, and you know it"? Moreover, firsthand experience has often demonstrated that the longer a woman with stepchildren waits, the harder it is for her ever to draw the line or be taken seriously as an adult with authority. I can attest to this fact. Because I was more or less a fraidy cat in the first year of my marriage, I had to be a tiger for the subsequent two or three years, as my stepdaughters still occasionally tried to walk all over me, just to see if they could. This was hardly their fault; I waited ages to take a stand about things such as snide remarks, dumping suitcases in the middle of the floor, and ignoring me.

Sometimes it *is* easier and smarter to ignore a stepchild's annoying habit, to decline to get involved in an emotion-charged discussion over her sweet sixteen party, or to be the voice of reason when planning her wedding. A number of women with stepchildren have found that "disengaging" is, in some situations, far and away the best strategy for them (see chapter 4). Other times, ignoring bad behavior just feels like being stepped on and creates a breeding ground for more resentment. And then what?

The culture at large is eager to gloss over women's anger in general, and advice for stepmothers in particular is full of warnings that if we express it, the consequences will be dire and irreversible. This strikes me as absurd. It would be the rare stepchild who never went through a phase of wanting to provoke his or her stepmom. Of course we lose our tempers, inevitably. And although it can feel catastrophic—What if they hate me? What if they think I'm wicked?—expressing our anger is, in my opinion, something we should do sooner rather than later. Otherwise, we risk setting the bar too impossibly high for everyone and creating a situation in which kids, teens, or even adult stepchildren go on pushing our buttons forever in an attempt to see where our limit is. Most of all, we need to learn as soon as possible — to experience firsthand — that being disliked is an occupational hazard for stepmothers, not a referendum on our worth. "Dad's girlfriend Laura yelled at us once in the car," my stepdaughter told me solemnly in our early days together. I didn't know exactly why she was telling me this, but I knew how Laura must have felt, and I admired her for letting the girls know when she thought they'd gone too far.

You're not my mother! Most of us fear that it is yelling or disciplining or losing our tempers or not being nice enough or patient enough or selfless enough that will keep our husbands' children from accepting us or drive them away. If only we had so much control. Instead, unrealistic expectations about blending and being maternal, difficult developmental stages, competition that is largely inevitable and unavoidable, misinformation about stepmothering, and a host of other factors play a bigger role in the way a reconfigured family group coheres — or doesn't. We are not, in fact, their mothers. Happily ever after and happiness all around are ideals — unlikely ones at that, even in traditional nuclear families. Eventually, we may find that we have arrived at a place of comfort, familiarity, and real pleasure with our husbands' kids. But if our happiness is contingent on his kids being happy for us, being happy with us, and loving us, then we have given away our greatest power and put everything at risk.

CHAPTER FOUR
"YOU'RE NOT MY CHILD!"

Anger, Jealousy, and Resentment

STORIES OF CRUEL STEPMOTHERS repulse, outrage, and fascinate us. A stepmother who excludes and persecutes her husband's children unsettles and reassures in equal measure: she is unnatural, and she is exactly what we have come to expect. A friend in graduate school told me, contemptuously, "My father's wife" — she often called her that, and to me it sounded thrillingly grown-up and distant, defiant, as in *She's not my mother, or even my stepmother; she's nothing to me* — "is so nasty. She just can't find it in herself to rise above the cliché of wickedness." My friend continued to describe how, when she was in college and her father and this wife, his second, moved to a different part of town, they did not give her a key to their new house. I was shocked by this act of "exclusion." It was her father's house. Didn't that make it my friend's house, too? Shouldn't she have the freedom to come and go as she pleased? How could a stepmother so blatantly and shamelessly surrender to the wicked stepmother script — acting jealous, mean, and petty and shutting her stepdaughter out? *She won't even let you have a key? And he goes along with it? Why?* Part of what fascinated me years ago about my friends and their stepmothers was the part of the story that I couldn't crack, even with all my questions: *How can your stepmother be such a witch? How did she get that way?*

Two decades later, I have a different sense of things. I see what my friend's stepmother did less as an act of locking someone out and more as an attempt to barricade herself in. Often stepmothers seem most alienating to outsiders precisely when they are feeling most vulnerable and weary and are taking steps, after years of feeling unappreciated, perhaps even attacked, to protect themselves. A step-mother who is seen to be shutting everyone out, who seems angry, jealous, and resentful, or just plain cold, I have learned, may very well be at the opposite end of an arc that began with her being another kind of person entirely. After years of listening to stepchildren tell us, literally and metaphorically, "You're not my mother," we may return the favor, feeling *You're not my child.* And acting that way. Our motives, it turns out, are more complicated than simple tit for tat.

All unhappy stepmothers are, in some way, alike. In large part, it seems, we have our gender to thank. Women are relaters. We aspire to be the carpenters who put the dilapidated house of stepfamily dysfunction back in order, the "fixers" who bring "ex-children" back into the fold, the good guys who charm recalcitrant and resentful stepkids into Best Friends Forever. It is more than a desire; to us, such reality-defying acts feel imperative. Why on earth do we take on such Herculean and thankless tasks, even when we know better? Because we must. Experts tell us that a woman's self-worth, and indeed her very sense of identity, are wrapped up in, even inextricable from, her success in relationships. Sociologist and family expert Virginia Rutter, Ph.D., summarizes: "A large body of research demonstrates that women's self-esteem becomes contingent upon relationships going smoothly; it holds in stepfamilies, as well." Simply put, we need to like and be liked, and anything less smacks of fault and failure.

Our need to solve problems in a stepfamily setting, our sense that it is up to us, is deeply ingrained — the legacy of decades of lessons imparted by parents and society — and may be nearly impossible for us to resist. As Elizabeth Carter, founder and direc-tor emerita of the Family Institute of Westchester and coauthor of *The Invisible Web: Gender Patterns in Family Relationships*, puts it, "Women are raised to believe that we are responsible for everybody. A stepmother sees the children as unhappy, or the husband as inef-fectual . . . and she moves in to be helpful. Women move toward a problem to work on it — whether it's theirs to work on or not." Stepfamilies, we know, have an abundance of such problems, interpersonal snags and aggravations, giving us plenty of material for self-doubt, self-blame, and feelings of failure. In fact, James Bray of Baylor University found that stepmothers are more self-critical and blame themselves more than any other member of the remarried family.

In this, we could not be more different from men. Studies show that stepfathers report much lower levels of engagement and involvement with their stepchildren — as well as significantly lower levels of conflict, stress, and guilt. And so it is likely that whether they are stepfathers themselves or not, our husbands will be rather bewildered, at best, by our need to knit and our keenly personal sense of devastation when we cannot. This gendered disparity in how women and men process stepfamily difficulty can act to drive the husband and wife apart, increasing the wife's sense of disconnection and failure. We all know the feeling Brenda, the mother of two toddlers and stepmother of a teenage boy, shared with me: "Sometimes I hate myself for not being able to handle it better, for not making us a family, for always fighting with my husband about his son."

Failing to connect, failing to fix, is something women take to heart. Maybe that explains why, during my interviews, several women with stepchildren told me the same story, or a version of it, repeating on each other's concerns in uncanny ways. It is a story about communicating and not communicating, about crossed signals and the intractable sense of frustration and resentment that so many of us find ourselves experiencing over and over — "Help! I'm stuck in a movie!" is how one woman with stepchildren described it to me — when it comes to dealing with his children and the uglier, more taboo feelings they sometimes elicit in us. The story goes like this.

A stepchild calls weekly, or a few times a month, and always leaves a similar message on the answering machine: "Hi, Dad, it's me. Hope you're doing well. I miss you. Give me a call. Bye, Dad."

In message after message, dozens of them, there is not a single hello for Dad's wife. It's her voice on the answering machine. It's her taking the message. (Okay, the stepchild doesn't know this, but still . . .). To make matters worse, she may have lived with the stepchild for a period of time, may have picked him up from the train station on alternate weekends and sent him birthday cards, or helped a stepdaughter plan her wedding, or otherwise rearranged her life and her priorities over and over, for years, trying to forge a bond in acknowledgment of the reality that her husband has kids.

She does not consider herself an overly sensitive person, the woman telling me this story, but she has to admit, the messages bother her. How can she fail to notice the fact that her stepchild does not so much as acknowledge her, again and again? The worst part is knowing that even thinking about it, even having feelings about it — about his kid never saying hi to her in the message — makes her seem petty. It is a classic stepmonster setup — nobody's fault, exactly, but somehow, because she has feelings about it, it becomes her problem. She can just imagine saying something to the stepchild the next time he or she calls: "Hi, how are you doing? Great. Listen, there's something I wanted to mention. I don't know if you realize it, but when you leave messages here, you never say hi to me, only to your dad. It feels a little . . . hurtful. I'm sure you don't intend it that way." She could never say this, she knows, because if she did, it would merely provide fodder for the rumblings about her she has already sensed — that she's a control freak, that she can't relax, that she has to stick herself into everything, that she is incapable of letting stuff go, that she's jealous.

No, she thinks, she won't mention it to her stepchild. Instead, she mentions it to her husband in passing, not wanting to start anything, just hinting, hoping that saying "Funny, every time Timmy calls, he says 'Hi, Dad' but never 'Hi, Jean,' even though it's my voice he's hearing" will be enough. Her husband nods. He seems distracted, or slightly irritated; he changes the subject. The messages don't change. And after a few months of it, or a year, the woman is tempted to stop giving her husband the messages at all.

Of course, she would never stoop so low — she tells me this part of the story in a rush, defensive, afraid that I might think she would actually do such a thing, suspecting that, in spite of the fact that I am a stepmother myself, I will judge her for even thinking, for one fleeting instant, about doing something so classically wicked.

She is frustrated and hurt, it's true, by this relatively little thing, which nonetheless feels, after all this time, like an intentional slight, a refusal (even if it is unconscious) to acknowledge her existence. But she *is* an adult, and she decides to be emotionally mature and direct rather than passive and resentful. Rather than letting it simmer and fester and become a bigger deal than it really is, she will speak to her husband about it again. Of course he will understand, she tells herself. Surely, he will tell his child that this "oversight" is a little odd and that it is only appropriate to say "Hi, Dad. Hi, Jean. Timmy here" when he hears his stepmother's voice on the answering machine.

"This again? You're making a big deal out of *nothing*," her husband responds instead, suddenly angry and defensive. "He's hardly ever here, and yet you still find a way to be critical of him. You're so *sensitive*. Why can't you just let it go?"

"I'm just pointing out his behavior. Why attack *me?*" the woman counters, surprised, disappointed, disoriented. Is she really so critical? She thought she was just expressing her feelings, asking for his help. Why are they once again divided as a couple at the mere mention of something his child has done? And are her feelings irrelevant, self-indulgent? Is what she's asking for unreasonable? She doesn't think so, but now she's not sure. Why is the burden on her, she wonders, to overlook and deny and pretend when his child does something she finds rude or hurtful?

The argument, even if it is short, feels lethal. It is their oldest, least productive dynamic, the fight they have over and over, the issue they never resolve. How can they be here again, back at square one? The woman married to the man with children begins to panic. She feels misunderstood, taken for granted, angry. Angry at her husband and angry at his child. Again. Again! It feels like a losing battle to be revisiting this wasteland of the bitterest emotions, the ones they forget for months at a time but that are apparently always there, even when things are going well. All over a stupid little message on the answering machine. For a moment, briefly, she hates her husband, hates his child, hates being a stepmother. She feels bitter. Then she wonders, *How did I get this way? When will it get better?* Psychotherapist Jamie Kelem Keshet writes of these feelings:

> *When a stepmother feels she has reached out to a child, the child's failure to reach back to her can be very painful. In some . . . cases this rejecting may cause her to question her worthiness as a person . . . Most stepmothers have ambivalent feelings about their stepchildren. A woman who is trying to acknowledge only her loving positive feelings toward the children and deny her angry and resentful feelings would be open to projecting her negative feelings onto them unconsciously.*

We need to allow ourselves to be less than all-loving all the time and to forgive ourselves for responding like human beings rather than saints to the par-for-the-course slights and oversights from our stepchildren that often feel deliberate. "I feel like, to succeed as a stepmother, you have to be either really assertive about not being stepped on or incredibly self-abnegating," a woman whose twentysomething stepdaughter veered from being prickly and standoffish to blatantly hostile told me. "I'm not really assertive, but I'm also not the kind of person who can say, 'Oh, his daughter's treating me like shit again. It's not personal. Whatever. It doesn't matter.'" What the woman with stepchildren seldom hears is that her feelings matter as much as anyone else's in the family. Indeed, sweeping them under the carpet or tamping them down, as we are so often urged to do ("Just let it *go* already!"), does more harm than good, exacerbating irritation and annoyance until it festers into full-blown, sometimes even explosive, resentment.

How do we stop the cycle? To begin with, we might simply acknowledge that, whatever their ages, our stepchildren do, in fact, frequently try to exclude us. They do things — consciously or unconsciously — that make us feel overlooked, left out, unappreciated. They send subtle and sometimes not-so-subtle signals that they wish we simply didn't exist, that they'd like to erase us from the picture, or from the message on the answering machine. I heard one story of a woman who was not invited to her stepdaughter's wedding, after nearly two decades of marriage to the young woman's father, "because it will be too difficult for Mom." Her husband told his daughter that they would attend together or not at all, but the stepmother never really recovered from her hurt and, not surprisingly, ceased making efforts with her stepdaughter for a long time. Another woman, visiting her stepson at sleep-away camp, noticed that he had taped family photos up on the wall next to his bunk and meticulously cut her face out of every one of them. She told me that the pain she felt was made worse by the fact that her husband failed to notice and then made excuses for his son.

My husband said, "Oh, really? Maybe he just did that because he knew his mom was visiting." Maybe. Still, I had put a big effort in with my stepson by this point. And he wasn't six; he was sixteen. I was surprised and hurt by the way he literally edited me out after all we'd been through together. After that, I realized that no matter what I did, no matter how nice I was, my stepson wasn't going to embrace me with open arms or consider me family. I can't blame him. It's true; I'm not exactly family. Anyway, after that I realized I should probably focus on myself and my marriage more and put myself out a little less where he was concerned.

At other times, as we've seen, our stepchildren may seem to be masters of splitting the couple, shutting us out and manipulating their fathers. Taboo it may be, but anger is a logical and normal response. It grows as we discover that our stepchildren have an uncanny aptitude for making us look bad when they are the ones misbehaving. Ayelet Waldman nails this aspect of stepmothering in her novel *Love and Other Impossible Pursuits*, the story of Emilia, who has lost a baby of her own and struggles to warm up to her husband's precocious, sometimes perfidiously emotionally savvy five-year-old, William.

One frozen afternoon, Emilia takes her stepson to see the Harlem Meer, a pond in Central Park. On this, the first day they have actually managed to have some spontaneous fun together, he slips near the water's edge, muddying his boots in the shallow water. Running into her husband, Jack, in the lobby of their building a few minutes later, Emilia knows that she is in trouble and that William will milk this for all it is worth. She is right: the boy wails dramatically as he recounts the story of his stepmother "throwing me into the lake." Emilia protests her innocence, but this is not, by now, the point. At issue is her husband's perception that she just doesn't like William or care about him. As father and son walk down the hall of the apartment to put the boy in the tub, Emilia feels shut out and set up and decides she has to say something.

> *"Aren't you going to tell him . . . he shouldn't get so crazy over a little mud and water? We were having fun, Jack!"*
>
> *Jack narrows his lips into a thin line . . . "You don't even give a shit. He's cold, and scared, and you couldn't care less."*
>
> *"I do so care. But he wasn't scared. You know William, he's just being dramatic."*
>
> *[Jack] leans toward me and says in a low voice, "You have no idea what your face is like when you look at him, Emilia. You are colder than the fucking Harlem Meer."*
>
> *He jerks the door open and walks through it, slamming it shut behind him. Before, I was warming to his son, I was. But now his words and those unsaid have spilled over me like liquid hydrogen. It is his words that have frozen me, made me brittle and immovable. Colder than he even knows. I am white with cold.*

Emilia's feelings — that her husband is taking his son's side; that she is unjustly accused but somehow ends up looking like a heartless, callow stepmonster who has mistreated his poor kid; and mostly her desperate fear and loneliness in this moment — are something many of us will recognize. What is not said to us and among us, what is not often enough acknowledged, what gets buried in the "you should's" and "you must's" and "you're the adult, so let it go's" is the simple fact that stepchildren are not always sweet victims like Snow White. Frequently, like William, they seem to be out to get us. Waldman gets at another unacknowledged but basic truth of stepmothering, too: it can feel like a betrayal when our husbands overlook or refuse to acknowledge something hostile a young or adult stepchild has done or said, or when they blind themselves to a stepchild's uncivil behavior, behavior that Dad would be unlikely to tolerate if it were directed at a stranger. (This phenomenon will be considered at length in chapter 6.)

William's melodramatic, divisive antics and his father's credulous response (the duped father) are nothing compared to some real-life stories I have heard: of a woman whose stepdaughter tried to push her down the stairs and whose husband accused her of "exaggerating"; of a woman who was literally beaten by her young adult stepdaughters before her husband intervened and told them they were no longer welcome; of a woman whose stepson spoke to her only in obscenities and whose husband told her he didn't want "to get involved in your problems with each other." Certainly, these are among the more extraordinary instances of stepchildren's unchecked hostility. But the combination of a child who misbehaves toward his or her stepmother and a father who fails to support his wife because he is passive or in denial about his kid's behavior, thus encouraging more such acting out toward Stepmom, is unfortunately all too common.

One option, of course, is to stick up for ourselves when our husbands don't and to assert ourselves when they can't, but such a strategy frequently back fires, or plays into the narrative that we are wicked, something we tend to want to avoid at all costs. Laynie, a doctor and the mother of two and stepmother of a ten-year-old boy, describes it this way: "There's a holding back and a level of consciousness all the time that there isn't with my own kids. With [my stepson] Teddy, I have to think about everything. There's always another process going on at the same time. Like with my own kids, they annoy me, they get a time-out. With Teddy, there's that extra moment. Will I? Won't I?" We may fear that something as reasonable as a time-out will cause a flare-up between us and the stepchild, between us and our husband, between us and his ex. As stepmothers, we are expected to let it go, often for years on end. If we can't — if we complain, set limits, or tell our step-children they're not welcome if they can't treat us civilly — we are being petty, stereotypical stepmonsters. Caught in this setup, we go silent, then get angry and resentful, and finally lash out at his kids, completing the cycle, playing our role in a script we never wanted any part of. Brenda, who always considered herself a fun, likable person, found herself trapped in this dynamic. "I don't know how it happened," she confided to me miserably, describing the downward spiral. Her stepson acted surly and provocative; she responded by complaining to her husband; he minimized her feelings and blamed her ("What do you expect — his parents are divorced!" "It's hard for him; you should be more understanding!"); and she became angrier and more snappish toward her stepson every time he exercised his unchecked power, power that had the effect of rubbing her nose in her own lack of authority in the household. Even if your situation is not as extreme as Brenda's or the ones I described earlier, such dead-end stepfamily dynamics can drive a stake through the heart of your marriage.

Our husbands, often either oblivious to our travails or critical of how we handle them, seem to live for, to relish, these small increments of time with their children — the very increments we sometimes find ourselves dreading. And this disparity between his experience of his kids and our experience of them builds what can feel like an impossible-to-scale wall between us. Inevitably, we are confronted with the simple fact that unless we are extraordinarily lucky and circumstances are just right (see chapter 9), we cannot like his children without reservation as he does, we cannot always feel enthused about their visit or the fact of them, and it is not always easy to disguise it. Paradoxically, admitting these charged truths will likely not lead to more problems but instead will lower the bar and our blood pressure significantly, bringing a much-needed sense of relief to what can feel like an endless struggle. Acceptance can also set the stage for us to explore just exactly what's under these feelings that can seem so overwhelming, feelings that may sometimes seem to threaten to blot out the rest of the world.

JEALOUSY

We know that stepchildren feel threatened, displaced, hurt, and scared. Less often do we hear how the stepmother experiences this reality: stepchildren, for all kinds of reasons beyond their control (and a number that are not), are also frequently angry and jealous, and they want us gone. Just as the wicked stepmother is a repository of the "bad parts" of the biological mother, a kind of splitting off, so the stepmother's "vengefulness and jealousy" toward her husband's powerless children may be a projection, one that allows stepchildren of all ages to disavow a deeper, more disturbing truth. Feeling decentered and enraged, envious of the woman who is now so important in the father's life, a stepchild may transform his or her own fantasies of revenge into a sense of victimization. "Rather than acknowledging 'I'm angry and jealous,' they tell themselves and anyone else who will listen, 'She is a jealous, angry bitch,'" New York City psychoanalyst Stephanie Newman told me. In other words, these intense and disturbing feelings are so hard for the kids to cope with that they frequently put them on the stepmother. "When I hear a story about a horrible, irredeemably jealous, petty stepmother from a patient, that is my clue to guide the patient toward understanding her own feelings of jealousy, anger, resentment, and envy," Newman explained.

None of this means that stepmothers don't feel jealous themselves. Sometimes, living up close with our stepchildren's jealousy and resentment, or coexisting with it for a weekend or a holiday, we begin to feel its corrosive force ourselves. "Those jealous little brats," one woman reported thinking jealously when her six-and eight-year-old stepdaughters sat on her husband's lap and told her, "Daddy likes us best!" In other cases, the jealousy is already there, spooling out from our own childhoods, our own personalities and pasts. Jealousy is the most shameful feeling stepmothers experience, the one we refuse to acknowledge and chastise ourselves for having in private. There is nothing quite so taboo, quite so ugly, or quite so clichéd as a jealous stepmother. Yet underconsidered and shameful as it may be, our jealousy is real.

Psychoanalyst Melanie Klein, in her groundbreaking work on jealousy and envy, defines jealousy as the feelings of anger, betrayal, and hurt that arise when we lose, or fear losing, a relationship that is central to us. The hallmark of jealousy, Klein says, is the three-way, or triangular, relationship — one person is jealous of the loved one's relationship with another. In distinction, she defines envy as the malicious, angry, destructive feelings we have when we believe someone else possesses a quality that we prize yet feel we lack. The qualities we envy in others, Klein writes, are tied to the way we define, or wish to define, ourselves.

Borrowing from and elaborating on Klein's theories, psychologist and stepfamily expert Elizabeth Church notes that whereas stepchildren are likely to experience both envy and jealousy of the stepmother, stepmothers most frequently report feeling jealous. Church's contribution to the discussion of stepmothers and jealousy is, first, to consider it at all. For as she herself points out, although jealous stepmothers are rampant in folk literature and clinical research about stepmothers, there has been almost no analysis of *why* this might be the case. Based on her own work with forty-two stepmothers, Church suggests that fairy tale portrayals of stepmothers are very far from the experience of real stepmothers, but these images do have a considerable impact on how stepmothers feel about being jealous and envious.

The real surprise in Church's findings is that jealousy turns out to be less a thing in itself and more a marker, a kind of detour by which one feeling masks another. Specifically, Church says, a stepmother's jealousy is usually "a response to feeling — and being — powerless and disregarded within relationships." Exacerbating the problem of acknowledging and processing jealousy are the stereotypes about it, Church notes: "Many stepmothers felt silenced by the image of the wicked stepmother. Some saw themselves as wicked, particularly if they were jealous of their stepchildren." Church discovered that jealousy in a remarried family system is really impotence turned inside out, a feeling of being shut out or excluded, and unable to do anything about it. A stepmother who feels jealous, Church suggests, probably actually feels disempowered but cannot articulate this even to herself. "It is important to remember," Church notes, "that this may not just be a *feeling* of powerlessness, but the person may in fact *be* powerless" (italics in original).

How so? What exactly is stepmother powerlessness? Church suggests that a few scenarios lead to powerlessness experienced as jealousy: feeling second best, feeling like an outsider, and feeling like a rival due to interactions involving our husbands and their kids and us. In many cases, such dynamics can be undone with simple psychoeducation — that is, information about what is within the range of normal in stepfamily life and steps we can take to ease situations that aggravate. I once observed a family — a man, a woman who looked to be his partner or wife, and his nine-year-old-or-so daughter — at the movies together. It was clear that the child was from a previous marriage not only from physical appearances but mostly from how they interacted. As they sat down, there was a kind of shuffle, an awkward momentary pause as the adults contemplated who belonged where. The man arranged things so his daughter was on the aisle, he was in the next seat, and his partner was on the other side of him. *Well, that's better than plopping your daughter between the two of you,* I caught myself thinking. Once comfortably ensconced in the middle, the man looked toward his partner with a sheepish grin, then took her hand in his right hand and his daughter's in his left. The woman

gave him a look — a halfhearted smile that masked resigned irritation — which I instantly recognized. When he and his daughter got
up minutes later and left without a word to his partner, presumably
to go to the concession stand, she turned to watch their retreating
backs, shaking her head. Upon their return — happy, voluble, laden
with treats — the man looked bewildered at his partner's reserve
and refusal to make eye contact, and I knew a complicated but predictable story was unfolding.

For an outsider witnessing the scene, it might be hard to fathom
what was going on; one might even think that the woman was making a big deal out of nothing. But consider that this kind of thing
had likely happened again and again. My best guess was that, like a
lot of stepmothers, this woman felt, for the hundredth time, like an
intruder on her husband's date with his daughter, and she wanted
to strangle both of them. Moreover, she was angry and disappointed
in herself for having such feelings. I wished, at that moment, that
there was a pamphlet I could hand the couple on their way out. It
would begin, "In a remarriage with children, the wife often feels
like a disregarded third wheel. Here's what husbands can do!"
Knowing that feeling stuck in insider/outsider roles is normal and
that jealousy comes from feeling and actually *being* shut out again
and again, rather than from being wicked and spiteful and essentially flawed, is a place to start.

In some cases, stepmothers bring something more personal to
the mix of normal stepfamily drama, and our jealousy won't abate
until we come to understand its very specific causes, which are often
obscured. Without therapy, my stepdaughters' possessiveness toward
their father and their feeling that I was a rival to be disposed of would
certainly have destroyed my marriage. After listening to me go on
in session after session about how competitive the two of them were
with me — the snippy remarks, the pointed taking of my place next
to my husband at the table or at the movies or in the car just as I was
about to sit next to him — and how that behavior enraged me, my
therapist helped me see the underlying dynamic that was making me
so furious. Their feelings of entitlement toward their father — *Daddy*

is ours, and we don't want to share him!* — were tapping into my profound and heretofore unexpressed anger that I had never had much
affection or closeness with my own father. Unconsciously, I felt that
my husband's daughters already had something I didn't have, had
never had, would never have: a father's love. And now here they
were trying to take away the only thing that I *did* have: my husband's
attention. I resented them not only for what they were doing (like
literally usurping my position when they stole my seat or refused to
let us have a moment alone) but also for what I had missed out on
when I was their age. Knowing this has helped me a great deal. My
stepdaughters are daddy's girls, which is not going to change — I
am stuck with it. But I am not, thankfully, quite so stuck with my own
deep, mysterious, and destructive emotional responses to this fact.

RESENTMENT

After jealousy — our own and theirs — our stepchildren's sense of
entitlement is perhaps the most frustrating thing of all, the expectation that goads us most. The presumption that we will be there
whenever they come back; that our affection for them is unlimited
and never-ending; and that we will simply turn the faucet of our
kindness back on, whenever they decide they're ready to drink its
waters, regardless of what has passed between us — this is what most
hurt and angered the women with stepchildren I spoke to. Cee-Cee,
a woman in her mid-forties who is the stepmother of an older boy
and the mother of a toddler, told me:

> *My stepson and I are quite close now, but when he was a teenager,
> he didn't speak to me for [many months]. He and his father had
> moved in with me, which is what I wanted. I wanted us to start the
> process of becoming a family. But the most galling thing was, here
> I was bringing home a paycheck and putting food on the table and
> paying the mortgage, and my stepson refused to talk to me. I mean,
> he would just get up and leave the room whenever I walked in. It
> was enraging. I wanted to jump out of a window. That was a long
> time ago, and we're through it. And I like seeing him, like that he*

*loves my son. Still, when I hear he's coming for the weekend, I often
think, Well, okay, but I'd have a better weekend if he didn't.*

The stepmothers I spoke with returned to this theme again and
again — the stepchild who does not feel or express gratitude, who
takes without compunction, and the fact that, though we understand that this is how children tend to be, we cannot help but resent
it. Sometimes this sense of entitlement and nonchalance about
what they seem to think we will tolerate, the one-way nature of the
relationship, is almost unbearable. This may account for the tendency stepmothers have to refer to their husbands' kids as "spoiled
brats," "black holes of taking," and "ingrates," in tones that sound
stepmonsterish to a non-step-mother's ears. In many ways, they *are*
ungrateful. They did not get down on their knees to propose to
us, and they do not feel obliged to honor and obey. This almost
makes sense, is almost excusable. Of course they don't love us — at
least not always or right away, and sometimes not ever. But what is
harder to understand and to forgive is that so many stepchildren of
all ages seem, like Cee-Cee's stepson, to want it both ways. Bizarrely,
we find that we are obliged to protect them from our own unmaternal feelings — feelings they have provoked in us with their refusal
to give back, sometimes, even so much as a "good morning."

Elizabeth Church points out that just as jealousy masks a feeling
of powerlessness for stepmothers, resentment of his kids and our
role masks a feeling of being overlooked and taken for granted.
The stepchild-stepmother relationship is, more often than not, profoundly unreciprocal. And given the tendency of women to derive
our sense of worth from the success of our relationships with others,
this can be difficult indeed. Unable to change our stepchildren's
behavior, we might do better by adjusting our own.

One woman's stepdaughter announced, for three or four years
running, that she had a gift for her baby sister's birthday, only to
show up each time with an "Oops, I forgot it." This same woman's
older stepson would say he was coming to the same birthday celebration, then cancel at the last minute. In general, psychologists

tell us, the stepchild's "gimme gimme" syndrome, her eagerness to receive, and her block about giving come from a sense of being deprived and a clumsy, childish attempt to set things right, as if doubling up on the gets could assuage the sense that something (a father, a family) has been taken away. By taking without giving, the stepchild turns herself into the center of a world she feels excluded from, thus reassuring herself that Dad's and Stepmom's love for her is not contingent on anything she does or gives in return. Likewise, the stepson who does not show up for the party can feel gratified that now the party is actually about him. Feeling decentered and dethroned, he puts himself back in the spotlight, paradoxically, by refusing to be there.

Knowing all of this, even understanding it, does not mean we shouldn't dislike this behavior or be annoyed by it. Denying ourselves the outlet of responding negatively will only backfire, breeding more resentment. The woman who told me the birthday party story vented to her husband about her frustration — luckily for her, he was able to hear it as more than just criticism of his kids, as he, too, was annoyed and hurt by the pattern — and then did some practical problem solving. She continued to invite his kids but didn't follow up with them in any detail. As her daughter got older, she never told the child that her older half siblings would be coming to the party, knowing that they might not show. She also opted out of what she called the "gossip sessions" when the relatives mulled over "why his kids might be boycotting." "I would just shrug and say, 'They're teenagers. You know how it is,' and walk away," she explained. By undercutting the drama, this woman put the focus back where it belonged (on her daughter) and also normalized the behavior of her stepkids, who after all were not being nasty or spiteful, just conflicted and self-centered.

A number of other strategies might help lessen our sense that the typical trying-too-hard stepmother things we do — cooking, gifting, planning outings — go unappreciated, in a way that often seems intended to hurt. Mostly, we can stop doing, not out of spite, but as a matter of strategy. For example, my husband cooks when his daughters show up. He likes cooking more than I do anyway, and if I don't cook, I don't set myself up for something stepchildren as a group cannot seem to resist: subtly criticizing and complaining about what we make in our (apparently presumptuous) attempts to feed them. In addition, most of us learn to be careful about birthdays. As one woman told me, "An e-mail card is just right for people who don't get around to saying thank you!" Cash is something kids of all ages seem to appreciate, and most of us have discovered that if we send enough to be helpful without going over the top, it is not so annoying when the recipient is too busy or distracted to acknowledge our gift.

Rearranging things on the inside can also help. Adjusting expectations and our level of effort seems to be the secret weapon of many women with stepchildren who succeed in overcoming resentment. For example, I have learned that a "friendly," out-of-the-blue phone call frequently presages a request for money. I am likely to get snubbed at a graduation or other big event if Mom is there — it's just too weird, and too hard, for my stepdaughters to interact warmly with me in that context. When there is a true crisis, the girls will always turn to him, not me, regardless of my efforts over the years. That makes sense: Dad is the parent, and I am not. The point in all these instances, it seems to me, is not to let it all go or be self-abnegating. We don't have to *like* being snubbed at events or being hit up for cash, or even to tolerate it. But we should expect it. And it's okay to withhold a little bit from them rather than to knock ourselves out and then feel rebuffed. In my case, I have become — contrary to my natural impulse, which is to be emotionally open and gregarious, as I am with my friends and my friends' children and my own children — emotionally cautious, even guarded, with my stepdaughters.

The risk is that in protecting ourselves a bit, we may unwittingly be turning ourselves into a stereotype — the emotional and financial skinflint of a stepmother. That may be a little sad, or a little funny, but it is also, we might remind ourselves, appropriate. We are, after all, their stepmothers.

DISENGAGING

Some stepmothers and therapists recommend a technique called "disengaging" as a way to reduce our anger and resentment toward our stepkids. Generally recommended in situations where there are extremely hostile stepchildren in residence and an extremely unsupportive husband, this technique may have applications for women in less dire circumstances as well, especially those with nonresidential teenage stepchildren and adult stepkids who are rejecting.

To disengage — to simply try less or stop trying at all — requires accepting a number of truths about being married to a man with children.

- They are not your children.
- You are not responsible for overcoming their upbringing or any emotional or social problems they have.
- You are not responsible for what kind of people they are. You are not responsible for what kind of people they become.
- These responsibilities belong to your husband, who will likely not raise his kids (or make interventions with his adult kids) the way you would.

Having accepted this reality, you then make a promise to yourself: *I will never give them the opportunity to treat me disrespectfully again.* Then you tell your stepchildren exactly what you will no longer be able to do for them: "I will not be able to drive you to school if you are rude to me. I will not be able to do your laundry if you will not speak to me in my own house. I will not be able to make dinner for you if you are hostile when I remind you to do your chores." Then follow through. If your stepson is rude to you while you're driving him to his soccer game, turn the car around and go home, saying simply, "I'm sorry you've decided to treat me disrespectfully. I must withdraw my offer to take you." With adult stepchildren, it might be enough just to tell yourself what you will no longer do: *I will no longer tell my husband that his thirty-five-year-old son should go to a psychiatrist because he is clinically depressed. Or, I will not be involved in the planning of my stepdaughter's wedding. It creates a loyalty conflict for her, and I will not be the object of her lashing out. Or, As long as he is not keeping me awake at night, I will not get involved with what my teenage stepson does while he stays with us over spring break. I will not "back-seat drive" my husband about my stepson leaving his room a mess, sleeping until 1 P.M., or leaving piles of dishes in the sink. I will leave everything as it is and let my husband deal with it.*

The goal of disengaging is to stop assuming responsibilities that are not yours and then feeling disappointed when no one appreciates your efforts. Once this happens, the anger, resentment, and other negative feelings will likely subside significantly. Tolerance and even affection will take root more easily, and grow stronger, in this terrain. And once you disengage, your husband can no longer be "the good guy" to your "wicked stepmother," and he will be more likely to step up to the plate.

Another benefit of disengaging is that the fewer the opportunities you give your stepchildren to resent you, the less likely you are to be a target. Advocates of disengaging insist that when we accept that this dynamic isn't precisely our problem, life gets easier. The overwhelming sense of "You're not my child!" may very well subside into something more like "This isn't perfect, but it can work."

CHAPTER FIVE

HIM

Understanding Your Husband

IF YOU HAVE STEPCHILDREN of any age, the most important person in your life is your husband. He is, quite simply, the person who in large part determines your happiness — or misery — in your step-situation. His actions and attitudes will dictate whether your quality of steplife will be extraordinarily stressful, basically tolerable, or even enjoyable, despite the inevitable difficulties and bumps along the way. Specifically, more than even you yourself, your husband is the person who will set the course of stepchild-stepmother relations, for good or for bad. By making it clear to you and his kids (whether they are four or forty) that your marriage is a priority for him, by backing you up in front of the kids if you have a disagreement with them (even if he disagrees with you in private later), and by showing them that you are loved, cherished, and here to stay, your husband can model for his children an expectation that they are to treat you with civility and respect at the very least. Belinda, age fifty-eight, is a retired stock analyst and stepmother of two. She told me what it is like to have a husband who is clear and without conflict about discipline and making his partnership with his wife a priority: "My husband was always on my side. Always. We were a team, and his kids knew it. The kids never did anything flat-out rotten to me. No frogs in my bed, nothing like that. But if they gave me any lip or anything, he would turn to them and say, 'That is *not* how you treat Belinda. Now apologize.' I didn't have a lot of the fights

93

that my girlfriends who married men with kids had to have, thanks to him drawing the line like that, early on and every time."

Your husband is utterly instrumental in enabling you to overcome the usual obstacles, such as your stepchildren's sense of divided loyalty, their resentment of you, and their anger that Dad has moved on. With him firmly in your corner, the two of you can even blunt the otherwise insuperable impact of an uncooperative and undermining biological mother. In the words of Sally, a retired psychotherapist and stepmother of two adults, "Dan always said, 'We come first. If we're not solid, everything falls apart.' Yes, it was really stressful when his ex was going crazy and calling us at midnight, and when his kids were going nuts and shoplifting and being angry at me and you name it. But I always knew Dan was in my corner and what his priorities were. I'm lucky, I know."

Belinda and Sally know they are exceptions and say as much. In fact, all too often the father who divorces and remarries is anything but firmly in his wife's camp. Conflicted, he may carom from corner to corner, now backing up his kids in their anger at his wife, now defending his choice to marry her. These conflicts are largely played out in his head and rarely communicated, but feeling torn between his wife and his children is nearly universal among dads who re-partner after death or divorce.

The truth is, this primary inner conflict may well be the best lens through which to view and understand your husband. Until he resolves this confusion, his dual role (at once your husband and their father) may well determine his actions, drain his energy, and color his — and your — happiness. The men I spoke with also described feeling conflicted about their obligations to two sets of children — either their biological children from two unions, or their biological children and their stepchildren. Men are especially prone to lingering, even debilitating guilt after their divorces. If they are stepfathers themselves, they struggle with the same role ambiguity that plagues stepmothers. Finally, while stepmothers often feel misunderstood, mistreated, judged, and "set up" in their role, the men married to them often feel paralyzed, fearful, and unable to do anything right.

POISONOUS PASSIVITY

The cliché of the dad who remarries is a familiar one: he is clueless, a formerly great guy who has been "kidnapped and brainwashed" by his new wife. The all-good, hoodwinked, browbeaten father is the flip side of the wicked stepmother. Each stereotype derives its symbolic potency from the other, and they become ever more intertwined each time someone like thirty-eight-year-old Annie speaks of her disappointment at how her relationship with her father has changed since his remarriage ten years ago. "My father just goes along with whatever my stepmother says," Annie said sadly. "He's a nice guy, and we used to be very close, but he won't put his foot down with her. He just doesn't get it. So I don't see him much anymore. She's in charge."

Many of the stepchildren I interviewed described their fathers as affable, easygoing, and manipulated by a second wife who takes advantage of these qualities, scheming to erect a barrier between him and his children so that she can "keep them apart" and "have him all to herself." As for the wives of these men, they also spoke in predictable and rather black-and-white terms about their husbands, portraying them as "suckers" for their manipulative adult children, whom they are too clueless to put in their place. Over and over, women with stepkids told me the same thing that sixty-year-old Florence, the stepmother of two, did:

> *My husband is not a confronting type. No matter how bad his kids act, he doesn't do or say much of anything. If they don't call for weeks or say thank you for a gift — he won't say, "Hey, how come I didn't hear from you?" He would never tell his kids to knock it off and treat him or me nicely when they were younger, for example. It's not in him. He won't even notice something like that, let alone talk to me about it when they've left. He tends to ignore problems.*

This portrait of the man with kids who divorces and remarries is a common one: not only does he "ignore problems," but he is conflict averse to the point of deafness and blindness. He is passive, the opposite of a knight in shining armor. Often a woman with stepkids feels that her husband is downright ungentlemanly, leaving her to "twist in the wind" when there is a conflict with a stepchild. In the early years of my marriage, I vividly recall wanting to brain my husband for the way he habitually ignored the occasional snotty remarks his teenage daughters made to me. Each time I mentioned it later, I was stupefied by his response: "Huh? She said that? I didn't even hear it." And he literally hadn't! My husband's response was typical of the man with children who divorces and re-partners: when he perceives that he is between a rock and a hard place vis-à-vis the interests of his children and his wife, he goes deaf. One woman on an Internet chat board wrote about her frustration with her husband, who seems to elevate this type of avoidance and apparently willful ignorance to an art form: "I'm sitting there saying it's not a good thing that his fifteen-year-old daughter is having sex at our house, and she's screaming at me to mind my own business and I'm not her mother and she doesn't have to do what I say. And I turn to look at him [so he'll back me up] and he's literally not there. He has actually left the room!"

Common as it may be, this passivity and avoidance is extremely corrosive of step-relationships. In many cases, feelings are flying fast and furious around the silent father/husband, who comes to appear as the calm in the center of the storm, a good guy besieged on all sides. But what is it really, this "inability to tell the kids to buck up and behave," this hesitation to "stand up to his pushy wife" who "won't let him see his kids as much"? Where precisely does it — this paralysis and passivity that he is accused of — actually come from? And, other than the key to your happiness and success with his kids, who is he really?

FATHERING, MORE FATHERING
Pushing through the thicket of stereotypes, we see a more complex reality taking shape. From research and everyday lived experience, an

unexpected picture of fathers who divorce and remarry is emerging: namely, these men face very real, very specific social and emotional challenges, and they feel just as deeply as their wives do, perhaps even more so. Indeed, in speaking to fathers who divorce and re-partner, as well as to the experts who study and treat them, I heard over and over that these men feel "conflicted" and "spread thin." Usually, the man with kids who remarries describes himself as feeling torn between pleasing his wife and pleasing his kids (who are presumably often at odds) and spread thin by his obligations — emotional as well as financial — to the children of both his current and his previous marriages. He may also feel overwhelmed, guilty, and fearful. "These men are being depended on and called upon by two families in lots of cases," psychotherapist Mary Ann Feldstein told me, "and that is a very, very tall order. At the same time, they usually do not get to live full-time with their biological kids. I don't think anyone who hasn't done it can imagine how difficult their lives feel."

All these feelings make more sense when you view them — and your husband — in context. At least two recent cultural shifts form the backdrop against which fathers who remarry are currently struggling — and suffering — more than ever before. Being a father now means being significantly more engaged with one's children. Gigi, who is sixty-five, marveled to me about the differences between fatherhood now and fatherhood when she was a young mother:

> *I can't tell you how different it is now. I mean, my stepson is down there on the floor with his kids playing with them in a way that my first husband wouldn't have imagined. My husband now, he's a fairly enlightened guy, mind you, but he calls his son "Mr. Mom" behind his back sometimes, not necessarily in a nice way. It's a gen-erational thing . . . Kids were strictly women's work when I was doing it. My husband didn't lift a finger; it was all on me. We [women] did it by ourselves.*

Gigi's peers echoed this sentiment in our conversations, expressing surprise and admiration about the degree of involvement their sons and stepsons, and a whole generation of men under age fifty, now have in their children's lives.

Their observations are right on target. According to a 2002 study by the Families and Work Institute, fathers ages twenty-three to thirty-seven now spend significantly more workday time caring for and doing things with their children (an average of 3.4 hours each workday) than did baby boomer fathers (who put in an average of 2.2 hours). The Institute predicts that younger fathers will continue this trend and show perhaps even more involvement. The president of the institute, Ellen Galinsky, notes, "This is one of the strongest trends we've seen . . . Men are really different now. It really is a change." She attributes it to factors such as younger men seeing their parents give all to companies that eventually downsized them, technology that allows fathers to work from home, and a "my family comes first" attitude since 9/11. As she says, "The 'Cat's in the Cradle' song that this generation grew up with really meant something." For this relatively new breed of fathers, more daily interactions with their kids lead to stronger ties, more meaningful bonds, and more grief than ever before in the event of a divorce.

This new generation has been silently facing a bewildering challenge: how to maintain a strong relationship with their kids when they don't have primary physical custody. Sam, a fortysomething stepson and the father of a three-year-old, seems shocked, in retrospect, by what happened after his parents divorced when he was nine years old. "I could never do what my father did in the divorce — leave like that," he told me. "He didn't want to see us more than every other weekend. That was enough for him. When I look at my daughter, the thought just kills me. She needs me so much. I can't understand it, I really can't. How could he do that?" Today's dads are far more likely to agonize over the distance their own fathers assumed was reasonable and to do everything in their power to make up for the fact that they are likely no longer a daily presence in their children's lives. As thirty-four-year-old Ella told me, quoting her husband, whose kids live across town with their biological mother, "You don't know what it's like not to be able to kiss your children and read them a story and tuck them in every night. You have no idea of that pain."

CHILD-CENTRIC CHILD REARING

Our new fathering expectations coincide with, and also stem from, a relatively new, more child-centered form of child rearing. Kendra, a custodial stepmother of a teenage girl, described it well:

> *Things seem to be much more about what the kids want, versus what makes sense for the adults, which is how it was with me and all my friends growing up. We're chauffeuring [my stepdaughter] every Friday and Saturday night, then staying up late waiting for her to come back home. A cranky husband waiting up late and fighting with his daughter about her curfew constantly makes it tough on us as a couple. And it's been a stress on our marriage, just not having those hours — when he's waiting up for her or arguing with her — for 'us time' anymore. My husband would never tell his daughter that she can stay out late one weekend night but not two. He would think that was selfish on his part. What his daughter needs and wants — that's kind of first.*

This is not exclusive to socially active teens. Indeed, as Stephanie Newman of the New York Psychoanalytic Institute told me, "Child rearing is now focused, in many cases to a fault, on the needs and demands of the kids, often at the expense of the couple relationship. Parents feel more compelled than they ever did before to always engage and to be perfect parents all the time." In the 1950s and 1960s, in contrast, housewives were told they should give their kids — and themselves — time alone. Who among us of a certain age doesn't remember playing in the backyard more or less unsupervised, or amusing ourselves in our rooms while Mom chatted on the phone, did the dishes, or even watched a soap opera? Such an approach to parenting, explicitly recommended at the time by pediatricians and other child-care experts including Dr. Benjamin Spock, may have had the downside of physical and emotional distance. But it gave parents and children alike time to recharge, to feel and to be independent. Perhaps most important, it gave children the sense that their feelings, needs, and problems were not necessarily something for adults to constantly fix. In marked contrast, today's parents, whether they work or not, are far more likely to "hover" and engage in every activity, from watching *Sesame Street* to doing a puzzle to helping with homework — and to feel intensely guilty if they do not. The term "helicopter parenting," which came into use in the 1990s, aptly describes the impact that this new sense of obligation has on parents' behavior. "We feel the need to show our kids we are always there for them," Newman said. "Pressures on parents today are tremendous compared to how things were just a generation ago."

And this pressure doesn't end when kids leave home. Parents are keeping in touch with their kids more often, and for longer into their adult lives, than ever before. Whereas in the past, long-distance rates and a single phone on a dormitory floor made contact between kids in college and their parents a weekends-only affair, the recent telecommunications revolution — and its aggressive marketing on college campuses — ensures that parents and kids are now in remarkably close contact. This technologically abetted, often daily contact, protracted into the late teens and early twenties, has a profound impact on child development, according to experts. Peter Crabb, Ph.D., a psychologist at Penn State University, says that constant contact between kids and parents "promotes immaturity and dependence" during just those years when achieving separation and adult independence and separation are the goal. For good or for bad, the net effect of this technologically driven change in communication is that children are staying in a childlike relationship to their parents longer. Cell phones and e-mail are just one piece of the puzzle, however. A number of other factors conspire to create a landscape in which separation is not as clear-cut as it used to be and adolescence is prolonged, in many senses, even into one's thirties (see chapter 10). Child-centric child rearing can last for decades, and fathers are part of it in ways they never were — and never would have been expected to be — before.

But while all these social shifts have increased fathers' involvement, their sense of obligation and investment, and the duration and intensity of their parenting experience, custody arrangements have remained stubbornly unchanged. In virtually every state, mothers are dramatically more likely to be granted primary physical custody than fathers. Even when joint custody is the norm, it is usual for children to live with the mother, according to Texas divorce lawyer Stewart Gagnon, who told me, "If a father lives a town or more away, joint custody may in effect still be the mother having primary physical custody and the father relegated to alternate weekends and holidays."

Forty-eight-year-old Harry's custody tribulations, and their emotional fallout, poignantly illustrate the struggles that fathers who divorce now face if they want to remain an active, everyday presence in their children's lives. A financial consultant and father of two who divorced and remarried a woman with two children of her own, Harry persuaded his ex-wife to move from Florida to the Northeast when he and his wife did. This way, he and his ex-wife could share joint physical custody of their son and daughter. Not entirely unrealistically, Harry imagined a big, inclusive household where his kids and his wife's kids would have the opportunity to spend lots of time together. But the informal agreement — and Harry's fantasy — unraveled when Harry's ex-wife changed her mind and decided to stay put in Florida. Several months later, after much pleading and a threatened court action, Harry and his wife had no choice but to follow through on their plan to move to the Northeast, since he had found a better-paying, steadier job there. In spite of the fact that a court action subsequently determined that his children had been in imminent danger while living with their mother, who was an alcoholic, and court-appointed professionals had clearly stated that the kids needed to start living with their father as soon as possible, things became bogged down in court, where Harry and his ex-wife's dealings became vitriolic.

When I spoke to him one holiday season, Harry, normally upbeat and optimistic, was struggling with what he called his "difficult position" — helping his partner raise her kids while pining away for his own children, who were hundreds of miles away. Harry felt that custody bias was at play, and it frustrated him, especially because he knew that he was a great father not only to his own kids but to kids who weren't his own as well. He told me, "There's this immense prejudice that still remains from the old, traditional gender roles. It puts me at a disadvantage. I love my stepkids, and it is a sweet relationship. But here I am, raising someone else's kids, while their biological father has no responsibility. And I sometimes have to force myself to be present with my stepkids when my mind races off in sadness, due to missing my kids."

Family court systems have yet to catch up to the new social reality of dads who want to parent on the frontlines. Until a sea change in our attitudes puts an end to custody bias, fathers will be in pain — and that will have an impact on how well they are able to function as husbands, partners, and stepfathers. "What I've found in my practice and in my experience is that most men take their obligations to their children very, very seriously," Mary Ann Feldstein told me. It follows that the pain of divorce is often devastating for them and that "just moving on," as their own fathers may have done, is simply not an option. In fact, it is inconceivable.

THE FEELINGS HE MAY NOT EVEN KNOW HE HAS

We know from the psychological literature, and from our own experience, that men tend to be poor communicators compared to women. They are also generally more hesitant to examine and more likely to disavow their own feelings and those of others, and they are more conflict averse in their marriages and partnerships. These tendencies can be as much a prison sentence for the men themselves as for their wives who attempt to talk with them about difficult topics.

In spite of the clichés about men being "less emotional" (and their bravado, which sometimes seems to prove it), the research on men and their feelings tells us something else entirely. Men are lonelier than women, it seems. Their rate of remarriage after either the death of a spouse or a divorce are much higher than women's. It is harder for them to spend an extended period of time alone: men tend to remarry within thirteen months after a divorce or the death of a spouse, while women average four years or more. A 2002 Penn State study found that childless, unmarried elderly men are at greater risk of depression than unmarried elderly women with no kids, perhaps because they have less social support and fewer friends.

This risk is not limited to older men, however. A study funded by the National Institute of Mental Health (NIMH) of cortisol levels in 124 young men and their female partners recently found that relationship conflicts actually stress men more than women. And for men in stepfamilies, the risks are considerably amplified. In fact, researchers Kirby Deater-Deckard and colleagues found that men in stepfamilies are more depressed than men in traditional families, while those in stepmother families (men with kids who divorce and remarry) are the most depressed of all. We might be surprised to learn that our husbands even suffer from something like postpartum blues. In the Deater-Deckard study, when divorced and remarried men and their partners had a baby, the men's rates of depression shot up dramatically. Clearly, stepfamily life can be hazardous to the mental health not only of stepmothers but also of their husbands.

Why might this be? We do know that men with children who divorce and remarry often experience tremendous stress and feel unable to talk about it. Among the greatest pressures men who divorce and remarry experience, to hear them tell it, are their obligations, both emotional and financial, to so many people — children, wives, ex-wives, and sometimes stepchildren. Jonathan, a successful fifty-one-year-old entertainment executive, good-naturedly described the financial challenges of having two twenty-something children from his first marriage and two children under age four from his current marriage:

I'm like the ATM when my older kids are here staying with us — and when they're staying with their mom, too. Ski trips, clothes, books. I pay

*for half their rent and their incidental expenses [while they're in gradu-
ate school, after paying for all their college tuition]. And now with
the kids [from my current marriage], there's nursery school tuition
and then private school tuition and all those other things. Plus the
mortgage. My wife works, but her income is nowhere near mine. I like
being the provider, it's a good feeling, but it's a lot of money and a lot
of pressure to take care of everyone. I don't always sleep so well at night.*

It is frequently said that women suffer more from divorce financially
than do men and that in many cases men actually benefit financially.
In 1987, sociologist Lenore Weitzman, then at Stanford, famously
wrote that the standard of living of mothers declined by 73 percent
one year after divorce, while that of fathers increased by 42 percent.
But Jonathan's sense that he has never been under greater financial
pressure jibes with what researchers have subsequently discovered.
Most concur that Weitzman's estimate was greatly exaggerated from
the outset, with some asserting that divorced fathers suffer financially
as much as, or even more than, divorced mothers when maternal tax
benefits and direct expenditures by fathers on children are factored
in. If Jonathan had daughters rather than sons, he might have an additional hurdle. Linda Nielsen of Wake Forest University, who headed a
fifteen-year study of college-age women, found that girls discriminate
against Dad, "treating him as a critical judge and a bank machine."
They are unlikely to give him the same chance they give Mom to talk
about personal matters or to express sadness and grief. Nielsen notes
that this tendency is exacerbated in the case of divorce and remarriage. Many young women, she found, take their mothers' side and
make little effort to stay in touch with their fathers, yet expect their
dads to continue to help with their expenses into young adulthood.

Harry described how the financial and emotional pressures
increase and grow in complexity when the dad who divorces and
remarries has stepchildren as well:

*It's certainly a big responsibility. I'll add a funny male thing: I got
twinges of jealousy when my stepdaughter's father sent her money*

*for her birthday, saying how much she means to him. Meanwhile,
he's out there being the quintessential playboy with not a care in the
world, and here I am raising his kids. This is the deep stuff, the
raw emotions I'm trying to get at for you. I wouldn't change places
with him for anything. I'm happy, but this is a very stressful period
for me. We moved to a new house in a new state, I have a new job,
and my partner and I are in a new relationship playing father and
mother rather than just dating.*

As a noncustodial father and custodial stepfather, Harry feels pressure to "father" not only his own kids but his wife's as well. The existence of his wife's ex at the margins of the picture — and his assertion that his kids are his kids in spite of his lack of involvement — is deeply unsettling for him.

Mitch, a fiftysomething banker, is the father of Jeffrey and Robbie and the full-time stepfather of his wife Jackie's son, Martin. He told me about another stress, which he dubbed "the stress of even-steven." Mitch began our interview by telling me that he has never called his stepson a stepson: "To me he [is] my son, that's it. I have tried to treat them all the same." But just a few minutes later, he told me that on some level, this isn't really possible and that trying to force the issue had nearly wrecked his marriage:

*Jackie got so furious at me one time, early in our marriage, maybe
we'd been married for a year or two, over parent-teacher conferences.
She felt I didn't spend enough time at Martin's parent-teacher conference. Well, I had my own two boys and so that parent-teacher
conference time was already cut in half so the teachers could talk to
me about both of them. And I can't split a conference for one that's
[been] split into two further into three. These are short periods. I
can't be everywhere at once . . . I was trying to do that every day, be
everywhere all the time, be everything to everyone, and plus I was
working my ass off. It was a tough time, trying to cut my body into
three pieces. It didn't work. Three pieces isn't as good as a whole. I
was pulled in so many directions. I'm not Solomon.*

Mitch's image of himself "cut . . . into three pieces" (one for each son/stepson) dramatically demonstrates the sense of conflict — of being "torn" and even "torn apart" — that men can feel when they have so much responsibility toward so many. The stress of even-steven — the expectation that he should love all the kids in exactly the same way and that they should all get the same "amount" of him — contributed to his sense of being stretched to the breaking point. A counselor eventually helped Mitch and Jackie with their dilemma by dispelling the myth of the blended family, telling them that Jeffrey and Robbie were always going to be Mitch's children, and Martin would always be Jackie's child. While Jackie and Mitch could have great, strong relationships with their stepkids, the counselor explained, they needed to remember that the biological parent is the *parent*. Mitch told me, "[The counselor] said, 'Martin doesn't want you to be his dad. And Jeffrey and Robbie don't want Jackie to be their mom. Why are you guys trying to make this impossible thing happen? Why are you trying to force a bond that's not there?'" Mitch was "thunderstruck, like, What do you mean?" and described this moment as "an epiphany. An absolute lifesaving epiphany. It was such a relief. He made something that felt so horrendous seem so normal and matter-of-fact!"

This insight was a godsend for Mitch and Jackie, allowing them to give up the fantasy of being just like biological parents to their step-kids and all the pressures and disappointments that came with it. They found they fought less and felt better after they made a pact to parent their own kids, while working to build a special but nonparental relationship with their stepkids. Other people in their lives, however, were not so comfortable with this arrangement. In fact, there was a great deal of confusion around rituals such as Martin's bar mitzvah, as Mitch explained:

First of all, [Jackie is] not Jewish, his dad is, and I am. And Martin wanted a bar mitzvah, so fine. We split the cost with Jackie's ex, and all that was fine. But the rabbi didn't understand it. He said, "Okay, so at this point in the ceremony, the mother and father will

come up . . ." And Jackie and her ex-husband and I all interrupt[ed]
him and [said], "No, not the mother and father. We want you to
say, 'All the parents.'" And the rabbi looked so confused, and he just
couldn't wrap his mind around it even when we explained it to him.
And people were so uncomfortable at the actual bar mitzvah with
all of us together.

The father who divorces and remarries, especially if he marries a
woman with kids of her own, is likely to be dogged by the very same
role ambiguity that stepmothers experience. Harry seemed at a
loss when he told me, "I'm living with them and paying for their
school and everything, which is great. I feel good about that. And
yet I'm not sure I could even make a decision about medical care
for them in an emergency. There are things on the legal front that
I'm not clear about yet." Harry is experiencing the classic bind of
the stepparent: responsibility without authority. For stepmothers,
the responsibility is to feel, act, and be maternal; for fathers who
are also stepfathers, it is often to provide for both children and
stepchildren. In some fortunate families, it may be easy for the man
to provide for everyone financially, but doling out love and affection can be more of a challenge. Harry, still in the midst of the same
dilemma that dogged Mitch precounseling, said, "I can see my kids
and her kids, when we're all together, watching very, very carefully
to see how I give out my praise and my love. They want to make sure
nobody is getting more than anybody else!"

This same sense of being spread thin by obligations to two sets
of kids, and the fantasy that they should all be treated the same, sur-
faces for Jonathan (the entertainment executive with four children,
two from each of his marriages) every year when it's time to choose
a holiday card to send out.

My sons are grown — they're young adults — and my daughters
are little. My sons don't even live in the same state with us — we've
never all lived together. Every year, my wife and I talk about a holi-
day card that's a picture of us with the two girls. But then I feel, Am

I excluding my sons? So I say, "Let's get a card without a picture of the kids and just sign it." The next dilemma becomes, Can I just sign the card from me, my wife, and the little ones? Is that fair to the older ones? Or do I sign it from them, too? That's kind of odd, since they've got their own lives and have never lived with us and [my wife] Julia's not their mom. I go through this every year. I finally suggested we just sign it "Jonathan, Julia, and family." My wife said fine, but she also said, "That doesn't exactly sound warm and fuzzy, does it?" I guess I haven't resolved something.

It is hard to imagine Jonathan's older children caring as much as he does about the holiday card, which, he told me, they are unlikely even to see. In fact, he acknowledged that, given geography and their busy schedules with graduate school, travel, and girlfriends, getting his sons to show up to do a "whole family photo" would be a logistical impossibility. The issue, as Jonathan himself suggested, is his own and is likely one that Mitch and Harry would recognize and understand. As for Mitch precounseling, for Jonathan the "whole family" is an unrealistic fantasy, but a remarkably potent one, imparting guilt and stress that are all too palpable. Jonathan does not want to appear to have "moved on" to a "new family" and fears that a card with only his younger children would give that impression. Yet taking on the impossible task of creating an idealized reality in which every child is somehow "equal" or "the same," in spite of differences in age, where they live, and who their mothers are, is a recipe for emotional exhaustion.

THE FACE-OFF THAT NEEDN'T BE: WHEN IT'S YOU VS. HIS KIDS

Jonathan, Harry, and Mitch have all felt, at various times, torn, overwhelmed, and conflicted by their obligations to two sets of children — whether biological children from two marriages, as in Jonathan's case, or their biological children and their stepchildren, as in Harry's and Mitch's cases. The most disastrous scenario for a man with kids who divorces and re-partners, however, is feeling torn between his wife and his kids from a previous marriage. This conflict is remarkably common, yet it is a terrible stress not only on the father but also on his partner, their marriage, and the entire family system. My subjects reported that their biggest, most dramatic blowups, as well as their longest-simmering, most poisonous resentments, had to do with situations in which a husband or wife felt that it was "her versus them" when it came to his kids. Mitch told me about the moment the honeymoon was over, both literally and figuratively, for him and Jackie:

> *After the wedding, we went away for two weeks. And then we came home to an instantaneous family that both of us didn't recognize or understand the dynamics of. And this was the hard part. Putting aside what I feel about Jackie and what she feels about me, we had three kids. And I had to get to know Martin. And she had to get to know Jeffrey and Robbie. And Jeffrey and Robbie had to get to know Martin. And Jackie and I had to get used to each other. And all hell broke loose. To boot, someone gave Jackie a cat as a wedding present, and the cat just wouldn't go in the litter box. Nothing was working out right. The boys were fighting; the cat was going to the bathroom on the floor. And I like to be in control; I like to know where the ship is going. Oh, it was torture.*

The problem, Mitch went on to explain, wasn't just that the boys were fighting with one another, but that he and Jackie were being drawn into it. "Jackie was defending her son, and I was defending my sons" whenever there was a spat, he said. The entire tone of the household was coming to be defined by this division, and Jackie and Mitch were increasingly polarized.

> *I began to see big problems: attitude problems that my sons had never had before, discipline problems that my sons had never had before. They began to act out, do obnoxious stuff at school — breaking the rules and things like that. I hardly recognized my boys. All of a sudden, the perfect world isn't so perfect anymore. Jackie and I*

go from happy-go-lucky and laughing premarriage to more serious yelling-and-screaming-type things. Robbie doesn't want to listen to Jackie when she says please don't put your finger in the serving bowl, please don't ignore me when you're saying good night to your father and I'm sitting right next to him, and so on. And she's mad at me for not telling him to toe the line with her.

All the chaos and fighting weighed heavily on Mitch, who, by his own admission, likes to be in control. Mitch recalled the terrible moment when he feared that he may have made a mistake. "Things got so bad in our household, one day I asked myself, did I do the right thing? Maybe it's better to not have a wife, to have a household where there's no mother, but at least to have a peaceful household."

The conflicts between Robbie and his stepmother were, of course, quite typical. But for Jackie, these slights were all the more aggravating because Mitch didn't intervene in small, simple ways to nip them in the bud. As for Mitch, he couldn't be bothered with these "small issues" because he was so distressed and distracted — consumed really — by the alarming adjustment difficulties his sons seemed to be having. Witnessing the way things seemed to be spiraling out of control just after he and Jackie set up house together, Mitch assumed that the boys' waning performances at school and their acting out must be due to the marriage. By pursuing his own happiness, Mitch suspected, he had selfishly deprived his children of theirs. He was guilty, in short, of prioritizing his desires over their needs. And here was Jackie, the (albeit unwitting) source of these problems, harping on him to yell at his sons, who were obviously in distress, about some bullshit thing like manners. Thus the terms of the face-off were set: it became "my wife versus my kids," as in so many other step-households across the country.

Luckily, this state of affairs and Mitch's tormented misperceptions did not last for long. The counselor Mitch and Jackie consulted explained that initial adjustment difficulties for all stepfamily members are the rule rather than the exception and that teenagers are almost always a pain; they would likely be having problems if Mitch *hadn't* remarried as well. "And then," Mitch told me, "the counselor said, 'The real issue is that they're being more of a pain in the ass than they might otherwise be because you're trying to put together a bunch of relationships that can't be forced.'" In essence, Mitch and Jackie were told to lower their expectations and to accept an "unblended" family model. They would parent their kids separately, while making it clear to everyone in the household that *their* partnership was airtight and primary. That way, there would be no "holes" in the family structure, and there would be no question that, though their family was not "traditional," the grownups were in charge. "After that," Mitch told me, "everybody felt a little better. I think kids are like dogs. They need to know the hierarchy in order to relax. Before it was like, they were always testing to see who's the alpha dog, this new stepparent or me? Not knowing was too confusing." Husbands tend to feel better, too, when it's not "my wife versus my kids" but "my wife and I, the adult partners, together trying to guide this thing as best we can."

Not every couple is as lucky as Mitch and Jackie, who knew they needed counseling and found a psychologist who was clearly knowledgeable about stepfamilies. Brenda, the mother of two toddlers and the stepmother of a teenage boy whom we met in chapter 1, is married to a man who cannot move beyond his sense of conflict about his loyalties to his wife and to his child. As usual, such an inner conflict has deep roots. When Brenda first met Avi's seven-year-old son ten years ago, she got the sense that Avi's parenting was not what her own would be.

> *I was a camp counselor, and I was very involved in the raising of my younger siblings, so I was pretty good with kids. But I didn't know how to deal with my boyfriend's son one-on-one. Little by little, as Avi and I got serious, I started to see that Avi and his ex-wife were really permissive. They let Jamie have ice cream, cotton candy, and soda whenever he wanted. At seven, he was allowed to watch R-rated movies. There was rap music and going to bed at one A.M. To me, all this was just crazy. I don't think it's right. And I don't think kids like it.*

Brenda never slept at Avi's house on the weekends when Jamie was there; Avi thought it was "wrong," even two years into their relationship, which had become very serious. Like the permissiveness about rules, this unwillingness to have Brenda over was an indicator of Avi's inability to put his own needs on a par with his son's. Brenda, fearful of seeming petty and selfish, said nothing. "I guess Avi thought it would be unfair to Jamie to have me sleep over while he was sleeping there, that I would be taking away his dad's time from him or something," she explained. "I thought it was weird, but I wasn't a parent myself, so I didn't feel I could say much."

Shortly after this period, when Jamie was ten, Brenda discovered that he still slept in the same bed with Avi. She was dumbstruck not only by the arrangement but also by Avi's nonchalance about it. "I said, 'He's ten, and he *sleeps* with you?'" she told me. "He said, 'Yes, and with his mom, too. What's wrong with that?' He was very defensive about it when I said this isn't normal and that I thought kids need boundaries and rules and independence. The family bed — that was a *big* point of contention. It took me two years to get my stepson out of my then boyfriend's bed!"

Avi was, perhaps unwittingly, setting his girlfriend and his son at odds, projecting his inner conflict about having a romantic relationship outward. Unable to separate from his son, he left it to Brenda to fight with him about it, insisting on something he felt too guilty to consider, let alone implement, himself. Although Jamie eventually moved out of Avi's bed, the dynamic whereby Brenda did Avi's psychological dirty work for him persisted. And so the "Jamie versus Brenda" dynamic was born and eventually set in stone. Misreading having a relationship with a woman as a betrayal of his son, Avi set up a false choice for himself. He then accused Brenda of making him choose between her and Jamie. Brenda and Avi's situation was extreme, but it typifies, in a heightened way, the dynamic of a stepfamily with a guilty father/husband.

After Avi and Brenda were married, Avi's sense that he could not integrate Brenda into his relationship with Jamie — that it took precedence over his marriage — continued. Brenda reported:

My husband, our two kids, and I are not allowed to go on a vacation if Jamie [who is now seventeen] can't come with us. Because Jamie's school schedule is so different from my own kids' school schedule, we have never had a vacation without Jamie, who often doesn't even want to come along anyway. The little ones are on break from school, and we're not leaving town because my husband feels too bad to tell Jamie he can stay at his mom's for a few days [while his school is still in session and we go on vacation]. I resent that. What's worse for me is that, even though we can't ever take a vacation without my stepson, Avi takes his son on a special one-on-one vacation twice a year. For a week each time! I'm left home alone with two kids under the age of four.

Avi's guilty ministrations to his son only made Brenda's tortured sense of being an outsider in the family worse. This feeling intensified, and her marriage reached a crisis when Brenda told Avi that she didn't want to be left alone with the kids for two weeks a year. She asked him if one week of vacation with Jamie might suffice. Because she had so much built-up resentment about it, Brenda told me, "I sort of demanded it." Avi exploded. Still seeming bewildered and hurt, Brenda reported, "He said, 'Don't *ever* come between me and my son, because I will choose my son!'"

It is hard to imagine Brenda's marriage surviving her husband's misplaced anger and the unnecessary schism he has created in the family. It is equally difficult to imagine Brenda being able to have a relationship with Jamie, who in spite of her best efforts over the years, seems to have been set up again and again as her rival due in large part to Avi's sense that his son must somehow come "first" in order for him to be a good father. Knowing that his father finds him so "special" that Avi can't even draw the line gives Jamie an inappropriate amount of power. According to Brenda, he talks to adults as if they're his peers, deals drugs, and ignores any rules, however reasonable, she tries to set. Despite his feeling that Brenda should be "nicer" to his son and "just back off," Avi has largely orchestrated the unhappy state of affairs that prevails in his household. His guilt over his divorce and remarriage, and his fear that his son will walk away if he sets any rules, have blinded Avi to the need to form a partnership with Brenda, poisoning his marriage and the family well.

FEAR: THE DRIVING FORCE

Talking to men with children who divorce and remarry, I got the sense that, to a surprising extent, fear is the province of men. In the psychological literature, and in their conversations with me, these men say that they fear that the divorce — whether they initiated it or not — has harmed their children. There is also the fear that remarriage is "selfish" and will damage the kids, shaking things up a second time.

And then there is the biggest fear of all, the fear that they may lose access to their children. It would be hard to overemphasize just how truly terrified many men are that, custody agreements notwithstanding, their exes, if angered, will attempt to poison the children's minds against them, manufacture excuses to interfere with visitation, or actually begin an action for sole custody. This dread seems entirely justified after hearing so many stories of ex-wives suing for sole custody when their ex-husbands remarry or have other children. Too often, it seems, custody and visitation are used as leverage by ex-wives who want more child support or simply feel angry.

What are the consequences of these different types of fear men feel? How does fear affect their day-to-day lives and their marriages? Over and over, women described to me how their husbands' fear of losing custody rendered them incapable of saying no to their exes. Laynie told me:

> *She'd call when he was at my place and we were getting ready to go to a wedding or something, since my husband and his ex- know so many people in common. She'd say, "Can you bring me some money? I don't have time to go to the ATM." And he would do it, rather than telling her to get her own money. She had left him and taken the baby with her before, and he was terrified of losing contact with his son again. He simply couldn't stand up to her or say no to her about anything.*

Fear of losing their kids leads men to make other poor decisions as well. Because their time with their children may be so short and infrequent (often just weekends or even alternate weekends), many noncustodial dads opt out of discipline, as Avi did. As one man told me, "My daughter is hardly ever here. I don't want to waste our time together nagging her to hang up her towel or do her homework. I want our time together to be fun." The truth is, this man is probably also afraid that, should he cease being a "never says no dad," his daughter might stay away. Predictably, all this indulgent, fearful parenting creates problems for the couple. "You're turning your daughter into a spoiled brat," his wife might (understandably) complain, furthering his sense that "it's my wife versus my kid — my wife is so intolerant and so hard on my daughter!"

On top of everything else, fathers who divorce and remarry often feel fearful of displeasing their wives. You may feel that you are his last priority, but the fear of failing (divorcing) a second or a third time weighs heavily on your husband's mind. You say, "You've got to stand up to your ex!" or "Draw the line with your kids so they stop already!"

From his perspective, taking a stand might well mean losing his kids, while failing to do so may mean losing you. Doing nothing seems like a pretty good option when he feels as if he's in an interpersonal land mine zone and any misstep could result in an explosion. And so begins the paralysis of the father who divorces and remarries. This conflict-averse, passive, avoidant man is not acting this way out of willfulness; he is doing so out of fear.

Guilt, conflict, and fear are not just common features of your husband's emotional landscape; they are also somewhat shameful and "unmasculine." Disavowed and split off by your husband, these underlying emotions are transformed, and if ignored long enough, they can resurface, more powerful and destructive than ever, as conflict between you and him.

CHAPTER SIX
YOUR MARRIAGE

REMARRIAGE: THE HISTORY OF YOUR UNION

ALTHOUGH SOCIETY AS a whole may not endorse remarriage with children as "the way things should be," it is anything but uncommon. Approximately half of all marriages in the United States each year are remarriages for one or both partners, and 65 percent of those remarrying have children from a previous relationship. It's not numbers alone that make such unions business as usual, however. Remarriage with children also has deep historical roots in the United States. Far from a departure from the norm, remarriage with children has been common throughout American history.

Remarriage rates have actually changed very little in the past three centuries. A 1689 census for Plymouth Township, Massachusetts Bay Colony, noted that among the population of adults ages fifty and over, 40 percent of the men and more than one-quarter of the women had remarried at least once. This trend continued for the following two centuries. Psychotherapist and marriage researcher Susan Gamache, Ph.D., estimates that in 1850, half of all American children would have had a stepmother. These remarriages were virtually always formed after the death of a spouse. Owing to the production-centered nature of households throughout our early history, during which husbands' and wives' economic roles were utterly interdependent, these remarriages with children were essential to the continued well-being of families and entire communities.

In contrast, today 90 percent of those who remarry do so after a divorce, changing both the symbolic import and the lived experience of remarriage with children in fundamental ways. In contemporary remarriage, there is almost always an ex-spouse, for example, a fact that is likely to influence the children's behavior and greatly affect the outcome of the stepchild-stepparent relationship. In addition, a remarriage with children today is more likely to be viewed as optional, a choice — in some cases even a rupture of the moral contract if one spouse leaves the other for another man or woman — rather than an economic and emotional necessity for the good of the children and the larger community. To complicate matters even further, stepfamilies and remarried couples today confront what Johns Hopkins University sociologist and history of marriage expert Andrew Cherlin, Ph.D., calls a "lack of institutionalization" — the absence of clear norms, expectations, and rules about how to be a stepfamily or a remarried couple with children. This means dealing with ambiguity and biases great and small — everything from not being allowed to make decisions about a stepchild's medical care in an emergency to wondering how to handle parent-teacher conferences, from not knowing what a stepchild should call us to many people's unconscious and conscious assumptions that remarriages and stepfamilies are somehow deficient in comparison to first ones. In the absence of the broad goodwill and social support that remarriage met with in previous centuries — in the presence, as a matter of fact, of biases in public policy, legal status, and ideology that amount to stigmatization — a woman's marriage to a man with children is subject to extraordinary outside pressures. More than any other kind of marriage, it requires prioritizing, tending, and that most unreliable yet essential salve — true love.

UNDERSTANDING YOUR REMARRIAGE WITH CHILDREN: AN OVERVIEW

The divorce rate for remarriages with children was, until recently, thought to be about 60 percent, which is 17 percent higher than the overall divorce rate. Now, however, the eminent divorce researcher and clinical psychologist E. Mavis Hetherington suggests that the divorce rate may be as high as 65 percent for remarriages in which one partner has children from a previous union (a "simple" stepfamily), and a sobering 70 percent when both partners bring their own children to the picture (a "complex" stepfamily). The divorce rate for remarriages with children is 50 percent higher than that for remarriages with no children, and remarried couples rate children as the number one source of stress and tension in their marriages. Indeed, a mere 5 percent of Hetherington's 1,400 study participants reported that they considered their stepchildren an asset to their marriage. Simply put, the single greatest threat to a remarriage is the presence of children of any age from a prior union.

Why might this be? What accounts for the extraordinary pressure his kids exert on your partnership? As researchers Kay Pasley and Marilyn Ihinger-Tallman have noted, although children typically have no say in their parents' decision to remarry and form a new family, they do have incredible power to break it up. As we have seen, stepchildren can be a source of nearly constant conflict, especially early in the marriage, as the couple deals with their hostility toward Stepmom and issues such as discipline and what their expectations of his kids will be. As stepfamily expert and family therapist Patricia Papernow explains, the issue with his children is virtually structural: "The parent feels attached to, pulled by, nourished by, and connected to the same child that the stepparent [likely] feels rejected by, ignored by, jealous of, competitive with, and exhausted by." In addition, as discussed in chapters 3, 4, and 5, stepmothers are overwhelmingly likely to find themselves in partnerships with men who are permissive parents. In reaction, the stepmother may call for structure, setting the stage for the couple to fight about his kids. Papernow describes this common dynamic as "being polarized by parenting his kids."

As if this polarization over parenting isn't enough, other factors can make remarriage with children particularly challenging. First, these couples are confronted with a number of definitional tasks and burdens that other couples are not — there is simply so much to do. Each couple must find a stepmother role that everyone — husband, wife, and stepchildren — can accept, which often takes months or even years of painful, divisive trial and error. Second, if the woman brings children to the union as well, there is the task of merging kids from different households and family cultures — not to mention the draining work of putting out all the fires that are bound to erupt during the process. Third, the presence of an ex-spouse who may be uncooperative further complicates the picture. Even if the ex is cooperative, all of the adults still need to coordinate schedules — pickups and drop-offs, doctor's appointments, music lessons, sporting events, and the like — and deal with all the emotions that transitions between households are likely to stir up for children and adults alike. And because stepchildren are the links between the two households, they can create friction by making comparisons, passing along unkind messages, and even spying. With older children, the remarried couple must navigate fraught holidays, visits, and life events such as graduations, weddings, and births, as well as relationships with step–in-laws. All these logistics are likely to have strong emotional components. Lois Braverman, head of Manhattan's Ackerman Institute for the Family, told me, "Just schedule-wise, a remarried couple with kids involves many more people's involvement and approval. Day-to-day life can be an exhausting negotiation. This is something that is unique to stepfamilies, something you don't see in a first marriage."

It is no wonder, given all these daunting tasks, that the remarried couple often forgets to pay attention to the marriage. As Ella, the Manhattan mom of three young kids and stepmom of two, told me, "It feels like a zero-sum game sometimes, trying to find time for just my husband and me." Somehow, the husband and wife have to establish and maintain a close couple relationship, despite the presence of kids who are likely to feel unenthusiastic and even antagonistic toward the union and their stepmother, often into adulthood.

MARRIAGE FIRST
With the cards stacked against it, your marriage needs more than mere tending. Battered by issues and dynamics not found in a first

union, yours will not survive unless it is given special priority by both you and your husband. This will not likely present a problem if your husband is in his late fifties or older. Such men tend to adhere to the cultural script of their generation, leaving "kin-keeping behaviors," such as close relationships with both young children and adult children, to their wives and focusing their attention on their careers and their spouses. The upside of this tendency for stepmothers is that they are unlikely to struggle with the feeling that they come second. The downside is that adult stepchildren tend to hold their stepmothers responsible for their fathers' behavior, which they interpret as a choice. Even when they sense that their fathers are basically blindly following their social programming, several adult stepchildren I spoke to still blamed Stepmom for it. "He just lets her call all the shots," one stepdaughter said.

As we saw in chapter 5, today's increasingly involved dads have their own difficulties when it comes to balancing remarriage and fatherhood. Unlike men from previous generations, who simply left the child rearing to the women or moved on after a divorce, happy with a hands-off, every-other-weekend arrangement, "many of today's divorced and remarried fathers are trying to work with the notion of 'two firsts,'" Francesca Adler-Baeder, coordinator of the National Stepfamily Resource Center, told me. This point was really brought home to me when I interviewed a man with children who had divorced and remarried. Asked to rate certain statements from 1 to 10, with 1 being "not at all true" and 10 being "very true," he gave both "My marriage comes first" and "My kids come first" a 10. Like him, most men today feel more of an obligation to put both their kids from a previous marriage and their wives at the top of the list, and too often this results in an emotionally exhausting, lose-lose proposition. More than one divorced and remarried man with kids I interviewed said something to this effect: "For the first few years, I felt that everyone — my wife, my kids, my ex-wife — was mad at me all the time." Patricia Papernow told me that one of her patients lamented, "I'm the meat that everybody wants a slice of. Nobody sees I'm bleeding."

The belief that everyone in the family must have "equal standing" and get the man's "equal attention" is confusing and stressful for everyone, regardless of whether they all live together, the kids are there only on weekends, or the kids are adults. In a successful and satisfying first marriage, the partnership is the foundation of the entire family system. Without it, there is no family. Things are different in a remarriage. Especially in the first five to seven years of a remarriage, psychologist James Bray and others have found, the relationship between father and child — reaching far back in time, soldered with that intense intimacy a divorced parent can achieve with a child when they spend exclusive quality time together — is likely to be stronger than the relationship between husband and wife. And so from the outset, the hierarchy of the stepfamily system is unclear. This creates confusion ("Do I have to be nice to her?" "Is she here to stay?" "What will Dad do if I just ignore her or if I'm rude to her?" "Who is my husband going to side with, his kids or me?"), which in turn leads to power struggles. Children who have become very tight with Dad during his single period might actually believe that they can "veto" Stepmother or treat her as an intruder. This perception becomes more entrenched the longer Dad hesitates to convey to them the primacy of his marriage, as if to spare their feelings and shield them from the fact that they're no longer the only ones in his life. Far from protecting them, however, he is putting his wife and marriage in the line of fire, while inflating his kids' sense of power in the home and the world.

Rebecca, age forty-five, was living this problem when we spoke. She told me, with a shake of her head, that a few nights before, she had felt pressured by her husband to cancel a long-standing "couples night out" with old friends who were in town for just a few days. Her husband's young adult daughter — with whom he had been arguing — had called that afternoon saying she wanted to come by to talk. "When his daughter decides she wants to show up, we're supposed to drop everything," Rebecca remarked dryly. "That's pretty hard to take. We're supposed to cancel on our dear friends we almost never see so [he] can have a fight with [his] daughter or make up with her? It can't wait until the next day? But when I said I thought it was silly to cancel, he said, 'Don't you want me to have a relationship with my daughter?'" Rebecca sighed. "Of course I want him to have a relationship with his daughter. I just don't think our lives should screech to a halt when she feels like showing up."

Given such potential problems, stepfamily experts such as Emily and John Visher and James Bray advise that the partnership between adults must be strong and primary and that the couple must be a unified team in a stepfamily more than in any other kind of family. Summarizing the research, his years of experience as a psychologist and family therapist, and his position on the matter, Bray states, "Marital satisfaction almost always determines stepfamily stability. If satisfaction is high, tolerance for the normal tumult and conflict of stepfamily life is correspondingly high. If marital satisfaction is low, however, tolerance for conflict is so low that often the stepfamily dissolves in divorce." Given the incredible vulnerability of the couple relationship in stepfamilies, giving priority to this relationship increases the chances of keeping the stepfamily together. Translation: putting the marriage first is good for everyone.

What does putting your marriage first mean in practical terms? No one is suggesting shutting his children out or ignoring them when they're around. But to succeed, you and your partner must let the kids know that your relationship is airtight, rock solid, and important to you both. You can demonstrate this in small, simple ways, such as holding hands when his kids are in the room (if that's something you would normally do) or telling them about a regular couple ritual — "We make hash browns every Sunday morning because we love them" — and inviting them to join in. Dr. Andrew Gotzis, a New York City therapist, suggests that it might help to have something else going on when his kids show up — a chore such as planting the garden or dinner with adults your stepkids know or would enjoy meeting — rather than providing a big-deal red-carpet welcome every time they show up. Little things like this will give his kids the sense that you have a daily life together, whether they are there or not. That in turn will help make it clear that your relationship is primary, that the kids are not in control of the marriage or the household, and that Dad and Stepmom are in charge and in love. Knowing the order of things and where they stand in it, experts agree, is enormously reassuring for children. By contrast, constantly custom-designing weekends for his kids sends the message that you feel you should turn your life upside down for them. This puts a lot of pressure on you and on the kids, too.

Above all, putting your marriage first means thinking of yourself and your partner as a team. This might not be easy. As Patricia Paper-now has written, the course of development in a remarriage with children "involves wresting the sanctuary for nourishment and the seat of joint decision-making away from the parent/child relationship and establishing it firmly in the couple relationship." In most cases, stepchildren are likely to resent this realignment. In practical terms, a mantra such as "We're the team" can be helpful, especially when his kids live with you and conflicts about discipline and manners arise daily. Given that children are geniuses when it comes to sensing and exploiting marital discord, husband and wife must strive to present a united front, backing each other up in front of the kids no matter what. If you turn off the TV while Susie is watching because she hasn't loaded the dishwasher yet as promised, for example, and your husband disagrees with what you've done, it's best for him to zip it until the two of you are alone. Nothing empowers, confuses, or upsets children more than feeling that they — and not the adults — are in control. And nothing makes a stepmother feel more resentful, discouraged, or "degraded," as stepmother and author Cherie Burns has written, than being undercut in front of his kids when she is trying to appropriately assert her authority as one of the heads of the household.

The more opportunities you take to solidify the team and nurture it, the stronger it will be and the more natural it will feel to take on challenges together. Dr. Gotzis recommends that after a weekend visit with his kids, you both take a few hours off on Monday morning if possible. "It's a way of reconnecting and getting back into the mode of intimacy," he told me. For full-time stepmothers, time away as a couple is paramount. Make sure a childless vacation is a regular yearly occurrence. Feel free to make your bedroom a stepchild-free zone. A weekly date night will demonstrate to everyone, especially yourselves, that the marriage is a priority. It also will give you and your husband valuable time to be adults — not just co-parents — together.

Easier said than done, you may be thinking. *My husband won't do that stuff.* A husband confused about how to balance his bonds with you and with his kids would do well to hear that your requests are reasonable from an outside, neutral source, such as a book, a minister or rabbi, or a marriage counselor. Prioritizing your marriage is a condition you must insist on if your partnership is to survive the tumultuous early years of remarriage with children and flourish during the later years, which present difficulties of their own.

THE BIG ISSUE: A MUTUAL CHILD

In a remarriage with children, deciding whether and when to have a child together — a mutual child, in the lingo of remarriage experts — is often *the* issue the couple will face. Five of the women I interviewed for this book were already mothers when they became stepmothers and were not interested in having more children. Two others had no children going in and were happy to keep it that way. The rest told me that having at least one child together had been a precondition of their marriage.

According to Berkeley, California, stepfamily expert Anne Bernstein, Ph.D., roughly one-quarter of couples in a remarriage with children will have an "ours baby" within eighteen months of marrying. Many women may fantasize that a baby will be their ticket to the inner sanctum of a family where they have felt like an outsider, and in some cases, this may actually be the case. Having a child of our own, including the shift in priorities and energy that comes along with it, can in fact make an ex-wife's resentment or a stepchild's rejecting behavior less of an issue. A number of women told me that a great deal of their unhappiness and stress seemed to recede when they had a baby of their own. Brenda said, "It was like, when we had our son, my husband's ex finally realized this was for real. It finally got into her head to stop calling and bothering us all the time with little made-up things. And I didn't have time to second-guess how she and my husband were parenting my stepson. I was busy. I had a chance to do it the way I wanted now." Dora told me, "When I had Belle, the anger melted away. It was just gone." Many women also told me that when they had children of their on to protect, they better understood their husbands' indulgent parenting styles and refusals to hear any criticism of their kids. "Now I have my own child, and *I'm* that annoying parent who thinks she's perfect," Cee-Cee said with a laugh, recalling how frustrated she had been when her husband couldn't hear that his son was, well, imperfect.

Of course, having a baby is far from the answer to all stepfamily problems. It can create difficulties and stresses as well. For example, ex-wives feel more threatened by a stepmother's pregnancy and show their distress more often than do ex-husbands in parallel situations. Many of us know firsthand the annoyance of the asymmetry in which our blessed development, something we may have fantasized about for so long, something that makes us so happy, is someone else's worst nightmare, reactivating her anger and resentment. Having a baby will probably stir up problems with stepchildren as well. I vividly remember my stomach-dropping disappointment when we told my stepdaughters about my pregnancy and they began to sob. Over the next nine months, I sometimes could not help but feel that they were trying to sabotage what I had (naively) imagined would be a time of perfect bliss for my husband and me. Of course, from their perspective, I was ruining their lives.

Although a baby's arrival can link "family" members in ways you had not imagined, bringing stepchildren closer and creating a feeling that you all have someone in common now, it can also bring out a kind of wild maternal protectiveness and paranoia, an ugly urge to push stepchildren away. Sarah told me that she grew enraged at her ten-year-old stepson when he observed, "The baby looks like an alien." The baby *did* look a little like an alien, but no mother wants to hear such a thing. It did not help that the stepson's tone was laced with the kind of hostility that comes from the fear of being excluded, or that the boy's father said nothing in response. Sarah told me she got over it quickly but noted, "Ever since Rosie was born, a part of me wants to build a little fence around me, her, and my husband. It sounds petty, and I can't tell anyone else this, but sometimes I want it to be just us." In this regard, Sarah is more typical than she might imagine. A little-spoken secret of stepmothering is that we love our own children more and may occasionally fantasize about life as "the only ones." In my case, in spite of a rocky start, I felt more tolerance for my stepdaughters — they were, after all, getting older, more charming, and more interesting every day — after my first son was born. And I was amazed that their affection for him transcended their early resentment toward me. In this way, my son really was a kind of stepfamily salvation: my stepdaughters gave him a chance, which made me want to give them one.

Of course, many couples struggle with the issue of whether to have a child together. When a husband already has children, what feels like an imperative to his wife can feel optional to him, and such a fundamental difference in agendas and feelings can be devastating. More specifically, men who divorce and remarry often feel deeply ambivalent about having more children, suspecting that doing so will harm the children they already have and fearing that this marriage also may fail, leaving them juggling custody and visitation issues with two sets of children. Regardless of what they may have said before the marriage, many men may balk when it comes to actually having another child. Not surprisingly, these negotiations are often remarkably charged, and they almost always touch on other issues, such as stepfamily dynamics, feelings of being excluded, and financial pressures. This is the situation one of my favorite subjects, Kendra, found herself in.

Kendra: "I Thought We Would Be a Family"

Kendra struck me as upbeat, sunny, and energetic the day I first met her. She had prepared a wonderful lunch and immediately put me at ease with her warmth and solicitousness. On the wall near the table where we sat in her dining room was a framed display of mementos from her wedding — the vows; an invitation; photos of Kendra, her husband, and his daughter, who looked to be about ten. Kendra surprised me by telling me, right after cheerily offering me a plate of hummus, that her marriage was "at a crisis point" and she was considering leaving it soon. She explained that she felt that her husband, Donald, didn't give their marriage the priority it deserved, that there was strain over finances, and that there were arguments over whether to have a child together. For Kendra, all these issues were inextricably linked.

"I thought we would be a family," she said. "My husband is Mr. Mom. He was always very maternal. So shortly after he and I were married and it suited her, his ex-wife decided she didn't want her daughter living with her anymore. She had this boyfriend Sadie didn't like. And she told us, 'I'm leaving, and Sadie wants to stay at her [current] school. You should get a place for her here.'"

It was a stretch for Kendra and Donald to get a place in the expensive town where the girl wanted to stay. Donald was in debt from the divorce, so Kendra used the proceeds from the sale of her own home and her life savings to buy and renovate a place where they could all live together. Donald subsequently lost his job, and now she was working a sixty-hour week to pay Sadie's private school tuition. She felt "burned" on many levels.

"If I have a complaint about my husband, it's that I'm still not first," she said. "Sadie lives in the same house with me, yet she never even says hello. Donald could have put an end to this long ago. But he won't ask her for even that. And now her mom is suddenly interested in her moving back with her — after years of not doing anything for Sadie or with her."

When I ask Kendra whether there was ever a conversation about Sadie moving in with them, or whether they might enroll her in public school, she laughed and said:

Oh, no. No one asked me how I felt about it! And I didn't know what I was in for! We were married when she was ten, and she was with us several nights a week and we were a family. Tickle trains and braiding-hair sessions and unconditional love kind of things. Now she's a teenager, and this is her home. She wants her own space; she wants to separate. I understand, but the way Donald lets her act — I'm not on the same page with him! And about school — my husband would never do that. Better for us to suffer than for her to have to switch. That's pretty much how it is around here.

Just then, Kendra's stepdaughter came in the house. She grunted in response to Kendra's greeting but offered me a dazzling smile before slamming the door on her way out again. Kendra smiled wryly. "Usually, there's not even a grunt hello," she said. "See, Donald's almost afraid of her. So he hasn't said, 'First priority is to treat Kendra with respect and make sure that because she does all this stuff for you — drives you to school, pays your allowance, helps with your homework — you at least acknowledge her presence when you walk into a room where she's sitting.'"

It was clear to me that Kendra felt exploited and was frustrated that her relationship with Sadie was so unreciprocal. She struck me as remarkably hands-on, and I wondered how much of her frustration stemmed from this fact. Might it reduce her resentment, I wondered, if she started doing less? I remarked that she seemed to feel like part of the woodwork. "Oh, yeah!" she replied. "I'm paying the bills, and that's what bothers me. I feel very ignored. And the problem is that she's never gotten into trouble. *I really wish you wouldn't do that, but I will let you* is my husband's attitude pretty much. So Sadie rules the roost."

When I told Kendra that her situation sounded stressful, she paused, then nodded and said, "I'm wondering if I can handle it, or if I want to. Sadie's living off of me but not doing anything for me. I feel so . . . underappreciated. Early on, I would ask him, 'Are we ever going to get married?' Joking around. And he would say, 'When Sadie is ready.' At the time, I liked his devotion to his daughter, but now . . . now I realize that I get the short end of the stick a lot. That's why I say to you, I'm number two."

Kendra took a deep breath and seemed to be considering whether to go on. Then she plunged ahead. "I married my husband because I loved him, not for the money. But all these years later, I think only women who marry wealthy can do this! If Sadie can go to camp for the summer, or if he can afford to whisk you away on a vacation when you really need one, that would really help. As it is, I feel my husband is living off me but not protecting me from his daughter, who I'm also supporting!"

Feeling exploited and unsupported by her husband and disrespected by his daughter had had emotional repercussions, Kendra explained. For quite some time, she had felt no love or sexual desire for Donald.

> A couple of years ago, Sadie said to Donald, "If you and Kendra have a baby, I will never spend another night in this house again." And I think that Donald remembered that. He knows our finances haven't been good, but . . . somehow in May of 2005 I got pregnant. I guess my birth control failed.
>
> When I told him, he said, "What did you do? You did this behind my back!" I said, "No! It was an accident." I didn't know how much he didn't want to have a child until that moment. I married him under the impression that we were going to have a baby. That's important for you to know. I would never have married him without [the agreement of] having my own baby! Our vows are right up there. In his vows, he says [we're] the two most important women in [his] life, and hopefully a little boy to come.

I was struck by Kendra's invocation of their marriage vows, especially the part about "the two most important women in [his] life." Kendra's dilemma seemed to be intricately tied not only to their financial problems but also to Donald's inability to prioritize his marriage, to set Kendra apart. Kendra told me that she refused when Donald told her he wanted her to have an abortion. But she ended up having a miscarriage, and in some corner of her mind, she wondered whether losing the baby was caused by the psychological stress of their fighting. Shortly thereafter, she began thinking about divorcing Donald.

> *I think I realized from that day that he accused me of getting preg-nant on purpose, I didn't want to have a baby with him, would not have a baby with him. We didn't have a lot of money, and we still don't, but the money wasn't all. What mattered was his daughter feeling that way. And this is what was going to dictate the fact that he and I were never going to have a baby. That's how it is around here. This child has a lot of power.*
>
> *For a time, I tried to tell myself that I could do it, I could parent this girl and not have a child of my own. But is this the authentic life that I want? For me? I have no control over how she ends up and how she lives her life and how she appears to be to everybody else, because I haven't been allowed to parent in the way that I could and [that] could benefit her. And so I feel like I am wasting my time.*

Kendra told me that she understood the other reasons that Donald didn't want to have a baby. At nearly fifty, he was tired and wanted to put the days of diapers behind him. But she also felt manipulated by how he presented his take on the matter.

> *I feel like, I know you've had enough sleepless nights and you're tired, but at one point you were going to do that for me, and now you're not going to do that for me. With no discussion. What about me? I didn't get the baby and the bonding and the good stuff?*
>
> *He talks about how "there's nowhere to put it." I say, "Come on, we could build over the garage, or somebody would give something up for a baby. That's the least of it!"*

Kendra told me she was going to spend the next weeks trying to figure out whether she could afford to have a child on her own. If she couldn't, she might just stick it out with Donald. But mother-ing wasn't the only thing on her mind. She seemed to feel equally frustrated about not being able to "parent" her stepdaughter the way she would like to. As I was packing up to go, she shook her head and said, "This could be a failed attempt at trying to be the best stepmother in the world and not being allowed to. That's how I see it."

FIGHTING AND COMMUNICATION

Beneath all of Kendra and Donald's issues — finances, the decision whether to have a child, Donald's ineffectual parenting, Kendra's feelings of being unappreciated and second-best — lurked the biggest problem of all, their "meta-issue": not knowing how to fight. According to stepfamily experts, not having this skill sinks more remarriages with children than anything else, but with it, you can beat even the worst odds.

The first thing you should know, and probably already have learned, is that there will be fights — knock-down, drag-out fights that are virtually Wagnerian in their intensity, epic sweep, and, perhaps, decibel level. Stepfamily researcher James Bray found that the first twenty-four months of a remarriage with children are characterized by intense conflict and unhappiness, even in couples that will later become harmonious and happy. Patricia Papernow has found that the settling-in period for remarriage is four to seven *years*. Some couples, she notes, will take as long as twelve years to reach a more serene stage of stepfamily development.

Contrary to what most people think, however, fighting does not doom a relationship, or even necessarily indicate big problems. In fact, according to marital experts, it's not fighting itself or even the frequency of fighting that leads to marital instability. It's the way people fight. Some fighting styles can destroy a marriage, while others can actually strengthen it. The good news, then, is threefold: you can learn how to fight; it is not so scary to fight when you know you are a team; and fighting well can actually solidify your relationship.

By contrast, not fighting, or fighting the wrong way, is bad for you and for your marriage. In a study of almost four thousand men and women in Massachusetts, 32 percent of the men and 23 percent of the women said they suppressed their feelings during a quarrel.

Bottling up their feelings did not seem to have a measurable health impact on the male study participants. But for women, holding it in increased the risk of dying over the ten-year study period to four times that of the women who always told their husbands their feelings in a disagreement. Another study, at Western Washington University, demonstrated that such "self-silencing" increased the risk of depression, eating disorders, and heart disease for women. And researchers in Utah found that the way a couple interacted in an argument was as important a heart disease risk factor as smoking or high cholesterol. In this study of 150 couples, men's risk of heart disease increased if their arguments with their wives involved a battle for control. ("Why can't you just admit that I'm right?" and "We're going to do it my way" are examples of a controlling argument style.) It made no difference whether they or their wives were the ones making the controlling comments.

Why Remarrieds Fight

Everybody who is married fights, and the health and mental health risks of fighting the wrong way are clear. But remarried couples with children probably fight more than other married couples. Why is this so? Mostly, it seems, because differences assert themselves so quickly and so undeniably in this type of partnership. This is because, as family therapist Lois Braverman told me, "going from being a couple to being a couple with a child adds a level of complexity and introduces a dimension that creates differences: How much attention should a child have? What is too much attention, and what is too little? How much independence should they have? And so on. It also introduces judgment."

Usually, the addition of a child comes over time, after the partners have hammered out differences or agreed to disagree about them. Introduce a child who belongs to only one spouse at the outset, however, and the differences, judgments, and stresses are remarkably compounded. For example, Sue Johnson, Ph.D., author of *Hold Me Tight,* told me, "Couples in a remarriage with children face powerful issues of belonging, which can create tremendous uncertainty and stress." Your husband may feel that he's a bad father for asking his kids to deal with change and accept you. You may feel shut out if the kids always seem to come first with him, unsure whether you count and whether he really needs you. Such basic fears compound the fact that kids create stress and make intimacy harder to achieve from the second the two of you come together. "It's almost universally true," Braverman said, "that when you watch someone else with their kid, the kid seems indulged. It's one thing to watch your girlfriend with her kids for an hour on Saturday and tolerate it for the afternoon. It's another thing entirely to live with it. Then you feel you have to say something!"

How Remarried People Fight

Remarried couples with children do not just fight more often. We fight in unique ways, and knowing what they are can help you in your quest to argue effectively. First and perhaps most important, we fight harder and sooner. Psychoanalyst Michael Vincent Miller, Ph.D., has written that marriage, like childhood, has developmental stages. After a giddy romantic period, he theorizes, comes a period of disillusionment, when members of the couple feel disappointed about the discrepancy between what they had hoped for and what they have, and perhaps even feel deceived by their spouses. Often this period of disillusionment brings up feelings of failure, which are so upsetting that we tend to lash out at our spouses rather than acknowledge our fear that things might fall apart, as well as our own role in bringing this state of affairs about with our unrealistic expectations. In a remarriage with children, this period of disillusionment arrives especially quickly and forcefully, shattering the honeymoon period — in which first-marrieds may luxuriate for years — before it has even taken root.

All heterosexual couples are likely to experience what Anne Bernstein calls the gendered overreacting/underreacting dynamic, as well as what E. Mavis Hetherington and couples researcher John Gottman, Ph.D., call the pursuer/distancer dynamic. Remarrieds with children are no exception. "Your son is being so rude to me," a woman might begin. "He's just a teenager," her partner, the boy's father, responds. "It's not that bad." Bernstein explained to me what happens next: "Now the woman has no choice but to amplify, in order to convince her partner that her concern is important and that she is not irrational." How often have we found ourselves yelling at our husbands, ratcheting up our affect in precise reverse proportion to his flat and terse replies? Gottman explains that the dynamic in which women pursue and persist while men distance or withdraw may actually have a physiological basis. He found that in disagreements, men get more aroused more quickly than women do, experiencing a steep rise in heart rate and blood pressure. Fearful of losing control, they withdraw, feeling that it is the "safest" option for decreasing the conflict they are experiencing. Imagine a man's surprise and frustration — not to mention his sense of being unfairly badgered — when retreating only increases his wife's desire to make her point. And imagine — this is probably easy to do — her sense of being abandoned as he retreats into a silence punctuated only by the occasional, lacerating accusation "You're irrational!"

This dynamic is present in all marriages, but because remarried couples with children have more to fight about and fight more often, it is more obvious and more difficult for them. As one woman with stepchildren explained to me, "I want to talk, and he wants me to shut up. Believe me, while we were dating, I never thought we would turn into the Lockhorns. It's such a cliché, and I hate it."

In the case of remarrieds with children, there may be a twist to this gendered dynamic: in bringing up a problem with the children, the wife herself becomes the problem. "How many times has he said, 'It's not a big deal, but you're turning it into one,'" Greta said to me one day, describing how her preteen stepdaughter pointedly and aggressively ignored her whenever the stepfamily was together. Greta's husband may actually have been trying to comfort her initially — *Don't take it to heart; it's not a big deal* — but it sounded like a dismissal, as if he were minimizing Greta's torment. Later, it turned into a criticism. Greta felt shut out twice, both ignored by her stepdaughter and misunderstood and censured by her husband for having feelings about being ignored.

A particular type of emotional censorship is more common among remarried or re-partnered couples than among first-marrieds. James Bray describes it as a tendency to communicate — by pointed inattention, impatience, and changing the subject — that one partner does not want to hear about the other's previous relationship. In this type of communication breakdown, the person simply does not want to know anything that might undermine his or her romantic view of the relationship. The problem with this approach is that in subsequent marriages especially, letting a partner communicate about the past can clear the way to a less problematic present. For example, a man might find that his wife does not want to hear anything about his ex. Yet by not listening to him talk about his prior marriage, she will miss the opportunity to learn about his fears and might misinterpret his behavior. This dynamic can go both ways.

David did not want to hear about Mandy's previous relationship with a man he considered unworthy of her. Without realizing it, he shut Mandy down every time she began to talk about feeling shunted into a babysitter role when her ex went out — often all night long — while his kids were there. By doing this, David missed an important clue as to why Mandy — otherwise so competent and self-confident — panicked and became furious if he so much as wanted to run to the grocery store while his seven-year-old twin boys were at their house. Had he not censored Mandy, he would have learned that for her, being left alone with her ex's kids had meant being exploited; she was frightened that this might happen with David as well. Listening gave David an opportunity to assure her that he understood and would never take advantage of her, but that sometimes a trip to the grocery store is just a trip to the grocery store.

Remarrieds with children might find themselves embroiled as well in what Anne Bernstein calls "conflict by proxy," a dynamic in which one person in a family takes on another's emotional work. A stepmother is likely to experience conflict by proxy in two ways, and recognizing it is her best way out.

First, conflict by proxy may be the way a twosome avoids direct conflict. For example, a divorced mother might enlist her children to carry her pain and anger at her ex-husband, so that they act out toward their father or, more often, his wife. Or children, even adult children, may provoke their stepmother, which feels safer than confronting their father, who is likely more loved and more feared.

Second, in addition to functioning as a kind of "free-fire zone" in detoured parent-child conflicts or in conflicts between ex-spouses, women in remarriages with children frequently find themselves "drafted" to act as proxies for their husbands. While I was interviewing my subjects and talking to psychologists, it became clear to me that it is common for a woman to act on a man's unvoiced issues, essentially having his feelings — which he may find frightening or inappropriate — for him. For example, Bernstein notes that sometimes when a stepmother and a stepdaughter fight, the father has actually unconsciously orchestrated the tensions so that his wife and daughter can play out *his* anger and fear. As they go at it, he recedes into the background, very likely telling himself that "women are crazy."

This was precisely the situation with Bernstein's patients Nell and Ken. Ken's young adult daughter, Darla, made it clear to Nell that she wanted nothing to do with her stepmother by ignoring her, grunting in response to her questions, and generally treating her badly. Ken, who felt embarrassed and put on the spot, did nothing when Darla acted this way. Understandably, Nell felt furious and abandoned. But all the conflict between Nell and Darla, and between Nell and Ken about Darla, was a distraction, it turned out. Ken didn't like the way Darla was acting any more than Nell did. But he was afraid that asking Darla to change would drive her away or make her behavior worse. Once he stepped up to the plate and asked Darla to treat Nell better, Nell stopped feeling so angry toward Darla and toward Ken, at which point Ken realized that *he* had issues with his daughter, issues he had heretofore "handed off" to his wife to fight out for him.

Bernstein describes yet another factor in remarried couples' fights, called "the vicious cycle." In this dynamic, the wife complains about a child's behavior; her husband ignores her; she persists, feeling unpartnered and unsupported; he feels that she is a witch who is on his kid's case all the time. If you ease up, Bernstein suggested when I interviewed her, he may see the problems himself and warm up to you for seeming tolerant toward his child.

And what of the father who doesn't have a disciplinarian bone in his body? To break the vicious cycle, it may help to tell yourself, "I can't come into a dysfunctional family and change everything," Lois Braverman suggested to me. You might even tell yourself, "It's not my problem, and that's a luxury." However, both Bernstein and Braverman were quick to point out that "checking out" should never mean being a doormat. One way to break the vicious cycle, Patricia Papernow suggested, is to ask your husband very calmly to tell his children, "I can't tell you how to feel, but when you're here, I expect you to be polite to your stepmother. You don't have to like her, but you may not treat her like a piece of furniture. Say hello and look her in the eye when she speaks to you." If you ask him to do this in the right way and at the right time, refusing to escalate or take the bait should he hem, haw, or accuse, he is unlikely to deny you so reasonable a request.

More specifically, Papernow suggested a communication formula she calls "soft-hard-soft" when making a request of your spouse on a charged topic. For example, rather than saying, "You let your kids treat me badly, and I've had it," try saying it another way: "I know it's hard for you that there are sometimes tensions between your kids and me [soft]. But could you ask them to respond to me when I walk into a room where they're sitting and I say hello to them [hard, but in the form of a request, not a criticism]? I don't like to put more pressure on you, because I know you're trying so hard. I really appreciate that. It's just that it hurts my feelings and makes it difficult to keep on trying when I feel ignored or treated badly by your kids [soft]." When remarriage with children feels complicated, a simple formula like this, one that cushions a hard request between two loving acknowledgments that the situation is difficult and you appreciate your spouse, is easy to remember and may save you untold aggravation.

Two other skills — putting it off and putting it away — can also help temper even the most passionate and hopeless-feeling conflicts. First, scheduling a time to argue sounds crazy, but it makes a certain amount of sense, marriage experts say. If your partner shuts down a discussion or says, "Not now, I'm busy," take a deep breath and say, "You're right. We're not having much success talking about this right now. What time should we discuss it?" Difficult as it may be to keep your cool when your husband seems to be shutting down, it's well worth trying this trick, which can help a wife seem more rational in her husband's eyes and will increase the likelihood that both partners will be calmer when the hot topic is discussed later. Second, knowing when to walk away from a fight is one of the most useful weapons in your arsenal. Walking away is not the same as stonewalling or bottling up your feelings. It means making a conscious decision to let certain things go so that you can focus on the issues that really matter to you. One woman told me, "He finally told his kids, after five years of me asking, that if they couldn't be nice to me, they shouldn't come over. And they got more polite. He did what I asked, and so I don't ride him about the little things his kids might do. He's done his part."

The Four Horsemen and the Good Fight

Sometimes it helps to have analysis boiled down to its essence, advice reduced to its simplest form. The next time you and your partner are having "the big fight" over his kids — the one you have over and over — consider that things *can* go differently. Psychoeducation — learning what is normal and what helps — is the key, couples experts say. John Gottman has studied more than two thousand married couples for more than twenty years and discovered four attitudes that predict dissolution of a relationship. Gottman explains that each of the "four horsemen" paves the way to the next. Avoid these four ways of fighting, and you and your partner will dramatically increase your chances of remaining together (relatively) happily ever after.

> **Criticism** = Attacking your partner's personality or character (rather than something he has done), usually with the intent of demonstrating that you are right and he is wrong. Using phrases such as "You always . . . ," "You never . . . ," and "Why are you so . . . ."
>
> **Contempt** = Being insulting to your partner or openly disrespecting him. Employing insults, name-calling, hostile humor or mockery, sneering, or eye rolling.
>
> **Defensiveness** = Denying responsibility, making excuses, meeting one complaint with another, or not paying attention to what the other person is saying. Using phrases such as "Yes, but . . ."; "That's not true, you're the one who . . ."; and "I do *not* . . ."
>
> **Stonewalling** = Refusing to respond, withdrawing, or physically removing yourself from the conflict. Far from being "neutral" or helpful, this tactic is provocative. Men tend to engage in it much more often than women do.

Gottman's research also concentrates on precisely what happens when successful couples fight. According to Gottman, these couples make five positive remarks about their spouse for every critical comment they make during an argument; do not escalate or "kitchen sink" (throw more and more issues into the argument, such as "You don't like my kids? Well let's talk about your stupid mother and how nasty she was last Thursday!"); break the tension with jokes and distractions; and always make repairs after an argument.

According to Sue Johnson, remarried couples, given their very specific challenges, must do one thing above all others: "Sharing basic needs and fears — about being an outsider, about creating stress for your kids by remarrying and feeling divided in your loyalties, about wanting to know you count — is what helps more than anything else in weathering the storm of creating a new family." For women with stepchildren, that may mean swallowing your pride and making yourself vulnerable just when you feel most misunderstood and betrayed. But it is also likely to open the door to greater emotional closeness and a partnership that beats the odds.

PARENTING IN YOUR MARRIAGE

There are kids who are not your own in this partnership, rendering it qualitatively different from others. Recognizing the unique characteristics of a remarriage with children and knowing that the everyday aggravations actually have a name might help stepmothers see that they are not alone and that their "families" are not so unusual or abnormal. And tackling these issues as a team can actually solder together a couple that they are threatening to pull apart.

The Dripolator Effect vs. the Percolator Effect

Anyone who has ever lived with a sullen teen or preteen knows that if you're not careful to separate your moods from your kid's, he or she can render the tone of the whole household stressful and lugubrious. Family therapist James Bray has noted that this effect is intensified in remarriages with children, with the normal order of things turned on its head. In a first marriage, a troubled child may affect the marriage to a small degree, but a troubled marriage will greatly affect the child. Bray calls this the top-down, or "dripolator," effect. Unhappy parents make bad disciplinarians and poor confidants, and high levels of marital conflict are known to contribute to a wide range of emotional and behavior problems in a child. By contrast, a strong and healthy marital bond in a first marriage has a positive effect on a child, instilling feelings of confidence, well-being, and security that all foster an ability to adapt.

But in a remarriage with children, Bray notes, the interaction between marriage and parenting flows in the opposite direction — from the kids up to the couple. He calls this the bottom-up, or "percolator," effect. In a remarriage, marital happiness has little effect on the adjustment of a child, who very likely has little invested in his or her parent and stepparent staying together and often harbors fantasies that they will divorce so that his or her parents can reconcile. Yet the child's moods, tantrums, and issues are likely to have a great impact on the couple, virtually determining, in too many cases, whether the marriage is happy or not. The reason, according to Bray, is this: "When an unhappy child acts out, he doesn't just make the mood of the household miserable; he begins to divide the stepmother, who is likely to become increasingly critical of him, from the parent, who is likely to become defensive and increasingly annoyed at his wife's criticisms of his child."

Like so many of us, Cee-Cee — whom we met earlier as the easygoing and affable mother of a preschooler and stepmother of a teenage boy — walked directly into this trap. Shortly after her husband and his two boys — who were nine and eleven at the time — moved in with her, she decided to take on the issue of the boys' table manners. "I just thought, *I refuse to eat at a table with pigs!*" Cee-Cee told me. But the more she pushed, albeit politely, the more the boys seemed to resent her, responding with sullen grunts and even getting up and walking away from the table when she spoke. Although this may not be entirely surprising, Cee-Cee was unprepared for her husband Ned's response. "Ned basically said, 'Get off their backs already!' Like I was being some kind of harpy. I'm a real 'get along and let the little stuff go' type of person. But their manners were atrocious, and I didn't feel I had to put up with it." Part of the difficulty was likely that Ned felt criticized. It was as if every time Cee-Cee asked her stepsons to please not grab a piece of meat off the serving platter with their hands, her husband felt that she was saying, "You didn't do a good job raising them!" Like Cee-Cee, we often feel unfairly stereotyped as wicked for wanting something as simple as minimally good table manners. After a number of these experiences, whenever our stepchildren act sullen, we may relive the injustice, experiencing all over again the feeling of being misunderstood. During the final stage of this cycle, we may find ourselves in a worse mood than the children were when they acted out.

But it is possible for couples to change this dynamic so that the stepmother is seen not as a shrew but as a powerful ally to her husband — and his kids. Psychologist Lauren Ayers told me one day in her office, "I've often told my patients here for family and couple work that I wish every kid had a stepmother. Stepmothers usually have higher expectations for their husbands' kids than their husbands do. And that can be really motivating, healthy, and helpful for the kids in the long run."

When it comes to "interventions" about a stepchild's behavior, a suggestion posed as a neutral question ("I think the kids are old enough to load the dishwasher themselves. What do you think?") can make a world of difference in your husband's receptivity, Lois Braverman of the Ackerman Institute for the Family told me. "It's the difference between feeling put on the spot and feeling supported," she said. An attitude of "we're in this together" on the part of the couple also has the benefit of restoring the correct flow of power to stepfamily relations and blunting the impact of a child's negativity.

Stepmother and author Cherie Burns recommends reversing the percolator effect by never pandering to a stepchild in a black mood ("What's wrong? Are you mad at me? Did something bad happen?") and by refusing to take it personally. Being busy and acting as if you don't even notice are the best policies, she suggests, to avoid creating a "stepchild-dominated environment." Kids may think they want to be in charge of the home and its moods, but in reality the most reassuring thing for them, Burns says, is the reassertion of the rightful order of adult-child relations. That means showing them that their rotten mood or nasty attitude will not sink the family ship. Even if you don't feel it, things will go more smoothly when you convey the attitude "We'll all sail through this just fine."

The Biological Force Field and Middle Ground

When you marry a man with children, you are not just setting out to forge a relationship and a world with someone you love. You are also entering into a web of habits, preferences, inside jokes, problems, hopes, antagonisms, rituals, and history that precedes you and very likely excludes you. The sensation of being an outsider, a feeling that things are set up to preclude intimacy, particularly in the first one to three years of a partnership with a man with children, is something many women experience. Lotte, a forty-three-year-old writer, told me that she was shocked to discover that the family computer — used by her new partner's ten-year-old daughter and fifteen-year-old son — was in his bedroom, the most heavily trafficked room in the house. When she told him she would prefer that the bedroom be a more private space, an argument ensued about her "not understanding kids," and it was months before the couple agreed to move the computer to the dining room. Olivia told me that her three adult stepdaughters "had an amazing ability to make me feel like a guest in my own home when they were over." And Lorna marveled that her then fiancé had let his nine-year-old son decide that she would not be allowed to sleep over on "his" weekends with Dad.

All these adult partners had run up against what psychologist James Bray calls "the biological force field," a strong bond between a parent and a child that can feel like an actual physical force keeping us at bay, repelling our efforts to be part of the family. But we seldom comment on it for fear of seeming petty. (This problem may be less severe for women who bring their own children to the marriage. In these cases, the woman is not so clearly an outsider in her husband's "mini-family," having a mini-family of her own.) The biological force field will ebb over time if husband and wife are committed to making theirs the central relationship in the family system, actively building what psychologist Sonia Nevis has termed "middle ground." Without this commitment, as we've seen, the married couple will likely remain the weakest relationship in the web of stepfamily relations.

"It was a process of coming together as a couple for a long time after we were married," Jonathan, the entertainment executive we met in chapter 5, explained to me of his partnership with Julia. (Remember that Jonathan has two older sons from a previous marriage and two younger daughters with Julia.) "My wife felt hurt when my older son [Mark] did things to show her he was here first. Mark would intentionally talk about things that had happened before Julia came along, so she wouldn't be able to participate in the conversation at all." On more than one occasion, Julia simply "zoned out" during a long, intricately detailed conversation about old times to which she could contribute nothing more than "That sounds like it was fun," over and over. In private later, Julia told Jonathan, with irritation, that she was tired of the dynamic in which he allowed Mark to put her on the outside — and keep her there. Time was part of the cure for what ailed Jonathan, Julia, and Mark, but there was also a commitment on the part of Jonathan and Julia to use that time to strengthen their own relationship. "Over the years, Julia and I made our own history, with Mark and his brother and apart from them," Jonathan said.

The "apart from them" part was crucial, because it helped Jonathan and Julia forge the "middle ground" that Patricia Papernow describes as "paths of easy connection where the partners don't even need to think about it." Unlike first-marrieds, Julia and Jonathan and other remarrieds with kids do not automatically have a lot of middle ground — whether it's going to the opera, reading the paper in a certain order on Sunday, or loving karaoke — before the introduction of kids, who tend to erode middle ground. The more Jonathan and Julia made a priority of "couple time" — which could mean just a half-hour alone together while Mark was visiting or a whole weekend together when his sons weren't around — the more middle ground the two of them shared, the less exclusionary the biological force field felt, and the better Julia could weather Mark's attempts to exclude her. Jonathan told me, "Eventually, Mark just stopped focusing on the past so much. I think he got a clear sense that there was a present with Julia now and that he could enter that."

Papernow notes that "much of what is needed to strengthen the partnership in a remarriage with children is counterintuitive." When Jonathan's sons heard Julia urging him to take them out to dinner one night every weekend for several weeks in a row while she stayed home to catch up on work, for example, their stepmother stopped seeming like quite so much of a "Dad hog." And Jonathan got a realistic sense about one-on-one time with his sons, particularly Mark. He enjoyed it immensely but saw that Mark, like all teens, was not always easy to be around. He began voicing some of the realistic criticisms of his son's behavior that Julia had felt herself but that Jonathan couldn't bear to hear from her. And in this way, over the years, Julia often found herself more able to take the role of supporting the boy rather than feeling compelled to point out his flaws or nasty moments to a defensive Jonathan. Predictably, this shift endeared Julia to Jonathan even more.

Julia also made a point to socialize one night every week with her friends from before the marriage. At first Jonathan protested, but Julia insisted that sometimes she needed to be with people who made her feel like an "insider" instead of an outsider. Her friends put her at ease, understood her, shared lots of middle ground with her, and made her feel less consumed by the difficulties inherent in life with stepchildren. Papernow explains that this is one more way that second partnerships with children are different from first partnerships: "If the husband is coming from a first-family model, he is likely to say, 'That's not good. If she can't spend time with our family, something is wrong.' But second marriages with kids are a different thing entirely. You can't use the map of the first family with a second family. Time away with friends, stepping out for the evening without your husband or his kids, can actually make this second marriage with kids work better. It's rejuvenating and prevents stepparent burnout." The surprising bottom line: sometimes surrendering to the biological force field, or stepping out of it for an evening, can strengthen the couple bond and build middle ground.

The Ex Factor

In previous centuries, remarriages occurred almost exclusively after the death of a spouse. With the rise of remarriage after divorce, however, a new and confounding variable has emerged: the ex. The presence of an ex-spouse is not a happy thing for the women

I interviewed. In contrast, a fair number of the men I spoke to described their wives' exes on the spectrum from "uninvolved, so not really a problem" to "fine" and even "basically a standup guy." These sentiments echo an interesting finding from comprehensive studies on divorce and remarriage with children: an ex-wife generally spells more trouble than an ex-husband.

In spite of a recent trend toward more involved fathering, mothers are generally thought of, and generally act as, "primary parents." They are more likely, for example, to have custody and to be the daily presence in a child's life. As such, mothers are more likely to make appointments and take children to them, to interface more regularly with teachers, and to have strong agendas, wishes, and expectations regarding how things such as homework, laundry, and lunches are done. In short, compared to a male ex, a female ex is likely to be more involved in the details of her children's lives and more involved with her ex's remarried family — and to feel that she should be and should have the final say. All this involvement translates into increased opportunities for conflict. Often the step-mother, because she is a woman and so presumed responsible for child care, will bear the brunt of the ex-wife's expectations about or disappointment over how things go during a stay with Dad. One woman reported to me that her husband's ex had called her in a fury after her twelve-year-old daughter had been there for a weekend. "Why aren't you making sure my daughter wears deodorant when she's with you?" the ex had demanded. The stepmother observed, "I'm not allowed to set limits about her TV habits or what she wears on a cold day, because her mom goes nuts if she hears about it and says I'm overreaching. Yet I'm somehow to blame for her personal hygiene?" She was clearly outraged — and understandably so — by the typical stepmother conundrum: the husband's ex who wants to have it both ways, giving us responsibility but not granting authority.

Many women find themselves in much worse situations. E. Mavis Hetherington found that resentment is more sustained in divorced women than in divorced men. She also found that the remarriage of an ex-spouse tends to reactivate anger for women more than for men. In my interviews, I was told about ex-wives who were the first ones to call and congratulate the couple on their engagement or marriage, only to call back the next day to demand more child support. Women also told me, over and over, about ex-wives who wanted to renegotiate custody and visitation after the remarriage. Hetherington discovered the same tendency among her cohort of ex-wives. Mom's lingering resentment renders it nearly impossible for children to build a relationship with their stepmother, sensing that liking her would be a betrayal. This in turn creates stress for the married couple, a stress that no first marriage has to endure.

In contrast to ex-wives, ex-husbands (and here we're talking about your husband) are more likely to be friendly and welcoming to their ex's new spouse, paving the way for better relations between stepfathers and stepkids. Men have been shown to have more sustained attachments to their ex-wives, to nurture fantasies of reconciliation with them (until they re-partner), and to hope for smooth platonic sailing with exes who have re-partnered. Although this sounds good in theory, it can lead to some unexpected difficulties for their wives. Many women reported to me, often in chagrined tones, that their husbands still performed a variety of household chores for their unmarried exes. The men explained it away as a necessity: "If I don't fix the roof, it's going to leak on my kids." It is easy to understand how these chores could be used as tests or leverage by an ex-wife who is unreconciled to her ex-husband's remarriage, tends to like to stir up trouble, or wants to flex her muscles and demonstrate her ongoing clout to her "rival."

When husbands decide themselves or agree with you to cut back on their activities at their ex's home — to build what Anne Bernstein calls a "good fence" — there may well be a backlash. Usually, you are blamed and, with unfortunate frequency, denounced loudly in front of the children. The ex also may try to change visitation agreements out of spite and exhibit other vengeful behavior. According to Bernstein, "Letting go of old resentments is the most challenging part of working with post-divorce families." Sometimes, she notes, an ex-partner may continue to suffer in order to exact revenge on those she feels have mistreated her. For these ex-wives, Bernstein explains, doing too well — being able to fix a broken fuse box, laugh at a joke, or just have a civil relationship with her ex-husband — "is seen as allowing the person one feels injured by to minimize the consequences of his actions." That is, in her eyes, being happy or high functioning would let her ex-husband off the hook. So she continues to do poorly, motivated by a desire to prove that she has been deeply wronged.

Such "accusatory suffering," as psychologists Arthur and Elizabeth Seagull call it, may be an ex-wife's way of feeling powerful and has the added "benefit" of separating her children from their father after a remarriage, at the birth of a child in the remarriage, or during any other event that reopens her wounds. Just knowing that such a behavior has a name, however, can help the couple keep their balance. "Look," forty-one-year-old Lorna told me one day, interrupting her own monologue about her husband's vindictive-sounding ex, "it's always the same old story. She's the victim, and we're the bad guys. We don't believe it, and someday her own kid is not going to believe it anymore either. So we'll just wait it out."

Research shores up our commonsense suspicion that an ex-wife who does not remarry is likely to be the most troublesome, not only for us but also for her children, who may well feel that she is victimized and at a disadvantage as long as she is single and Dad is remarried. Simply put, children with single mothers have a harder time accommodating a stepparent, and knowing this may allow you to take their rejection a little less personally. Sociologist Linda Nielsen has outlined a number of additional factors that determine just how problematic an ex-wife will be. She found the highest levels of conflict when the biological mother was white, had a graduate education, and had a high household income. Why would these women — the ones who are likely to have better access to psychotherapy, as well as the luxury of time and energy to read about what's best for their kids — have the hardest time letting go of anger? Researchers suggest that it is a matter of social programming. Unlike women from other backgrounds, middle-class and upper-middle-class white women are less likely to have a tradition of sharing child-rearing

duties with adults other than a spouse and are much less likely
to subscribe to the "it takes a village" mentality. White women of
means also likely grew up with a very "possessive mothering model"
compared to women from lower-income backgrounds or from
other racial groups. They tend to feel more threatened and jealous
when it comes to their children having a close relationship with
another adult, particularly a mother figure. (In contrast, close, loving relationships between children and a variety of parent figures
are common in the West Indies, Polynesia, and Ghana, as well as in
the Pueblo, Navajo, and African American cultures in the United
States.) Adding to the difficulty, very educated white single mothers
with high household incomes are more likely to have permissive
parenting styles (high levels of warmth and low levels of control).
The parenting style of the residential biological parent can play a
large role in determining whether a child feels accountable for bad
behavior toward another adult — a stepmother — or not. And bad
behavior toward the stepmother makes for more marital discord
and more stress. In addition, a permissive mother makes a normally assertive stepmother with reasonable expectations seem like a
monster in comparison. Finally, if an ex-wife is a substance abuser,
mentally ill, has a personality disorder, or suffers from depression,
the stresses on your remarriage with children will be compounded
dramatically.

The ex factor can have a profound impact on the remarried
couple, especially when children are younger and visitation, child
support, schooling, discipline, and other issues are on the table,
"linking" the divorced spouses in fundamental ways. But life is not
necessarily easier for women who marry widowers. Although most
researchers have found that stepmothers, couples, and even children report better relationships in a remarriage with children when
the marriage ended with death rather than divorce, women who
marry widowers have challenges of their own. Florence summed it
up well: "My therapist said, 'The longer your husband's ex is dead,
the more sainted and powerful she'll become.' And that has definitely been the case."

Florence feels very close to her stepgrandchildren, for example, and goes to great lengths to travel to see them, to send them gifts, and to spend time with them when they are in town. But the fifth consecutive year she timed the sending of a gift to coincide with the day of her stepgrandson's birthday party and received no call of thanks or gesture of inclusion; she became angry and hurt. For the first time ever in their twenty-five-year marriage, Florence's husband called his son to the mat on Florence's behalf, asking why there had never been any acknowledgment of the gifts. Florence's forty-five-year-old stepson replied that she should stop signing her cards "Grandma Florence." "Their *real* grandmother is dead," he said. "Do you know what it means to me that she does that? How disrespectful it is of my *mother*, your first *wife?*" In spite of Florence's best efforts for nearly three decades and a relationship with her stepson that she characterizes as "not great, but pretty good," he felt that her desire to be a grandmother to his son was an infringement, a belittling — even a negation — of his mother. Acknowledging Florence's gifts, and her interest in having a loving relationship with her stepgrandson, was more than an issue of nomenclature for her adult stepson. It was actually a betrayal of his mother, for whom he reverently reserved the title "Grandma." Florence, meanwhile, said, "I don't care what they call me. I'm just surprised that my stepson is still so touchy. And I'm a little tired of it." She was happy when her stepson's wife recently sent her a Grandmother's Day card — exactly the acknowledgment that she had been hoping for and that her stepson did not feel comfortable extending.

Co-Parenting and Parallel Parenting

Depending on the age of your husband's children at the time of your remarriage and the level of conflict in his relationship with his ex, you may be drafted into co-parenting, parallel parenting, or just watching from the sidelines. The need for flexibility and negotiation is paramount, and until the marriage has built what Anne Bernstein calls "good fences and good bridges," working through the kinks can create stress for both the wife/stepmother and the couple.

Cooperative Co-Parenting: The "Best-Case Scenario"

In recent years, the concept of co-parenting has taken center stage in the discourse of divorce and remarriage. An essential component of what psychologist Constance Ahrons terms "the good divorce," cooperative co-parenting is an ideal practice in which divorced parents put their differences aside in order to form a parenting coalition in the best interests of their children. For example, they may call each other to make sure homework is getting done, agree to attend a child's sporting events at the same time, and coordinate household rules and child-rearing practices. They may get together for holidays and children's birthday parties. At the extreme end of the spectrum, a very few divorced couples may have an arrangement whereby they themselves take turns living in the children's home a certain number of days each week, rather than having the kids change households. Highly cooperative co-parenting may be catching on. Lois Braverman of the Ackerman Institute for the Family has seen an increase in co-parenting in the past decades, now that parents have become more familiar with the literature about how beneficial it is for children and states have begun to require parenting courses for divorcing parents. She told me, "There's a trend toward people making that effort, trying not to be a high-conflict, contentious divorced couple, to cooperate on parenting issues for the sake of the kids."

Cooperative co-parenting is likely the best practice for everyone in the long run. From the stepmother's perspective, happier kids who have a strong bond with their father will generally be less threatened by her and ultimately less disruptive to her marriage. And if her husband and his ex are cooperative enough that the mother actually encourages her kids to give their stepmother a chance, the children's loyalty conflicts will diminish, allowing them to be open to having a cordial — or even close — relationship with her. Yet Braverman, who has spent decades working with families of divorce and remarriage, explained that although the prognosis for kids is very good when there is a high degree of cooperation between their divorced parents, such cooperation can be difficult for the wife/stepmother. "It can leave wives with the frustrating sensation that when it comes to their own lives and their own marriages, their hands are tied," she said. "So many people are involved in these decisions." This means that something as simple as trying to arrange a romantic getaway can become absurdly complicated or even impossible. In some cases, cooperative co-parenting may go too far not only for the taste of the stepmother but also for the health of the couple and the well-being of his kids.

Laynie was married to a man whose ex "thought we were going to be like one big happy family. She actually wanted us to go on family vacations together. I had no interest in that!" Making matters more complicated, Laynie's husband lived across the street from his ex, and Laynie frequently got the feeling that "it was just sort of one big house without a boundary," a situation she set about changing by insisting that they move. Other women told me of feeling pressured to do big "family" holidays with their husbands' exes "for the sake of the kids." But such arrangements seem to work for only a few. Just one of my subjects — a remarkably easygoing woman who had no family of her own and who also had the good luck to marry a man whose ex was as laid-back and good-natured as she was — wanted to spend her holidays this way.

It is crucial for remarried couples to start and maintain rituals and traditions of their own, leaving the door open for the children to join them and sending the message that both their marriage and their invitation are real. To my mind, this imperative to nurture and protect a remarriage — which has the odds stacked against it from the outset — outweighs the obligation many divorced fathers feel to repeat the rites of a past that no longer exists for the sake of their offspring (who may actually find it awkward) or to appease an ex.

Though well-intentioned, the increasingly widespread belief that remarriage with children should be as child-centric and change-free as possible can lead to stress for everyone involved. It is easy to see how it might be stressful for the woman with stepchildren. But research also shows that high levels of closeness and involvement between exes are as confusing and counterproductive for children as are high levels of conflict. Children are likely to wonder, "If you like each other so much and get along so well, why did you get a divorce?" and feel profoundly perplexed about what exactly makes for a good relationship. The movie *Stepmom* takes the expectation to an absurd extreme. In it, the stepmom, played by Julia Roberts, spends Christmas with her husband, her husband's children, and his dying ex-wife in her home and is overwhelmed with gratitude when the ex invites her to join them for a "family portrait." The good news, grounded in reality and not in Hollywood fantasy, is that although the outcome of remarriage with children is brighter when exes cooperate with each other, this needn't entail spending a lot of time with your husband's ex. Also remember that the need to coordinate closely with and get "permission" from his ex will lessen as the kids get older.

Parallel Parenting

If cooperative co-parenting is the ideal, parallel parenting is the norm. Texas family law expert Stewart Gagnon told me that although he has noticed "a shift in expectations, with more people now believing that the divorced couple should 'try to get along for the sake of the children' and even attend events like the children's birthday parties together, there has not been a huge shift in real behavior." Indeed, only about one-quarter of the participants in E. Mavis Hetherington's huge longitudinal study on divorce achieved what she calls "a cooperative parenting relationship" after breaking up. About half of the divorced parents she followed adopted instead an arrangement of more or less ignoring each other. Called "parallel parenting," this arrangement basically allows each ex to do his or her own thing regarding child rearing. One parent might send an e-mail announcing an intention to attend a school event rather than make a phone call, for example, and leave it to the ex to decide whether he or she will also attend. With parallel parenting, each household may have very different rules, but researchers have found that hearing "This is how we do things here" just once or twice is enough to clear up a child's confusion.

Hetherington found minimal overt or persistent conflict between exes in these arrangements. They often work quite well for the stepmother, because they allow her to have more of a voice in the child-rearing practices in her own household, especially rules about cleaning up and courtesy, which tend to be the biggest sticking points. As for the children themselves, Hetherington reports being surprised at how well they were able to adjust to the apparent contradictions of parallel parenting. Often they may have not only a sense of "two sets of rules" but also of "two homes" and even "two sets of parents." My own younger stepdaughter has always been impressive — and perhaps also typical — in her flexibility in this regard. Before she left boarding school for college, if she called us from her mother's and we asked where she was, she might say, "I'm at home." Yet she often fills out forms requesting a home address by giving ours. Sometimes when she's on the phone with a friend while staying with us, she says, "I'm hanging out with my parents in New York City."

However, kids who grow up with the parallel parenting paradigm may also develop less healthy coping strategies — namely, ways to "game the system." Accustomed to Mom and Dad not communicating, they can be manipulative about issues such as money, homework, and curfew, to name just a few. "I'm all done with my math. I did it at Mom's," your stepson might say when he simply doesn't feel like doing it. With no communication between his parents, no one will check, and he may develop the sense that there are no consequences for being dishonest. These tendencies stress a stepmother's tolerance, as she is less likely to see the child through rose-colored glasses or assess his behavior through the lens of paternal or maternal guilt. One woman reported discovering that her adolescent stepson was asking both his mother and his father for money for the same school trip. "It was a lot of money," the woman told me. "We only figured it out by happenstance, since my husband and his ex don't speak. I know he learned [to use this behavior] because his parents aren't on the same page in all kinds of ways. But I like him less when he does this stuff." A stepmother who brings such behavior to light with the intent of helping a stepchild become a more honorable and trustworthy person is likely to incite fireworks rather than change. No one likes to hear his or her child criticized, least of all a father who feels guilty for divorcing the child's mother and secretly suspects that he himself may be at the root of the child's behavior or character problems.

Whether your husband and his ex settle on a strategy of cooperative co-parenting — and do the attendant emotional and logistical work — or stumble into parallel parenting by default, each of these approaches to handling children from his previous marriage will have an impact on you. On the days when the difficulties feel insuperable, it may help to remember that co-parenting only lasts for so long. Children grow up, depart, separate from their mothers, and see things in a new light in many cases. Coordinating schedules, sporting events, holidays, drop-offs, pickups, and the like will slowly fade from your calendar, your life, and your mind. Your partnership, on the other hand, in spite of all the statistics and stresses that seem to indicate otherwise, can be forever. In spite of the distractions, dramas, and sideshows in a remarriage with children, your relationship with your husband is the center that holds.

PART III

PERSPECTIVES

CHAPTER SEVEN

SOCIOBIOLOGY

What the Birds, the Bees, and the White-Fronted
Bee-Eaters Can Teach Us About Stepmothering

A S IS CLEAR from the many insights of therapists and researchers that inform this book, psychology has produced knowledge about stepmothers that is at once illuminating and extremely specific. There is a wide range of discourses beyond psychology that, while having much to offer in the way of reframing and explaining step-realities and step-struggles, has seldom — if ever — been brought to bear on the topic. How might we bulwark the discoveries and contributions of psychology and counter both its inward orientation and the misapprehension of some therapists that we can "fix" most of the problems of stepparenting? (This bias is explored in depth in chapter 9.) Certainly, the historical and cultural pieces of the stepmothering experience, often considered by the best family practitioners in their work with stepfamilies, can help us to see contemporary stepmothers in a broader context, offering new ways to understand and perhaps resolve dilemmas that might otherwise seem purely interior or interpersonal. But other disciplines may allow us to widen our field of vision even further — into prehistory, for example, as well as into other worlds (or at least other cultures). The fields of evolutionary biology and anthropology do more than simply allow us to see stepmothering in a new way. They urge a fundamental reconsideration of what a stepmother is, and what having stepchildren means, by exploring just what might be informing our social behavior other than psychological drives or psychodynamics.

When Harvard entomologist E. O. Wilson published *Sociobiology: The New Synthesis* in 1975 he set off a controversy that continues to reverberate in some quarters even today. His contention that natural selection acts not just on our bodies but also on our social behaviors, attitudes, and emotions touched a nerve. By and large, the outrage stemmed from the belief that Wilson and other sociobiologists were suggesting that animal (including human) social behavior is determined by our genes. Nor did many people like the implication that behaviors — especially unsavory ones — might have been selected for because they were evolutionarily advantageous or adaptive. Wilson was not the lone proponent of sociobiology. His colleagues and collaborators included biologists, zoologists, primatologists, and anthropologists, such as Robert Trivers, William Hamilton, and Sarah Blaffer Hrdy. Of course, sociobiology was ultimately indebted to and expanding on Charles Darwin's theories. The main assertion of sociobiology was that natural selection would favor those individuals who acted to improve their fitness — their ability to survive and produce strong, healthy offspring, who would in turn survive to reproduce.

Three decades later, those who are interested in the biological underpinnings of human social behavior tend to call themselves human behavioral ecologists. Whatever name they go by, these scientists are paying more attention to context than ever before, emphasizing the complex interplay of biological, social, cultural, and ecological factors that likely underlie specific human behaviors such as taking care of our young. These scientists suggest that such practices, far from being preprogrammed by our genes, have likely been informed by millions of years of natural selection but will express themselves in different ways depending on the situation. A devoted mother bear may be assiduously maternal by letting one of her two or three cubs die, for example, rather than committing to all of them under unfavorable conditions and increasing the odds that none will survive. The main conceptual underpinnings of behavioral ecology and sociobiology — concepts such as fitness, altruism, reproductive tradeoffs and maternal retrenchment, parental investment, parent-offspring conflict, and kin selection — seem ready-made for helping us think through just why stepparenting might be at once so challenging and so widespread.

Oddly, one of the best ways to understand stepmothers, and the internal and external conflicts in which they find themselves mired, may well be to take a look at what sociobiologists and human behavioral ecologists have had to say about mothers. Even more oddly, what a few of them have had to say about mothers of species other than our own may shed the most suggestive light on the conundrums of contemporary human stepmothers. Though admittedly a circuitous path, this one does afford a uniquely comprehensive perspective, reaching back into prehistory while linking us to our closest animal relatives — as well as some that are not so close. For example, birds.

LACK'S BIRDS: INDIVIDUALS, MOTHERS, AND TRADEOFFS

In her masterful book *Mother Nature: Maternal Instincts and How They Shape the Human Species,* which informs this chapter and the next in fundamental ways, sociobiologist Sarah Blaffer Hrdy calls David Lack, an adviser to the British Trust for Ornithology in the early 1940s, "the first reproductive ecologist." After World War II, Lack organized hundreds of amateur birders in Britain to help him compile information about banded swallows and robins, among other birds. They observed nests, carefully counting and weighing eggs, then continued watching as chicks hatched and fledged.

Lack wanted to know: How many eggs were produced? How many hatched? Of those that hatched, how many actually successfully fledged? And why? How to account for the discrepancies? For example, why would a mother bird lay three eggs but fledge two chicks? Or only one? Why did some bird mothers fail to rear any young at all in some breeding seasons? Lack's interest from the outset was to investigate certain assumptions about what birds "just do naturally" when it comes to parenting. When the massive amount of data was in, Lack realized that there were significant differences when it came to individual birds' breeding success: some mother birds seemed to be better at it than others. He also noted that bird mothers did not adjust their fertility to benefit the species or the group, but rather, as Hrdy puts it, "they managed their reproductive effort" — their egg laying, nest guarding, incubating, and provisioning — "so as to make the best of their own particular circumstances." Far from "greater goodists" — a term coined by scientist Helen Cronin to describe the misapprehension that evolution was about the survival of the species — these bird mothers were acting out an individual's agenda.

And it was all a great deal more complicated, Lack realized, than it might have seemed. For she who produced the most eggs in a breeding season or even over her lifetime, or attempted to incubate and rear every egg she laid, or provisioned the chicks most tirelessly, did not automatically win the evolutionary jackpot and fledge the most chicks. What made some bird mothers successful in this undertaking and others less so? How come some fledged more chicks than others? For the answers, Lack looked to the phenomenon of staggered egg laying. In species such as eagles and gulls, the females lay their eggs a day or more apart. But the mother begins to sit on her eggs as soon as they are laid, and thus the first-laid egg hatches days before the next. The inevitable consequence is that the first chick has the run of the nest — and several meals — by the time the next hatches, easily beating it out for food and thus all but guaranteeing that if provisions are in short supply, the unfortunate second-born will starve. During this struggle, mother bird will not intervene on behalf of the beleaguered younger sibling. But if there is no scarcity of food, she will take steps, aided by the simple fact of bounty, to ensure that the second sib will survive the elder's attempts to rule the roost.

By laying more than one egg, then allowing the firstborn to reduce the size of the brood if necessary, the mother bird tries to bring her family size in line with the food supply. Abundant food and happy ecological conditions mean two or more chicks; tougher circumstances ensure that there will be only one and that Mom will not deplete herself too much in her efforts to feed her young.

These mothers, it seemed to Lack, were far from birdbrained. They were hedging their bets, taking the measure of circumstances around them before deciding how the drama in the nest would unfold. Would a mother incubate all her eggs or let one fall to the side? Would she provision all the chicks, investing equally in each of them? Or would she allow the oldest to extinguish the younger one(s)? Lack's birds were, in Hrdy's words, "highly discerning mothers" (weighing their options, assessing prevailing conditions), "whose commitment to their young was contingent on circumstances."

Taking it all in, Lack struck on an idea: there was a fundamental tradeoff in the life of these avian mothers. It was *Should I have more chicks and invest less in each, or have fewer chicks and go for broke each time?* Lack paved the way for later scientists to explore the notion that mothers might "trade off" reproduction in the present against the possibility of doing even better in the future. This female discretion — this deciding what to do — meant a number of things. First, some mothers would be pretty good at hedging their bets, while others would fail. Such variation meant they were open to selection pressures: that is, better maternal strategists would produce young who would in turn reproduce themselves. The variation in success rates also suggested that a mother's interests were not always identical to those of her brood. Bird mothers might stand aside and complacently allow one offspring to peck its less fortunate later-born sibling to death or starve it out. Or they might rally all their energies in the service of incredibly draining efforts to ward off intruders who threaten their nestlings' lives. In short, it all depends. Nothing about mothering, Lack's work suggested, was "rotely nurturing" or "automatically maternal." These mothers were "flexible strategists" (Hrdy's term), more closely resembling film noir dames coolly assessing their options than June Cleaver. Their dedication to their offspring, their "instinct" to nurture, could not be separated from a facility for logic that might turn lethal. The charged truth that motherhood entails calculation and strategy — Is what's good for my chick going to be bad for me? Do I give this chick my all or reserve my efforts for what might be a more robust chick or, better, more plentiful conditions down the road? — seems more charged still when biologists suggest that precisely such tradeoffs inform maternal behavior in other animals as well — including bees. And humans.

HAMILTON'S BEES: INCLUSIVE FITNESS AND KIN SELECTION

Lack's strategic mothers, assessing conditions and making tradeoffs in each breeding season over a lifetime, with greater or lesser success, and adjusting their efforts to best increase their individual fitness, suggested further avenues of inquiry. Scientists now began to wonder, *What are the other ways animal mothers adjust maternal investment in line with ecological conditions?* And if Lack's bird mothers and other animal mothers were deciding (in some sense) how many young to care for in a given season, just as other animal mothers were also adjusting their maternal investment in line with varying and variable contexts, what to make of a species in which females would forgo motherhood? Not just for a breeding season, or even two or three either, but for their entire lives, dedicating themselves instead to the task of raising someone else's offspring. What could possibly motivate an animal to be so apparently selfless as to forgo reproduction altogether?

This was the question facing anyone with an evolutionary bent who studied honeybees, ants, and wasps, known as a group as "hymenopteran social insects." Honeybees, living in what appears to be a kind of utopia (biologists call their living arrangements "eusocial," or "perfectly social"), seem to be the ultimate daycare providers — tireless and self-abnegating — or the devoted stepmothers of our dreams. Toiling in the service of the queen bee, they busily tend to her young rather than having their own. Why?

It seemed to fly in the face of Darwinian evolutionary thinking, an exception to the rule of individual fitness, until a scientist named William Hamilton proposed a theory about just what might be going on in these highly cooperative breeding colonies, "where only one in tens of thousands of females ever becomes a mother herself." Such insects, Hamilton asserted, care for the queen's offspring rather than their own because they are extraordinarily closely related to her. So closely, in fact, that they would be less related to their own offspring than they are to hers. Chicago Zoological

Society biologist and primatologist Dan Wharton explained to me how this bizarre (to us) situation comes about: "Among honeybees, females have two sets of chromosomes (diploid) while males have just one (haploid), resulting in haplodiploid reproduction. And in such haplodiploid-reproducing organisms, two sisters with the same father have more common genetic material than mothers and their own offspring." In other words, when it comes to Hamilton's bees, what seems like the ultimate in self-sacrifice is actually keenly self-serving.

With such creatures in mind, Hamilton argued that the notion of fitness should be expanded to include not just the individual but also his or her closest genetic relatives. In other words, Lack had been right that it was about the individual rather than the group, but sometimes, as in the case of these honeybees, the group was actually a closely related extension of the self. "Inclusive fitness," Hamilton suggested, was the individual's fitness plus the fitness of his or her closest kin sharing genes by common descent. Altruism would evolve, Hamilton said, when its cost to the giver (C) was less than the fitness benefits (B) obtained by helping another individual related by r, a letter designating the proportion of genes the two individuals shared by common descent. The phenomenon — often termed "kin selection" and expressed in the formula $C < Br$ — "underlies the evolution of helping behavior in all social creatures," Hrdy writes. It also explains the universal human pattern of favoring kin over non-kin.

Behavioral ecologists are quick to point out that they are not claiming that there is a gene, or even a set of genes, that influences people to prefer kin to non-kin, only that, among animals (including humans), the preference seems to be universal. Initial experiments with jewel wasps and other insects proved that inclusive fitness was real; later studies of humans seem to prove the universality of kin selection as well. But how might kin selection actually work? Hrdy suggests that "in humans we can only assume that our powerful predisposition to prefer our own kin derives from very ancient emotional and cognitive systems, such as learning to recognize people familiar from a very early age and having a lower threshold for altruism in our behavior toward them. This is the simplest explanation for our similarities with other social creatures in this respect."

According to human behavioral ecologists and evolutionary biologists, then, we live in a "kin über alles" world. We will do more for our kin than for our non-kin, with the reverse being true as well. Which begs the question, What, exactly, is kin? What is a cost? And how, precisely, are we to define "benefit"?

TRIVERS'S FAMILIES: COOPERATION AND CONFLICT

William Hamilton got a renegade sociobiologist named Robert Trivers thinking. If inclusive fitness explained how shared genetic material might lead to cooperation and altruism between close relatives having common agendas, could it also explain differences in agendas between closely related individuals? Mothers and their offspring, Trivers noted, are not genetically identical. Was it not reasonable, then, to suppose — based on the theory of kin selection or inclusive fitness, as well as Lack's observations — that a mother's interest is not always identical to that of her offspring? From the perspective of the offspring, the same might be said as well. A baby of any species, for example, is related to itself 100 percent. But it shares only half its genes with its mother and half with subsequent offspring, if all have the same father. If they have different fathers, the degree of relatedness is 25 percent. Yet the mother, Trivers noted, is equally related to all her offspring. And so it is inevitable that the relations between mother and offspring, and offspring and offspring, should be not only cooperative, but also conflictual. In short, the wants and needs of mothers and their children do not perfectly coincide. Logical and reasoned as this observation sounds, its implications are profoundly subversive of our dearly held notion that mother and child live in a kind of mutually agreeable symbiosis.

Au contraire, as Lack taught Trivers and others who came after him: reproductive effort — gestation, delivery, provisioning — is costly and depleting. Any effort a mother puts into one offspring detracts from the effort she can put into another. It also detracts from her ability to have more offspring herself. Trivers had a theory about that, too, one he called parental investment. Parental investment, Trivers asserted in 1972, is anything that a parent does to promote the survival of an offspring that also detracts from the parent's ability to invest in another offspring. Now, with Hamilton's insights about kin selection in mind, and the notion of potential conflict underscored, the question became, How much and for how long should a mother care for her offspring? When did this tiny, dependent being become less an extension of her own agenda and more of a drag against it? Trivers wrote, "Parent and offspring are expected to disagree over how long the period of parental investment should last, over the amount of parental investment that should be given, and over the altruistic and egoistic tendencies of the offspring."

To make this theoretical argument more concrete, Sarah Hrdy explains how the phenomenon of weaning exemplifies the way Trivers sought to reframe family members as at once cooperative and competitive: "Weaning conflicts epitomize for Trivers the disagreement over how much and for how long a mother should provision her offspring . . . Just after birth, when suckling is essential for her infant's survival, a mother and baby are likely to be of one opinion . . . [but later] the infant is more motivated to suckle than the mother is to provide additional nourishment."

Across cultures and species, weaning is indeed accompanied by epic tantrums and titanic battles of will. Primatologists report screeching fits, angry displays, and even depression among baboons and chimps being weaned. These infants' objections to no longer being allowed to nurse were so reliable and consistent that Trivers actually advised fieldworkers attempting to locate baboons on the savannas of Africa in the early morning to listen for the weaned

baboons' screaming. In human societies characterized by prolonged nursing (or in societies with foreshortened nursing periods,
such as our own) such problems arise as well. When !Kung mothers are pregnant (the !Kung are hunter-gatherers who live in the
Kalahari Desert of Botswana), they tell their three-and four-year-old
children, "You can't nurse anymore. If you do, you will die." The
!Kung children whine and throw fits, insisting that they still want
to breastfeed. Many !Kung three-and four-year-olds go to live with
relatives in another camp during this contentious period, so great
are the stresses on mother and child alike. Indeed, most !Kung
carry the memory of their weaning with them into adulthood. In
Westernized cultures, we might hide our breasts from, or simply
attempt to distract, a toddler who still wants to nurse, or we might
encourage a diet of "solids" beginning at six months of age, acceler-
ating a process that in other cultures might take years, so that weaning can be accomplished by the comparatively early age of eight or
nine months, or perhaps a year.

"Sleep training" is another issue over which mothers and infants
in Western, industrialized cultures will likely come into the kind of
early, direct, and dramatic conflict that Trivers had in mind. At a
certain point, those of us who eschew the notion of the family bed
decide to up our expectations of an infant who has been hard-wired
by eons of evolution to fear being left alone. Into the crib baby goes,
to "learn to fall asleep on his or her own." Baby wants and needs to be
held (in order to feel secure); mother and father want and need to
sleep (in order to function). Hours of crying may ensue, for days on
end, depending on the temperament of the baby and the resolution
of the parents. This ordeal can be exceedingly stressful (one mother
told me that she developed shingles from the stress of sleep training
her infant), but our ambivalence and misery as we leave our children
screaming in their nurseries does not change the fact that our needs
and theirs come into fundamental opposition over the issue.

These different strategies to negotiate infant dependency, and
our feeling that we need to resort to them, dramatize the ways in
which, as Trivers pointed out, mothers and children might find

themselves at cross-purposes. And if something as basic as nourishing a child or reassuring him when he is (arguably) in distress and fearing that he has been abandoned, can be a site of such conflict and disagreement; if mother and baby are two genetically nonidentical individuals with agendas that are not always perfectly coordinated; if the relation between mother and child is not just one of synchronized, gentle, and loving interdependence but also one of occasional but very real struggle — what, then, might the relation between stepmother and a child *not* her own be? Suddenly, Lack's strategic avian moms, ever mindful of potentially perilous food scarcities, bring to mind those humans (fantastical or real) who might lead children deep into the dark forest to "chop wood" during a harvest failure, abandoning them there so that they no longer continue to empty the family larder.

EMLEN'S WHITE-FRONTED BEE-EATERS: JUST LIKE US?

Comparing birds and humans might seem specious, but it is not entirely without precedent — or rationale. Stephen Emlen, a behavioral ecologist at Cornell University with a special interest in human families, convincingly argues that we might learn more about ourselves from our feathered friends than from our hairy cousins. Primates, he concedes, certainly resemble us when it comes to cognition and mental capabilities, with their tool use, problem solving, and knack for learning sign language. But in the arena of families, there are more differences than similarities between us and our close simian relatives. For example, "chimpanzees live in troops where males do not help raise offspring, while gorillas and hamadryas baboons live in extended 'harems' of several unrelated females and a dominant male," primate expert Dan Wharton told me. Birds, by contrast, form mostly monogamous pair bonds, sometimes mating for life. Male birds play an active and engaged role in parental care. And some birds even live in "communities." What do all these similarities mean? That birds are uniquely instructive in thinking through what we ourselves do, some ornithologists and evolutionary biologists suggest. "Animals that live in very similar types of societies will have had long evolutionary histories of encountering the same types of social choices, and therefore will have developed very similar rules for how to behave," Emlen explains.

One particular "community" of birds piqued Emlen's interest several decades ago. He had heard tales of the white-fronted bee-eaters of Kenya, keenly social creatures living peacefully and altruistically in apparently utopian groups of three hundred or more. Sharing, caring, and selflessness, it seemed, were the norm. During food shortages, for example, these birds shared with their neighbors. Females and males split child-care duties and were monogamous 85 percent of the time (about the same as humans, Emlen notes). And grown offspring often stayed on to "help at the nest," assisting in the rearing of their younger sibs. Remarkably, they even "babysat" for neighbors. "The reason I went after Bee Eaters," Emlen explains, "is they were seen to have complex, nonfamily helping." This, of course, flew in the face of evolutionary theory, with its emphasis on individual fitness and kin selection.

What in the world was going on with the bee-eaters? How did all this helping others, nonrelatives at that, make sense? A sociobiologist through and through, Emlen thought he might just find in Kenya an exception to Hamilton's Rule about putting kin first. Perhaps, he hypothesized, this was an instance where another theory of evolutionary biology, "reciprocal altruism," might come into play. Reciprocal altruism occurs when someone performs a favor for a nonrelative, with the expectation that the act of generosity will be returned in kind someday. If it is not, no more altruism will be forthcoming from the spurned individual, and a social bridge will have been burned. Such behaviors have been observed in male olive baboons trying to build coalitions during aggressive interactions with other males, as well as among female vervet monkeys and among male lions attempting to overtake a pride. Were white-fronted bee-eaters doing something similar? What Emlen ultimately discovered was surprising — and, for stepfamilies, perhaps also surprisingly relevant.

Peyton Place in Kenya: Conflict, Cooperation, and Kin Selection

After thousands of hours of field observation on slippery mud banks in Kenya, Emlen realized that the white-fronted bee-eaters were *not* the exception to the evolutionary rule; instead, they *were* the rule. That is, they actually lived not in close quarters with strangers, but in extended, multigenerational families. Like Hamilton's bees, they were helping their relatives, and so helping themselves. Ostensibly self-sacrificing behaviors turned out to be, once again, fundamentally self-serving. Take, for example, those grown offspring helping at the nests of neighbors. As it turns out, they were aiding relatively close kin, and so improving their own fitness. If their own nests failed — if, say, the eggs were eaten by a predator — they might switch over to the nest of a sister and brother-in-law, aunt and uncle, or their own parents. Eventually, Emlen was able to use Hamilton's theory of kin selection to predict who would help out whom. "If a nest failed," he explains, "I should be able to predict the number two backup that gets the help" based on the percentage of shared genetic material. And, indeed, he was able to do so. Natural selection, it seemed, had done its job over the millennia, such that the birds had internalized complex "decision rules" for weighing the relative importance and closeness of different kin, and thus the potential genetic payoff for helping them.

But that wasn't all. The bee-eaters' "peaceful society" was something else altogether. Instead of being cooperative, caring, and devoid of conflict, it was a kind of avian Peyton Place, described by one nature writer as "a swirling soap opera of love, deceit, harassment, divorce, and adultery." Emlen, his wife, and their assistants, who had begun to recognize specific birds and keep track of precisely what they were up to day in and day out, were eventually struck by how "human" they sometimes seemed in their courting, trespassing, and sneaking off to achieve an "extra-pair copulation" far from home. And although it was true that grown offspring often stayed "home" with their parents, rather than move to their own nearby "apartments" built in adjacent mud banks, even this started to look more complex than it had at first. Sometimes parents actually aggressively pressured their young into coming back home once they'd moved out — for entirely self-serving reasons. For example, one day Emlen noticed a father "greeting" his son over and over again at the entrance to the son's nest. The greeting went on for so long and was so persistent that it had the effect of preventing the son from going into the nest for quite some time. Significantly, the son's mate was inside sitting on their clutch of eggs, and he couldn't get inside to feed her.

Over the course of his observations, Emlen realized that with this kind of coercion, parents could actually increase the likelihood that their own offspring's nests would fail. And — voilà! — the offspring would come back "home" to help Mom and Dad with their child-rearing duties. Dad had seen to it that those most closely related to him — his own offspring — had a better chance of fledging than those less closely related to him — the offspring of his offspring. And he had his nearest and dearest older kids as ultra-reliable "helpers at the nest." There was something in it for these grown offspring, too, of course. After all, if you're not raising your own kids, the next best thing is to raise your siblings, with whom you share 50 percent of your genes.

It didn't always work out so well, however. Emlen discovered that the busy bee-eaters had one more thing in common with humans. Pairs that were unsuccessful in their reproductive attempts had higher probabilities of what he and many ornithologists actually term "divorce." And in the event of a nest failure and subsequent breakup, they were likely to re-pair, choosing new mates. Emlen observed very closely when long-term bee-eater mates split up and chose new partners. What would happen? he wondered. Would everyone get along, or would there be tensions when a feathered stepparent came on the scene? Would the offspring from the original pair bond stay, or would they go? Based on Hamilton's Rule, Emlen had a hunch, and what he discovered did, in fact, jibe with the theory of inclusive fitness.

The bee-eater offspring of an original pair were much less likely to help raise hatchlings of one of their own parents and a stepparent than they were to tend to the chicks of both their parents. Consequently, the chances that they would disperse and go help at the nest of others in their extended family increased whenever a stepparent showed up. Emlen wasn't surprised: the offspring with a parent and stepparent shared the same amount of genetic material with a niece and nephew as with its half sibling (25 percent), making a move that much more likely. Nor was Emlen surprised to see that the likelihood of leaving the nest of the parent and stepparent for good increased. "The kids from the first pairing say, 'Thank you, no. I'm doing much less, provisioning much less. I'm going to spend much more time over there with my other family members," Emlen explains. Finally, when a new mate first came on the scene, tension and aggression shot up — for very specific reasons. "Sometimes, there is great interest between the son and his stepmother, while there had been none between the son and his mother, and great aggression as the father attacks the son, as the father guards the mate," Emlen observes.

But what does this all mean for humans? An adaptationist through and through, Emlen believes that the answer is, quite a lot. Being subject to selection pressures and having similar predilections (more or less monogamous, long-term pair bonds, divorce and re-partnering, shared care for offspring, and an evolutionary history of living in extended families), humans, he argues, have developed similar "decision rules" — those unconscious strategies that guide us in our social behavior. For Emlen, the bee-eaters are a lens of sorts, a lens onto a broad, comparative evolutionary view of families and family issues. In all stepfamilies, he suggests, we are likely to see much of what we see among white-fronted bee-eater families in Kenya: early dispersal (or "leaving the nest") for stepchildren; increased conflict and sexual tension in stepfamily households; and a preference for one's own kids, one's own parents, and one's full siblings. None of this is particularly savory, but neither is it terribly controversial. Based on studies and clinical work, a number of sociologists and psychologists have drawn many of the same conclusions Emlen has. Still, Emlen is quick to point out that none of these problems or conflicts is "genetically determined" or inevitable. Asked whether environment and culture play "second fiddle" to genetics, his answer is a resounding no. "Both genetics and environment are major fiddles," he insists. "There is no disagreement that most human behavior is strongly influenced by culture and environment. But there are biological underpinnings as well, and these underpinnings — our inherited predispositions — play a more important role in shaping our social interactions than previously realized." How so, exactly?

THE HUMAN CASE: ANGEL PARK'S POLYGYNISTS

A particularly elegant study conducted by behavioral ecologists William Jankowiak and Monique Diderich among polygynous Mormon families in the year 2000 nicely illustrates Emlen's point about the importance of biology in guiding our social behavior and shaping our feelings. Jankowiak and Diderich studied interactions and perceptions of closeness between full and half siblings in a Mormon community they call Angel Park. This particular community is unique even among Mormon polygynous communities in that the preferred ideal, relentlessly promoted in sermons, Sunday school lessons, and high school classes, as well as at home, is to live together in one "united and harmonious household" of one father, several wives, and their collective offspring. To this end, genetic differences in the polygynous family households of Angel Park are consistently and intentionally downplayed, while an ethos of family is emphasized. Kids of different co-wives live and play in common areas and are consistently told "we are all true brothers and sisters." This made Angel Park an ideal setting for exploring just how much genetic relatedness matters. Do people really feel as close and as attached to their half siblings as they do to their full ones? Will they bend over backward for half siblings as they will for blood kin? Put another way, is the degree of sibling solidarity in Angel Park (and perhaps in general) about biological kinship? Or, as sociologists and psychologists suggest, might other factors, such as being raised together and being close in age, play more of a role in establishing closeness?

For Jankowiak and Diderich, the big question was, Can people who are not related learn to love each other as if they are, with constant proximity and under ideally supportive conditions? It is not difficult to see just how relevant and instructive such questions — and answers — might be for stepfamilies, where unrelated stepsiblings, half siblings, and full siblings, as well as an adult to whom they are not related, may reside together, feeling compelled, to some extent, to "blend."

Focusing on thirty-two polygynous families, the study authors spoke to seventy individuals total, all with full and half siblings living in the community. They used a number of measures to assess perceptions of "closeness" and feelings of solidarity. Young kids were asked to "draw a picture of your family," on the theory that excluding someone from the drawing would be a strong indicator of negative feelings. If these young children resided in a home with two or more infants, they were also asked, "Who is your favorite baby?" Then they were asked, "Is that your birth mother's baby, or the baby of one of your other mothers?" Adults were asked whether they had recently loaned a brother or sister money. With outsize families the norm, there are perpetual cash shortages in Angel Park; this means loans are both necessary and carefully allocated. Researchers also asked the adults whether they had recently asked a sibling to babysit. With so many children around, providing child care is a significant and much-appreciated favor, neither requested nor conferred lightly. If the answers to these questions about loans and babysitting were yes, the respondents were further asked, "Was it a sibling through your birth mother, or another mother?" Finally, the authors analyzed who went to whose birthday parties and wedding receptions. Was attendance skewed more toward full siblings, they wondered, or split evenly between half and full sibs?

When the data was collected and analyzed, it revealed a dramatic difference in emotional closeness, degree of loyalty, and affection between full siblings and half siblings. Overwhelmingly, Jankowiak and Diderich found, there was more affection and attachment to full siblings, and a remarkably increased willingness to put oneself out for them. This held true despite the force of religious ideals, regardless of similarity in age, and notwithstanding the continued close physical proximity of half siblings as they had grown up.

This preference — a strong partiality for those who are closest kin — was revealed in at least two additional ways the authors had at first not thought to measure, but observed in the course of their interviews and other work in the community. First, if the father of a polygynous family was alive, adult siblings would meet at his home for weekly family dinners. But after his death, something interesting happened, and it happened quickly: half siblings dispersed, not unlike white-fronted bee-eater step-offspring abandoning the nest, and these family gatherings rearranged themselves in accordance with full blood ties, with the birth mother taking the dead father's place at the center of the family, if not at the head of the table. Second, virtually all the adults interviewed remembered at least an incident or two in which they had perceived that one of their father's co-wives had shown a preference for her own child over him or her. For example, they recalled a co-mother bending the house rules for her own child or giving her own child a bigger piece of cake. "Perception" is the key word here, and it is remarkable indeed that such perceptions can take root and bloom in an environment that has dedicated itself to their extinction, to promoting the notion of co-mothers and biological mothers loving children just the same, and biological and nonbiological ties being equivalent. What, we might wonder, would be the perceptions of children growing up in a culture that promulgates precisely the opposite?

The study authors concluded, with understatement, that "there is a pronounced clustering of feelings and affection in Angel Park that is consistent with inclusive fitness theory." Even in an environment where non–blood relatives and half siblings are encouraged to feel "just like kin," where this ideal is promoted tirelessly and kids grow up in close proximity from birth, in the end relatedness matters. Well might we want to share these findings with anyone who judges us wanting when our stepfamilies "fail" to "blend."

STEPFAMILIES: NOT SO CLOSE? NOT SO TRAGIC

Like the white-fronted bee-eaters and the Mormons of Angel Park, stepfamily members, while capable of great affection for those less related to them, nonetheless seem to be wired to feel closest to their own. For example, in a 1981 national survey of U.S. children ages eleven to sixteen, participants were asked, "Whom do you consider a member of your family?" Thirty-one percent of the stepchildren did not consider their residential stepparent a family member, and 41 percent of them did not mention their stepsiblings.

"His kids aren't coming for the holidays?" relatives, friends, and even acquaintances may ask, aghast. Or, "Why on earth hasn't your stepson come down from college to see the new baby yet?" The implication is that something isn't right, and the unmistakable insinuation, in many cases, is that the stepmother must be doing something wrong. She is failing at her culturally designated role as "family carpenter" or falling short in the "warm and maternal" department where her step-kids are concerned. The simple fact of the matter, confirmed in numerous studies, is that stepfamilies (as we saw in chapter 4) are different from first families. To reiterate a point that seems difficult for outsiders and sometimes stepmothers themselves to accept, they are less cohesive. And there is little empirical evidence for the assumption that they tend to become closer or more cohesive over time. The even bigger news is that as disorienting as this may seem to the uninitiated and to those who try to use a first-family map to understand the topography of step-families, they often function just fine that way.

Residential stepfamilies can have a college dorm/roommate feel that is likely to throw those who equate "family" with synchronized, super-close first-family dynamics. Stepfamily members — particularly when both members of the couple bring kids of their own — might eat at different times, put up two different Christmas trees, even elect not to take all their vacations together (all practices described by people I interviewed). When kids are older and not living together, even less "bondedness" is the rule. Some of the step-families with adult children I interviewed went months without seeing one another, as holidays did not provide an automatic pretext for getting together. With obligations to so many people, there was no assumption that Thanksgiving, for example, meant "all together now."

As off-putting and "wrong" as some first families might find such a reality, it may well be this very lack of proximity and closeness that allows stepfamilies to jell in their own way and to foster positive relationships. A number of researchers have noted that in stepfamilies, respectful behavior, flexibility, and lower levels of cohesion are not only more normal but also more adaptive, and so more predictive of a good outcome, than "tight-knit-ness." If the unrealistic yet unrelenting fantasies of uninformed outsiders about how things "should" be in our stepfamilies have become our burden, there is solace in the unlikely facts gleaned from evolutionary biology — from Angel Park and the Kenyan mud banks — worlds at once utterly apart from and unexpectedly adjacent to our own.

ROHWER'S AVIAN STEPPARENTS

If Emlen was interested in *how* family life in general and stepparenting in particular played out among his avian cohort, as well as among other animals including humans, a number of other biologists have been interested in *why*. Why does stepparenting happen in the animal world at all? Why would any creature — an anemone fish or a baboon or a yellow-headed blackbird or a white-fronted bee-eater (all of whom, it turns out, exhibit stepparental behaviors) — do anything so apparently altruistic?

Maybe, the early thinking on the topic went, they wouldn't. In 1975, in a paper titled "Mountain Bluebirds: Experimental Evidence Against Altruism," ornithologist Harry Power asserted that the presence or absence of what he termed "true altruism" — "the promotion of others' reproductive success while reducing one's own inclusive fitness" — could be gauged by how these birds behaved toward the offspring of others. He removed male and female mountain bluebirds from pairs during the nesting phase; the newly single birds found replacement mates. However, most of these replacement mates did not help in the raising of their step-offspring. This was an obvious outcome, Power suggested: an effort to raise someone else's offspring contributes to the proliferation of the genes of rivals rather the genes conducive to the development of altruism. Basically, Power asserted, stepparental "selflessness" makes no adaptive sense.

Like so many scientists whose work has a marked impact, Power raised as many questions as he answered. Ten years after he wrote his paper, another ornithologist, Sievert Rohwer, disputed its findings as well as its conclusions. After reviewing the literature on how birds behave toward the previously sired offspring of their new consorts, he discovered that avian stepparental care was not at all rare. Remarkably, among Cooper's hawks, peregrine falcons, western gulls, sandhill cranes, and Australian ravens, for example, females would actually incubate eggs and then raise young not their own. And males of a number of species, including hawks, gulls, chickadees, yellow-bellied sapsuckers, purple martins, and cactus wrens, ran the gamut from provisioning and guarding the incubating female to defending and feeding the brooded young, or even raising them altogether.

But why? There were, after all, other options. When confronted with these offspring not their own, birds could do one of three things, Rohwer noted. They could commit infanticide, tolerate the chicks without putting forth any effort, or actively assist in rearing them. Tolerance and care, Rohwer concluded, were actually more common than infanticide. But why? Wouldn't infanticide make more sense? Primatologist Sarah Blaffer Hrdy had already argued that, among a certain type of langurs in India, invading males killed infants whenever they could. Committing infanticide, Hrdy argued, gave the new males an advantage in siring offspring of their own, since the females would ovulate soon after they ceased nursing. Confronted with infanticidal males, female langurs had developed counterstrategies, such as fighting off males and copulating with a number of males in order to confuse the issue of paternity. But ultimately, it was in the best interest of the female to reproduce again, even with the male who had killed her first infant. After all, her own reproductive fitness was at stake as well. So went the adaptive, albeit gruesome, logic behind such infanticide.

Soon biologists found a similar strategy among lions. Males who took over prides killed the cubs in order to shorten the wait until the next breeding opportunity with the females. In some sense, then, Rohwer's discoveries about stepparental behavior in birds were extremely surprising. Might such behavior, he asked, be a misdirection of parental care, and so maladaptive? In other words, was it possible that the birds just couldn't tell that the offspring were not their own? Perhaps, like unsuspecting characters in a human soap opera, they had been intentionally deceived about their parenthood by their mates. Or maybe, Rohwer hypothesized, stepparenting could actually be adaptive. It might be a mating effort, a tradeoff in the classic Lackian sense: the payoff for raising offspring not one's own was future mating opportunities with the step-offspring's genetic parent.

Once Rohwer conducted experiments with yellow-headed blackbirds which confirmed that they could, in fact, detect which offspring were their own, he came down on the side of the "stepparenting behavior as mating effort" hypothesis. A bird would invest in the young of another under very specific circumstances, Rohwer noted. In certain cases, he reasoned, tolerance and even care of the new mate's previously sired offspring was the best possible mating strategy. As with Lack's mother birds, who could be selfless or heartless by human standards when it came to investing in a particular brood in a particular season, in this case, once again, it all depended on circumstances. The factors that would make it worthwhile to invest in step-offspring were linked to specific ecological conditions.

For example, using their unconscious internalized "decision rules," the birds would make various assessments, weighing their options in ways that might, in some cases, sound familiar. Were new, unfettered mates sufficiently scarce? That is, would it take a lot of time and a big expenditure of energy to find a mate without offspring, and might the bird risk not finding one at all if it didn't pair up with this potential mate right now? Could the newly formed pair, including a mate with previously sired offspring or a clutch of eggs sired by another bird, be expected to endure relatively long-term? If there were plenty of opportunities to sire or lay eggs of one's own down the road, it could make sense to wait out a single breeding season. Did the birds tend to divorce after a nesting failure? If so, the bird would only be putting itself at a disadvantage in creating a nesting failure by killing or not provisioning the previously sired young. Would an individual who lost its young quickly return to breeding condition, or would that take a long time? In the case of it taking a long time, there would really not be much cost in waiting out the fledging of a brood not one's own. Finally, was there time left in the breeding season for another clutch? If not, then ignoring, tolerating, and even provisioning the young would not cost the stepparental bird so much.

Summarizing Rohwer's work with birds, Canadian biologists and evolutionary psychologists Martin Daly and Margo Wilson write that "in circumstances . . . where breeding territories or mates are scarce, and are retained for a long time once they have been acquired . . . step-parental investment is evidently the price paid for future breeding opportunities with the genetic parent." Given these specific environmental and ecological constraints, Daly and Wilson note, not only certain birds but also monogamous fish such as anemone fish, as well as some baboons, "find stepparenting an acceptable courtship experience." Then, in a rather astonishing turn, Daly and Wilson hypothesize that much the same holds true for human stepparents:

The human case seems to us analogous. Stepparents are primarily replacement mates and only secondarily replacement parents. They assume their pseudo-parental obligations in the context of a web of reciprocities with the genetic parent, who is likely to recognize more or less explicitly that the new mate's tolerance and investment constitute benefits bestowed on the genetic parent and the child, entitling the stepparent to reciprocal considerations.

DALY AND WILSON: DISCRIMINATIVE PARENTAL SOLICITUDE

With their emphasis on tradeoffs and benefits in human stepparenting, and the suggestion that this is not a selfless undertaking but something more strategic (albeit unconsciously so), Martin Daly and Margo Wilson lead us down a darker path, one that might be strewn with Hansel and Gretel's pebbles and bread crumbs, those plangent semaphores of parental neglect — and worse. The husband-and-wife team, based at McMaster University in Ontario, wanted to know whether stepchildren were, in fact, disadvantaged relative to genetic children. To find out, they trained their sights on lethal child abuse perpetrated by stepparents (actually, stepfathers — more on this later). They didn't do this because they thought that most stepparents were killers — in fact, more than 99 percent of us are not. But lethal abuse, they reasoned, while the most extreme, was also the most undeniable and *verifiable* indicator of bias against stepchildren. After all, virtually every case of it would be reported, making it a more reliable measure than other forms of child abuse, which tend to be vastly underreported. After pouring over statistics, studies, police reports, and child abuse registries in the United States, Canada, England, Australia, Finland, and Korea, Daly and Wilson concluded that children who lived with one genetic parent and one stepparent were much more likely to suffer the most severe forms of child maltreatment. In fact, in a 1988 article in *Science,* they reported that a co-residing stepparent was seventy times more likely to kill a child under two years of age than was a co-residing genetic parent.

But were these lethal effects of living with a stepparent not perhaps just byproducts of other factors associated with stepparenthood, such as poverty? Might stepparenthood itself be a mere incidental correlate of abuse, rather than a cause of it? Daly and Wilson had already thought through this objection to their findings. They had conscientiously tested for poverty and a number of other potentially confounding variables, such as differences in parental age, differences in family size, and the traits of those who become stepparents, reasoning that the abuse might be explained by the population of remarried adults potentially including disproportionate numbers of violent people. Even when controlling for these other factors, however, they found that living with a stepparent increased the risk of all abuse, and specifically lethal abuse, dramatically.

In addition to increased frequency of lethal abuse, Daly and Wilson found that stepparents murdered their stepchildren differently than parents murdered their own children. Parents who killed their children, police reports and studies by psychologists showed, tended to be depressed. They often killed their children as they slept, by smothering or a gunshot, and frequently killed them under the delusion that they were somehow sparing the children from future hardship and suffering, rescuing them even. Such murderous parents were highly likely to kill themselves after killing the child. Stepparents, on the other hand, used what Daly and Wilson term "more assaultive means" to kill stepchildren: they tended to batter, kick, or bludgeon their victims to death. And homicidal stepparents did not kill themselves afterward. Perhaps most tellingly for their hypothesis, Daly and Wilson found that stepfathers didn't abuse and kill their own children nearly as often as they did their stepchildren.

These qualitative and quantitative differences in how stepfathers versus genetic fathers killed, and *whom* they killed, were dramatic and disturbing. But one of Daly and Wilson's findings is particularly notable. They discovered that, perhaps counterintuitively, the step-children at greatest risk of dying at the hands of their stepparents were infants. Why might this be? It was clear to them what a "difficult" older kid might do to elicit rage from a stepparent, however out of proportion and irrational that rage might be. But how on earth could a defenseless infant provoke such anger and resentment? It was here that evolutionary theory offered a way to understand something otherwise incomprehensible. Confronted with the unsettling realities of who killed and who was killed, and building on the work of Lack, Hamilton, and Trivers, Daly and Wilson eventually articulated their theory of "discriminative parental solicitude." This concept springs from Trivers's premise that parental resources are limited, as well as Hamilton's concept of kin selection. It also hinges on one of Lack's observations: in some species, birds could discern their own young, while in others they could not.

Daly and Wilson theorized, first, that successful discrimination of one's own offspring from those that are not one's own is a problem parents, particularly fathers (more on that later), have likely faced throughout our evolutionary history; and, second, that we discriminate in the degree to which we are solicitous of children: more so if they are our own, less so — perhaps not at all — if they are not. From an evolutionary perspective, given the intensive and protracted period of energy expended to raise a human child, there is nothing so mysterious about allocating one's investment to one's own offspring. Conversely, Daly and Wilson write, "indiscriminate allocation of parental benefits without regard to cues of actual parentage would be an evolutionary anomaly." Psychologists as well as biologists, Daly and Wilson go on to frame the issue in terms of feelings as well as behaviors: "If the psychological underpinnings of parental care have evolved by natural selection, we may thus anticipate that parental feeling and action will not typically be elicited by just any conspecific juvenile. Instead, care-providing animals may be expected to care selectively for young who are a) their own genetic offspring and b) able to convert that care into improved prospects for survival and reproduction."

DISCRIMINATIVE PARENTAL SOLICITUDE, NATURAL SELECTION, AND THE CONUNDRUM OF MALES

Babies could not be more vulnerable — or more demanding. They require constant care, monitoring, attention, and interaction, and they have evolved all kinds of ways to get it. From crying to clinging to gazing at a caregiver; from ample fat stores that render them plump and hence healthy-looking (read, worth investing in) to appealing round eyes and faces that we find adorable (under the right conditions, especially), infants have, as Sarah Blaffer Hrdy points out, evolved over the millennia a number of strategies to elicit love and care from their mothers, fathers, close kin, and caregivers. In fact, research has shown that, with exposure to our infants and even those not our own, if the circumstances are right, we do tend to fall under their sway — and how. Levels of prolactin — a hormone that elicits loving feelings of bondedness — increase in both fathers and mothers when they spend continuous time with their infants, and levels of testosterone in fathers actually decline when they care for their babies for several hours at a time. Humans, it is clear, can be "primed" by both biology and culture to care for their neonates.

What, then, of Daly and Wilson's cohort, stepfathers who lethally abuse children, usually those under age two? Why might the rate of lethal assault of infants be so high compared to the rates for older children and teens? First of all, Daly and Wilson are quick to point out, these murderous stepfathers are no infanticidal male lemurs or lions. There is nothing adaptive about murdering a child: the perpetrator will not increase his fitness or even reduce his costs by killing a baby. He will end up in prison, likely for life, and incur the wrath of an entire society. Even in our evolutionary past, Daly and Wilson emphasize, it is implausible that abusing or killing stepchildren would have promoted the assailants' fitness. A preference for their own offspring, however, likely would have been highly adaptive. And so evolutionary biology offers an explanation — one that is rather circuitous — for such bewildering behavior. The conundrum of the male mammal, as so many biologists have pointed out, is internal fertilization, a phenomenon that makes it particularly difficult — *The Jerry Springer Show* notwithstanding — to determine paternity with a great deal of certainty. And so unlike female mammals, who know that a baby is theirs, males just might get duped into caring for a child not their own. Owing to this uncertainty, evolutionary biologists believe, men and women evolved different reproductive strategies. Females tend to invest more in care, or parental effort, while males invest more in mating effort. This typical mammalian asymmetry means that males with babies have always found themselves facing a conundrum: Should I put my faith and efforts here in these offspring, or should I sire another or even several more offspring? Should I stay (and invest) or go (and inseminate another)? Or should I stay and inseminate again?

Given the sex-specific realities and strategies of our evolutionary history, it only makes sense that males, faced with constant uncertainty about paternity, would have evolved a higher threshold for parental care — that is, more of an ability to resist the charms of an infant attempting to elicit coos, cuddles, and more depleting forms of parental care from them. A woman, on the other hand, was unlikely to be confused about whether a baby was hers, as she had gestated it in her own body and pushed it out of her birth canal. Humans are not ungulates, so there was no possibility that someone else's offspring would climb to his or her feet, sidle up to another woman, and begin to nurse. Even if women were, in our prehistoric past, occasionally of the habit to nurse the babies of others (and there is a compelling argument to be made that we were), this was likely more for snacking than to provide sustenance, and the favor was conferred upon the baby of someone closely related. Thus, in a woman's case, falling in love with an infant can only be for the good, as she can be sure that the child is her own (or closely related). But a man cannot be entirely certain that even his partner's tiny, demanding creature is his issue. A higher threshold for feeling warm and fuzzy about a stranger's infant is a kind of protection — it decreases the likelihood of falling for a baby not his own.

What Daly and Wilson have unearthed — rather than some "rationale" for lethal child abuse — is compelling and meticulously documented evidence that, given eons of selection, unrelated males have evolved what we might think of as "emotional earplugs" when faced with a crying baby's unrelenting, unremitting need. Such indifference, relative to what a mother (or confident father) might feel, means, as Hrdy has observed, that there is in turn less of a barrier guarding against all the factors that lead to infant abuse — bad judgment, rage, and frustration. Elevated rates of abuse and violence, Daly and Wilson emphasize, are best understood as "non-adaptive byproducts of lesser solicitude." Babies, who will require intensive caregiving for years on end — that is, the most investment — are at maximal risk for abuse. For Daly and Wilson, the fact that those who are the most vulnerable and needy over the long term are in the most danger is virtual proof of their hypothesis about discriminative parental solicitude and adult resentment of pseudoparental obligation. From a biosocial perspective, what might create more resentment in someone "unprimed" to provide than a being not our own, a being who demands the most protracted, intensive, and committed forms of investment?

Daly and Wilson are careful to emphasize that most stepparent-stepchild relationships are *not* violent or abusive in any way. (In fact, Wilson told me that she had a stepfather, "a nice, nonabusive one!") They also note that lethal abuse is the extreme manifestation of discriminative parental solicitude — commonly, more benign effects, such as a stepchild leaving home earlier than a biological child is likely to, are the strongest evidence of discrimination. "Ideally, and perhaps typically," Daly and Wilson told me, "these relationships become somewhat like friendships, with genuine mutual interest in one another's well-being. In-law relationships are potentially problematic, too, but they are not ineluctably conflictual."

Still, they insist, discriminative parental solicitude is real and is likely the root cause of fundamental differences in agendas between genetic parents and stepparents, as well as between step-parents and stepchildren — issues such as how much money to give to which children and for how long, for example. Is there anything so controversial, they want to know, about suggesting that stepparents will not often, and certainly not automatically, come to feel the same sort of love and commitment as is ordinarily felt by genetic parents? "Might it not be helpful," they wonder, "if the stepparent's ambivalent and sometimes aggrieved feelings were acknowledged as normal and if the genetic parent were encouraged to express appreciation for stepparental investment, rather than to demand it as one's due?"

Most of Daly and Wilson's work centers on stepfathers. Residential stepmothers, they point out, are statistically rarer, and so there are fewer instances of lethal abuse among them. Nevertheless, they note, stepmothers are also greatly overrepresented in child abuse statistics, and they estimate the risks of having a stepmother to be comparable to having a stepfather. As evidence, Daly and Wilson report that the American Humane Association found more abuse in stepmother homes than in stepfather homes and that homeless adolescents in New York City are disproportionately from stepmother homes. In a study of Korean schoolchildren they cite, there were identical frequencies of being beaten among those from stepmother and stepfather homes, with both rates being substantially higher than those among children who lived with two parents. All of which suggests, Daly and Wilson insist, that discriminative parental solicitude does not discriminate against women.

But if women have evolved to have a lower threshold for eliciting care — and less to fear, as it were, from babies not their own — why wouldn't this ensure that we would be better stepparents for it? Does this lower threshold fail to buffer against discriminative parental solicitude because we virtually never get a stepchild who is a baby? Perhaps. Or perhaps discriminative parental solicitude simply overrides the other predisposition: once the "courtship" component is over and "courtship effort" becomes mere everyday effort — effort directed toward a child not our own, no less, and unlikely to be a baby who has evolved a repertoire of charms to elicit commitment — all bets are off. And so, this theory goes, we discriminate — not by beating and killing, the rarest of all instances of discrimination — but by caring and giving less.

Another possibility also presents itself: that the entire notion that stepparental behavior has evolved as an adaptation for anything is wrong. Richard Prum, chair of Yale University's Department of Ecology and Evolutionary Biology, takes a dim view of the notion that natural selection is acting to produce stepparenting behaviors of any sort, suggesting, in effect, that there is no there there. An ornithologist, he told me about a fascinating, classic photo of a male cardinal perched on the side of a concrete pool, stuffing bugs into the mouth of a . . . goldfish. "Why would we call that a misdirection of parental effort, or call the behavior of birds taking care of chicks not their own *step*parental effort that has been selected for, rather than just parental effort?" Prum asked me. The goldfish's open mouth elicited parental feeling in the male cardinal, suggesting that he had the qualities of a great dad, period. "The same qualities that make me a good father will lead me to wipe the nose of a kid I don't know on the playground," Prum explained. It's unlikely that such decisions and behaviors are subject to natural selection pressures, because, as Prum put it, "it may be that the parental behavior module in the brain cannot be so fine-tuned by natural selection." The failure of Rohwer's idea, and Daly and Wilson's, he suggests, "is to imagine that every component of phenotype is independently subject to natural selection." For evolutionary explanations of avian and human stepparental behavior to fly, it must be possible to select for specific aspects of reproductive behavior without also damaging others, and Prum, and evolutionary biologists like him, don't buy it. From their perspective, good parents will make good stepparents, and vice versa. Presuming that a stepparent who murders or abuses stepchildren can also be a parent who nurtures and loves his or her own children doesn't always make sense from an evolutionary perspective, Prum said. That's probably not how selection works. "When there is evidence of adaptive infanticide, it's not often associated with parental care," he explained. "A male lion may kill the youngest cubs when he takes over the pride, but then he provides little paternal care of his *own* offspring later on."

What, then, accounts for the difficulties? Nothing quite so convoluted as genes or selection or discriminative parental solicitude, according to Prum. Rather, stepfamily life is difficult because families are cultural systems. "The new parent is bringing experiences, expectations, and desires for social stability that are different," Prum said. "Plus, we're comfortable and stable in our natal families of origin and likely less so in others." Which all adds up to some degree of stepfamily tension and drama.

Daly and Wilson's reach extends to folklore as well, and with scientists' discerning eyes, they seize on an apparent paradox: although the absolute quantity of abuse perpetrated by (more numerous) stepfathers exceeds the violence by (less numerous) stepmothers, there are literally hundreds of stories in the folklore about wicked stepmothers and virtually none about wicked stepfathers. Why might this be? First, they explain that, as we saw in chapter 6, stepmothers have not always been rare. Historically, high rates of mortality in general and death during childbirth in particular meant that more stepfamilies were formed when fathers sought replacement mothers for their children. If stepmothers were common, one might surmise that mutual hostilities, as well as incidences of abuse, violence, or neglect, were likely proportionally higher than they are today.

Daly and Wilson suggest another reason for the popularity of wicked stepmother stories. If maternal death and paternal remarriage were common, they reason, the social purposes of storytellers must certainly be considered. Tales such as *Cinderella* and *Snow White*, with their vast folk traditions, were told to young children. The narrators were overwhelmingly likely to have been their mothers — mothers cognizant of the terrible possibility that they might die and leave their little listeners behind. "It is easy to imagine," Daly and Wilson explain, "why mothers might prefer stories whose subtext is, 'remember, my dears, that the worst thing imaginable would be for me to disappear and for your father to replace me,' over those that instead whispered, 'should your father ever die or leave us, it would be a terrible thing for you if I were to remarry." Human behavioral ecology suggests such fears — that those unrelated to our children might fail to put them first — are not the stuff of mere fantasy or legend, but rather based at least partly in fact. Since the beginning of time and in virtually all species, mothers have made tradeoffs, decisions, and what Hrdy terms "retrenchments in care" that might appear harsh and uncaring. If mothers can be accurately characterized as dry-eyed, strategic, and ruthless, as well as doting and devoted, what can and should we expect of stepmothers? If motherhood is "a burden seldom embraced unconditionally" (Hrdy's phrase), what might stepmotherhood be? This question suggests another one as well: if selective pressures have created a tendency to do more for our kin, how is it that, so often, so many women and their stepchildren accommodate each other so well?

CHAPTER EIGHT
STEPMOTHERS WORLDWIDE

Anthropology, Attachment, Context

LEARNING FROM NISA

Human behavioral ecologists tend to look to contemporary foraging peoples for clues about what everyday life, social behavior, and decision making must have been like in our evolutionary
past. Such tribes, they reason, are a time capsule of sorts. After all,
gathering roots, nuts, tubers, and berries — and, to a much lesser
extent, hunting — as our ancestors did during the Pleistocene era,
before the advent of agriculture or the domestication of animals, was
the way people lived for as much as 99 percent of human existence.
"The uniqueness of the human species was patterned — and the
human personality formed — in a gathering and hunting setting,"
anthropologist Marjorie Shostak explains. The story of Nisa, the vivid,
eponymous heroine of Shostak's bio-ethnography of a !Kung woman
living on the northern edge of the Kalahari Desert in Botswana, is
remarkable for what it tells us not only about one woman and her
people but also about family and stepfamily life in our collective prehistory. All current talk of a "divorce revolution" aside, Nisa shows
us that rather than a historical departure or anomaly, the stepfamily
form has likely always been with us. Worldwide, it is universal.

From her earliest memories, Nisa recalls the events of her own
life as inextricable from a web of kin who helped raise her, as well
as a dizzying series of love affairs, marriages, and re-partnerings.
Nisa's life was from the very start characterized by relative freedom
and self-determination. She could move between huts and relatives

(and later, lovers) more or less at will and would continue to do so, like most !Kung women, for her entire life. One of her first recollections involved being weaned at age three or so, on the early side for the !Kung, when her mother was pregnant with her younger brother. As all pregnant !Kung mothers tell their youngest who is still nursing, Nisa's mother informed her, "My milk is no longer any good for you, it will kill you." A bereft Nisa continued her attempts to nurse in spite of the admonitions, but her mother repelled her efforts with increasing force. Eventually beside herself with jealousy, and surely having frayed her parents' patience, she went off to live with first her grandmother and then her aunt for several months. She recalled, "When I was growing up, some days I stayed with my aunt . . . then went back and lived with my mother. After I moved on again and lived with my grandmother and stayed with her . . . They all brought me up. All of them helped."

This mobility among a network of close kin during childhood was typical of the !Kung before they took up a more agrarian lifestyle, and even more so of hunter-gatherer tribes such as the Efe Pygmies of the Ituri rainforest. Those who aid a mother in the care and rearing of her child in this way — generally but not always kin — are called "allomothers," a term invented by Harvard entomologist E. O. Wilson and deriving from the Greek *allo*, "other than." Thanks to such allomothers — who are common in the nonhuman primate world as well — mothers can work unencumbered, forage more efficiently, and in some cases even have more children more quickly than they might otherwise. Competent allomaternal care seems to benefit everyone: it generally increases a child's chances of survival, while also increasing the likelihood that the allomother's own eventual offspring (if she is pre-reproductive) will survive childhood and grow up to reproduce. Indeed, there is ample evidence that our more recent way of raising children — with the mother, largely isolated, taking more or less sole responsibility for the child's wellbeing day in and day out — is an anomaly. We did not evolve, evolutionary biologists increasingly concur, to do this all by ourselves, or even in a mother-father dyad, and it is highly likely that "cooperative breeding" — raising children in a group of responsible, invested kin or committed allomothers rather than within a single nuclear family — was one of the practices that allowed our species to flourish.

Most !Kung, Shostak tells us, experience one long-term marriage, but divorce is common and relatively uncomplicated. Divorced partners usually remarry within a year, and children generally live with the mother. With a keen eye, Nisa witnessed her own parents' marital transitions. Some 95 percent of !Kung were living monogamously at the time of Shostak's fieldwork; polygyny, though rare, was far from unheard of. A man might marry his wife's sister, should she lose her own husband, or his wife's widowed cousin. Occasionally, a !Kung husband might marry an unrelated or unknown woman — or try to. Once, for a period of two nights, Nisa's father had two wives. In Nisa's words: "My father told my mother that he and his brother were going to go and sleep at another village . . . He didn't tell her that he was also going to get Saglai, another wife." He returned to rather predictable results. "My mother was very angry . . . She punched my father with her fists and said, 'Is this your true wife sitting by the hut? Why didn't you tell me you were going away to get another wife, to get Saglai with the big vagina?'" Nisa's mother, Chuko, continued in this vein until Saglai became petrified. A day later, she left. Chuko had made her point. She insisted that she was angry because she had not been consulted: "If I myself had said to you, 'I'm getting old . . . so, go, get yourself another wife. She will get water and give it to me and get firewood that we can use and sit beside' . . . you, having listened to me, could have taken another wife. But you acted deceitfully and forced something on me."

Chuko did in fact have the right to protest and to make Saglai leave, and also to berate her husband. Why might this be so? The answer, most generally, is that it's all about context. More specifically, it's about economics. In gathering societies, women often provide as much as 80 percent of the family's daily calories. Meat, while relished and even preferred to the fare women provide, nonetheless is not the bulk of any meal, and unlike what is foraged, it is an unpredictable form of sustenance. The women provide, and so they can make demands and expect to be heard. "A co-wife is a truly terrible thing!" Nisa exclaimed. Fortunately for her, she lived in a society where she could refuse to have or to be a co-wife. In other contexts where most of the calories come from men's hunting or farming, life is more sedentary, interbirth intervals are shorter, and men are involved in tribal politics, things do not work out so well for women or their children (more on that later).

This relatively egalitarian state of affairs means that !Kung women have a fair degree of sexual autonomy as well (or did have before their way of life changed, when the !Kung became more agricultural and sedentary). Taking lovers, for example, is a common occurrence (Nisa's own love life, as narrated to Shostak, was astonishingly but not atypically complicated. She had dozens of lovers and at one point gave birth to a child by her husband's brother.) Nisa told Shostak of a family upheaval that not only reflects this sexual freedom but also paved the way for Nisa to gain a stepmother. While Nisa was still young, her mother left her father for another man — her own sister's husband, Toma. This was after a protracted affair and much family upheaval — including Nisa's brothers physically attacking both their mother and her paramour. In spite of the family's objections, one day Nisa's mother simply left with Toma. "[My younger brother and I] cried and cried. We just stayed with my father and cried," Nisa said. After several attempts to woo his wife back, Nisa's father, Gau, "finally let Toma have her." Later, he went for a trip and upon his return "brought an older woman with him. She was his new wife. Then he took us and we went and lived in her village."

Nisa did not mention much more about her stepmother. Her appearance, her personality, and other details about her go entirely unremarked. Years later, Nisa told Shostak, after the death of Toma, Chuko returned. Nisa's father refused to have her as his wife but said they would live next to each other, conceding, "The children we gave birth to, they will just live between the two of us, because they are both of ours. If I prepare something or if you gather, you'll give me and I'll give you." And what about Nisa's stepmother, Gau's second wife and Chuko's co-wife? Gau told Chuko, "Even the woman I married, my wife, she will give you food and meat to eat and beads to have."

How on earth, we might wonder, would such a situation play out in real life? According to Nisa, "My mother just stayed with us . . . [My brothers] and I would sit for a while by our father's fire, then get up and sit at our mother's fire. We'd eat with her, then go back to our father and eat with him. And we just continued to live." The remarkable (to us) flexibility of this arrangement, the porousness of households and boundaries in the wake of divorce and re-partnering, apparently did not strike Nisa as anything unusual. Nisa's nameless, faceless stepmother is not mentioned further in the book, and her absence is striking, given the detail and zest with which Nisa described all the interpersonal conflict and drama she had experienced. Had there been any set-tos between her and her stepmother, we certainly would hear about them.

Nisa did, however, tell a story about *another* stepmother. A woman she knew, Nisa recounted, had a very small baby. This mother died just after giving birth. The grieving father said he would kill the child, but others intervened, urging him to raise the child with an unmarried woman who had been his lover. They did raise the child together: "It grew and grew. Then it died." (Child mortality is high among the !Kung — all of Nisa's four children died before reaching adulthood, and she spoke to Shostak at length about the horrible ordeal of losing them.) There is no particular implication here that the stepmother of Nisa's anecdote had done anything evil. But there are other indicators of palpable stepfamily tensions among the !Kung. Nisa's second husband, Besa, married her after the death of her first husband, with whom she had children. When Nisa's young son Kxau addressed Besa as "Father" or "Daddy," Nisa's older daughter Nai protested: "Why are you calling someone Father who isn't? Call him Uncle the way I do." Because Kxau was young when she married Besa, Nisa explained, he called Besa Father and thought of Besa that way. Nai, however, had known her father. "That's why part of her heart refused to call Besa Father . . . That's also why she often spent long stretches of time living with my brothers and their families." It all sounds familiar: children who are closer to or more distant from their stepparents depending on the age at which the stepparents came into their lives; adolescents rejecting the idea of a parental bond with a stepparent, dispersing early, or perhaps deciding to leave the household entirely, electing to spend time with other kin.

Nisa was never a stepmother herself, but in her later years, having lost all of her children, she did become an "auntie," or allomother. Life came full circle, in a sense, when Nisa's younger brother and his wife were expecting their third child and wanted to wean their second, Nukha. Nukha refused to give up her claim to her mother's breast. Exhausted by the conflict and aware that Nisa had lost so many children, her brother and sister-in-law "loaned" Nukha to Nisa, saying, "Why don't you take care of her for a while?" While fosterage is common in Africa (as discussed later in this chapter), Nukha, at age three, was quite young for the practice, Shostak notes, and the arrangement was likely as much about Nisa's younger brother and sister-in-law looking out for her as it was about Nisa helping them. Nukha became intensely bonded with Nisa, and vice versa: "I am the one . . . she calls Mother. She says her real mother is just another person, and refuses to sleep in her hut . . . At night she lies down next to me. Taking care of her has made me very happy; it's as though I had given birth to her myself." Something between a mother and a special, favorite aunt in her post-reproductive years, Nisa cared for the child of her kin; this closeness mitigates against unspeakable losses.

In many ways, Nisa's family experiences parallel those in other preindustrial foraging societies. Anthropologist Barry Hewlett, an expert on child-rearing practices across the world, notes that anthropologists who study preindustrial peoples generally emphasize children's relationships with nuclear family members — their mothers, fathers, and siblings. He finds this bewildering and biased, since among farming and foraging populations, "seldom does a child stay with his or her natural parents throughout the dependency period."

That is, among preindustrial peoples, living with one's parents for one's entire childhood is the exception rather than the rule. This is in part due to high parental mortality rates — women dying in childbirth and men dying during warfare or while hunting or climbing trees to retrieve honey or palm nuts, for example. Of the ten Ache children between the ages of eleven and fifteen in Chupa Pou, Paraguay, where anthropologist Hilliard Kaplan did his field-work, only one was living with both natural parents. Anthropologist Napoleon Chagnon, who noted a similar trend among the notori-ously bellicose Yanomamo people of the Amazon, has called this effect "the decline of the family." But children in preindustrial societies also live in families formed by divorce and remarriage, and divorce rates are high indeed. For example, among the Aka Pygmies of central Congo, the divorce rate is 25 percent; among the Paliyan foragers of southern India, it is 35 percent. Proponents of divorce reform would pale at the marital practices of the Ache. Men average 10.8 partners in their lifetimes, while women move their hammocks an average of $_{11.7}$ times in their quest for Mr. Right. Children in these societies, then, are overwhelmingly likely to live with stepparents (or, in polygynous societies, with their mothers' co-wives). To wit: 55 percent of Paliyan households are one-parent or stepparent households. Among the Aka Pygmies, stepmother families may outnumber stepfather families: nearly a quarter of Aka kids ages sixteen to twenty live with their father and a stepmother, roughly the same percentage live with their mother only, and just under 20 percent live with their mother and a stepfather.

Divorce and remarriage with children, and gaining a steppar-ent (or other parent substitute) after a parent dies, are in no way particular to postindustrial society. A number of anthropologists have written about stepfathers, generally noting that they invest less than biological fathers in their stepchildren and that having one may be disadvantageous. But what happens worlds away when children get a stepmother or a woman gets stepchildren? Are the insights of sociobiologists and human behavioral ecologists instruc-tive? Do they hold water cross-culturally? Unfortunately, it is hard to know, since anthropologists have written little about children with stepmothers. Evolutionary psychologist Martin Daly suggested to me that this is because, exceptions like the Aka Pygmies aside, "stepmothers *in loco maternis* are truly rare," as most children live with their mothers after a divorce or with relatives in the event of the mother's death. If we want to know about stepmothering in these preindustrial cultures (and, by extension, in our evolutionary past), it makes sense to look at family forms that are comparable or analogous to modern stepfamilies. Just as the polygynous Mormons of Angel Park (see chapter 7) have much to impart to stepfamilies in the broader culture, so, too, might peoples in the Amazon, in Cameroon among women who "foster," and in the Dogon country of Mali.

WHEN SOME CHILDREN ARE MORE EQUAL THAN OTHERS: FAT, FLEAS, AND THE YANOMAMO

Folklore, fairy tales, and evolutionary biology all tell us that being a stepchild can be perilous. Many of us would like to dismiss such assertions as so much stepmother bashing. But biological anthropologist Edward Hagen of Washington State University discovered that in the Amazon region of Venezuela, having a stepmother can indeed be bad for your health. A decade ago, the indigenous Yanomamo people of the upper Orinoco were experiencing short-term food stress due to El Niño. Their gardens of manioc and plantain, two food staples, had been damaged by flooding, yet no one had starved, and the situation was already beginning to improve. These were ideal conditions for anthropologists to observe whether and how people adjust their investment in kin when resources are in short supply. Would resources go to offspring, mates, other kin, or themselves? Would certain children get less when food was tight, while others got more? Why would adults make the choices they did? To find out, Hagen and his colleagues set out to study "wellness" in thirty-six Yanomamo children ages five to fifteen. They decided that triceps fold thickness — indicating the amount of subcutaneous fat in a child's arm — would be a good measure of nutrition. The more excess fat, they reasoned, the better fed the child was likely to be. They also observed the ectoparasite load in the same children — the number of sand fleas on their bodies and the severity of any resulting infections — taking it as an indicator of their overall health.

The anthropologists wondered, Could the children's welfare and outcomes be linked to any particular family forms, as well as degree of kinship with their caregivers? As it turned out, the measurements and assessments told a clear story: food and care were distributed unequally among the kids, in some cases dramatically so. Especially notable were the effects of having a mother in a polygynous marriage versus a monogamous one, as well as the effects of being an orphan. Having a mother who was a junior (second or third) wife versus a senior (first) wife versus a monogamous wife made for a big difference in triceps fold thickness. Children whose mothers had a co-wife had less subcutaneous fat, and those whose mothers were junior wives had less fat still. Meanwhile, all the kids with high ectoparasite loads had mothers who were junior wives or were divorced, or else they were orphans living with grandparents or even more distant kin.

What do these findings about subcutaneous fat and fleas really mean? Basically, they suggest that among the Yanomamo (and likely among us all), relatedness matters: kinship is important when it comes to the distribution of food and care to children.

Interestingly, Hagen found that food was parceled out differently than care. Orphans living with grandparents or other kin had as much fat on their bones as other kids, but like the kids with mothers who were junior wives, they had higher parasite loads and more resultant nasty infections, too. Informants told the anthropologists that the orphans either spent too much time with the village dogs, known to have fleas; did not have access to the wooden needles villagers used to remove sand fleas; or slept on the ground because they didn't have relatively costly hammocks. That is, those looked after by more distant kin had less supervision (allowed to hang out with dogs) and fewer material advantages (needles and hammocks). They suffered because adults were not investing the time needed to remove the parasites from their bodies as a mother or father would. These clearly disadvantaged orphans did, however, have bigger triceps (and so, presumably, fuller stomachs) than did the kids living with co-wives. In fact, children whose mothers were junior wives were the worst off: they got less grooming time *and* less food than kids living with monogamous mothers, and they got less food than the orphans.

Hagen's findings suggest a number of questions. Were Yanomamo senior wives actually actively preventing some kids from eating more? Or was it simply the presence of other mothers and children in the family that kept the children from getting as much as their peers who had mothers in monogamous marriages? Did fathers have less of themselves to give to their children when they "spread themselves out" between two or even three wives? An entire subfield of anthropology focuses on just such questions about polygyny and its effects on women and children. Depending on the context, these anthropologists tell us, polygyny might arguably be good for wives and offspring — or, as human behavioral ecologist and expert on polygyny Steven Josephson has discovered, the offspring of one's offspring — or extremely disadvantageous. But what does this all have to do with us? Quite a bit, it turns out.

People in the United States and western Europe may well have what Josephson, who intensively studied a cohort of Mormons, terms "serial monogamy that is arguably slow motion polygyny." With marriage, childbearing, divorce and remarriage, and subsequent childbearing, our families resemble polygynous ones in more ways than we might want to admit. Certainly, we don't all live together, but there is increasing pressure for the adults, particularly ex-wives and wives, to "get along," to form cooperative parenting coalitions, and to help stepsiblings and half siblings feel like "true brothers and sisters." In such a family form, men do in fact have "two families" — it's just that they're divorced from one wife and married to another. This is all separate from what Josephson describes as "polygyny in all but name," in which men in the contemporary Western world — where we explicitly condemn polygyny but pass no laws against men cheating — secretly have two families who don't know of each other's existence. (Former French president François Mitterrand, U.S. congressman Vito Fossella, and high-ranking males like them are particularly prone to this type of polygyny, as is the case worldwide.) Perhaps, Josephson says, these examples suggest that when it comes to polygyny and our evolutionary history, "the software is still in there." Which is to say that the case of the Yanomamo kids is arguably highly analogous to our own.

Yet viewed in a broader context, these less fortunate Yanomamo "stepchildren" might, for all their disadvantages, be considered lucky. For in some places, having a co-mother is less a question of discomfort, infections, or eating less in the short term than a matter of life or death.

POLYGYNY AND FOSTERAGE IN CAMEROON

The tradition of fosterage in West Africa may be difficult for those of us from the United States and western Europe to fathom. In a culture where mothering is extremely possessive, exclusive, and exclusionary — that is, where we presume that mothering is a matter of one biological mother doing the heavy lifting and nurturing on her own, day in and day out, "loaning" one's child to others seems a strange, even incomprehensible practice. Yet fosterage, so seemingly foreign, may actually shed light on why some of our stepmothering arrangements are easier than others.

Fosterage is widespread in West Africa. In Cameroon, for example, nearly a third of all children between ages ten and fourteen live with someone other than their mother. Why is fosterage so popular? As many anthropologists have noted, there is a genuine love of children throughout much of Africa and a true desire to have them. One expression is "If you have a child you have a life." Unlike in the West, where we associate children with financial hardship, in Africa they are associated with wealth, prosperity, and happiness. Indeed, throughout Africa, Sarah Blaffer Hrdy has noted, "not wanting a child is incomprehensible."

"A child has many mothers," a Nso' woman of Bamenda, in northwest Cameroon, told anthropologist Heidi Verhoef when she inquired about fosterage. Why would those "many mothers" — be they sisters, grandmothers, more distant kin, or even relative strangers — *not* help in raising the child if they could? After all, it is an arrangement that benefits everyone in the end. In many West African countries, there is a belief that children are not only good company and good workers but also a kind of social security. Invest in one, and down the road, he or she will take care of you in turn. Strikingly, among the Nso' and in West Africa in general, children are never "fostered out" to stepparents. "Being outside the extended family network of obligations, [stepparents] are not thought capable of having children's best interests at heart," Verhoef explains. In fact, children tend not to live with stepparents in West Africa, period. Instead, Verhoef notes, "it is expected that parents who remarry will protect their children of previous unions by finding other relatives to raise them." A "grannie" who is not one, it seems, is preferable to a father's wife who is not the child's mother.

Fosterage is not a uniform or monolithic practice. Women who foster their children out do so for different reasons, depending on the context and their life circumstances. Some of the Nso' women Verhoef interviewed had fostered their children out under ideal conditions and were happy with the arrangements. Working women with good incomes, they said that fosterage was a way to provide their kids with positive social experiences. For example, one woman had only one child and felt that the girl needed to live among "sisters and brothers." (In West Africa, children are socialized by older children — relatives who have the authority to direct, teach, and reprimand them.) Another urban working mother wanted her child to experience the freedom of living in a large compound in the country. These women fostered their children out only to very close maternal kin — their mothers or a sister. They sent money for their children's upkeep, visited often, and had a clear understanding that the children would return home when Mom had shorter working hours or it was otherwise ideal for them to do so.

Other Nso' women had fostered their children out under very different circumstances and had entirely different outcomes than the more privileged women. These women were mainly unemployed or farmers, widows, or single mothers. Fosterage for them was a way to increase their children's standard of living by providing better education and medical care. These women fostered their children out to the children's paternal kin, their more distant maternal kin (an aunt), or, in one case, an unrelated guardian. And these poorer women did not have unfettered access to their children. In many cases, those who had taken the children in actually discouraged regular contact between mother and child. These foster mothers also expressed unhappiness about the hardships they endured due to mothers who couldn't make financial contributions. One woman grumbled to Verhoef, "My family just thinks that since I [have money], they can send anyone they want here and I will take care of them." When the gulf in status between mothers who foster out and those who foster in was dramatic, the birth mothers often gave up their rights to their children altogether, noting that it was sad but in the best interests of the child. For their part, the caregivers were explicit and frank that the children they fostered in should "earn their keep." One woman said of her foster son, "He carries water. He helps me to grind corn for my corn beer . . . stirring the corn beer when it is cooking. He helps me to carry the corn beer to the spot where I sell it. That's where I get the money to take care of him." There was also an expectation that should these children succeed in the world one day, they would remember and handsomely reward their foster mothers.

Depending on the context, fosterage arrangements among the Nso' can either hew to the proverb "A child has many mothers" or seem, to our Western eyes, disturbingly like *Cinderella* — children living with distant or even non-kin, sometimes resented and working for their keep. Viewed from the other direction, long-term care of a foster child seems to be linked to the expectation of a sizable return. Although West Africans truly value and love children, no one fosters a child in simply or wholly out of the goodness of her heart. Those hearts seem to be only so big for only so long, unless circumstances are just right. To wit, anthropologist Caroline Bledsoe, who lived among the Mende of Sierra Leone, found that if resources are tight and parents do not send sufficient gifts to care-givers, or if the fostered child is not a relative, he or she may end up getting less — scrounging for food, for example — and going without medical care.

Fosterage in Batouri, eastern Cameroon, gives a whole new meaning to "the best interests of the child." Here the native Kako people have what anthropologist Catrien Notermans describes as "a low social and economic position." Women do agricultural work, while men tend to work as bricklayers, carpenters, or mechanics. However, due to high unemployment, few men actually contribute much to the household. In spite of this, they seem unwilling to give up polygyny. In one of the town's districts, Mbondossi, 25 percent of the households are formally polygynous. As might be expected, such economic hardship leads to intense competition between co-wives for the money and sexual favors of their husbands. And fre-quently, it seems, children become an arena where co-wives play out their animosity toward one another.

A twenty-two-year-old woman named Sylvie is a case in point. She told Notermans that when she was a girl growing up in a polygy-nous household, her mother and her mother's co-wife fought so much that their husband, Sylvie's father, sent the two women back to their respective families for a time. Sylvie was left behind with her siblings and half siblings, who fought with each other as well. Throughout the interview, Sylvie referred to her mother's co-wife as "stepmother," translating it for Notermans as "bad mother," and asserted that her "stepmother used sorcery to [try to] drive my mother away, to kill her and even to kill us. She has always been too jealous." Eventually, Sylvie's mother and the co-wife returned, and shortly thereafter Sylvie was fostered out to relatives. Her mother stayed behind with her husband and co-wife, presumably better able to fight it out on her own once Sylvia was safely out of the house. Sylvie's case, with its outlandish-sounding accusations of sorcery and evildoing, seems to be typical of polygynous households in Batouri. Among the Kako, for example, there is a saying, "Children cannot develop in the hands of their stepmother." Such women are accused of using their co-wives' children as slaves, of not feeding them or attending to them if they are sick, and of generally attempting to foil them in progressing at school so that they will never be able to support their mothers when they are grown. Typically, Notermans notes, mothers fear that a stepmother will use witchcraft to kill their children. Fosterage, in this context, is a strategy to remove a child from a strife-filled and potentially dangerous household.

Fortunately for Sylvie, fosterage was an option. Her mother had sufficient autonomy to make this decision and the nearby kin to help her follow through on the arrangements and care for her daughter. Sylvie's mother may even have earned enough extra from selling vegetables from her garden to send money to her daughter's foster mother, ensuring that she would be properly cared for. So Sylvia's ending was a happy one. But what if fosterage was not possible? What happens when there is no such escape hatch, when kin are far away, for example, or one's mother is impoverished? What happens to children when co-wife conflict rages around them unabated?

THE WICKED CO-WIVES OF DOGON COUNTRY, MALI

The Dogon women of Mali could not have lives more different from Nisa's in the Kalahari of Botswana. Whereas in the past !Kung women enjoyed mobility, autonomy, and relative sexual and reproductive freedom owing to their high status as gatherers, the way of life of the women of the Dogon region of Mali can only be described as systematic oppression. Anthropologist Beverly Strassman, who lived among the Dogon in Sangui, Mali, along the dramatic Bandiagara Escarpment — essentially a village built into a sandstone cliff — notes that women's low status is everywhere obvious. For example, women spend 20 percent more time working than men, yet men spend nearly a third more time resting than women do. In spite of the burdens of lactation, child care, and heavy labor, women are not permitted to eat meat, only locally farmed millet and onions they harvest themselves from their husbands' gardens.

In this region of Mali, inheritance is patrilineal and residence is patrilocal — that is, men live among their kin and pass land down to their sons. Women share their husbands in households far removed from their own families, likely their only source of potential emotional and financial support. Worse still, they share their husbands with strangers. Among the Dogon, there is a prohibition against a man marrying sisters or even more distantly related women, and this has the effect of "dividing and conquering" co-wives who might otherwise be able to build coalitions based on kinship. To deal with the perpetual male problem of paternal uncertainty, the Dogon have devised effective ways to supervise and control female reproduction and sexuality. Women are required to repair to a menstrual hut during their periods, with the result that virtually everyone in the village is aware of who ovulates when. This strips a woman of the power of confusing the issue of paternity, in turn promoting absolute certainty that she has been impregnated only by her own husband. As added insurance, women's clitorises are removed, on the theory that decreasing their sexual pleasure will decrease the likelihood that they will "stray" and thus put a man at risk of misdirecting parental investment.

But as Beverly Strassman points out, perhaps the cruelest burden that Dogon women experience is a heartbreakingly high rate of child mortality. More than 20 percent of the babies in Sangui die before their first birthday, and an astonishing 46 percent of children die by the age of five. It seems that children succumb to impure drinking water, malaria, measles, and diarrhea. But is that all? During her fieldwork in the region, Strassman was part anthropologist and part detective. She wanted to unravel a mystery, to test a hunch: Could child mortality be linked to polygyny? And if so, how, exactly?

In the village of Sangui, 35 percent of the men had two wives, and 11 percent had three. During her fieldwork following 205 children,

Strassman learned that there was a dramatically increased risk of death for children whose mothers were polygynous. In the polygynous group, for example, 37 children died and 81 survived over the six-year study period. In marked contrast, in the monogamous group, only 3 children died, while 55 survived. Even controlling for other predictors of mortality — age of children, sex of children, and family's economic status — it was clear that polygyny was dangerous for the children of Sangui, particularly the boys. Parsing her findings further in search of clues, Strassman realized that the greatest risk was to those boys in "work/eat groups" with lots of other children. That is, if co-wives and their offspring worked the fields and ate together, more kids were likely to die. Was this, she wondered, due to increased exposure to pathogens from living, eating, and working in such close proximity to one another? Or was it due to a phenomenon known as "the dilution of wealth," in which a greater number of children end up getting less when all the goods are divided more or less equally? Strassman was able to rule these possibilities out and was left with a puzzle: the odds of death for a child, particularly the male child of a first wife, were nearly ten times greater in a polygynous household than in a monogamous one.

The Dogon women of Sangui told Strassman what they were sure was going on: women with few options and no power, hoping that their own sons would eventually live to inherit the millet fields of the fathers all the children shared, were poisoning their co-wives' sons. Particularly, they were targeting the sons of first wives, those who were first in line to inherit. This, the women insisted, explained it all, including the fact that sons died more often than daughters. Girls, after all, married out, while boys remained in the family home and competed for their fathers' land. Strassman notes that the Malian courts and newspapers are full of accusations of neglect, mistreatment, and fatal poisonings of children by competitive co-wives. Sometimes there are even confessions. Whether women are actually doing this or not, Strassman points out, it is tremendously stressful on a child's immune system to live in such a high-conflict environment. This factor alone could account for greater susceptibility to disease and in turn contribute to higher child mortality.

Why, we might ask at this point, don't the polygynous Dogon husbands put an end to this? After all, these are their children, too, and as any human behavioral ecologist would point out, their own fitness is at stake. Yet like Cinderella's and Snow White's fathers, the Dogon fathers remain on the margins of the story, an absence. Perhaps, like Hansel and Gretel's father, they simply stand to the side, allowing their wives to motor the plot toward its sinister conclusion. The fact is, it is not in the interests of the polygynous fathers of Sangui to intervene, and so they do not. If co-wives are at each other's throats, they will not have the energy to change or try to escape the dismal material circumstances of their lives, let alone build coalitions with one another to protest them effectively. And since these polygynous husbands have an average of two additional living offspring for each additional wife, they can afford to, and do, invest less in each child, with the same or even a slightly better fitness outcome than if they were monogamous. The boy children are caught in the crossfire. In other words, there may be enough of them to spare. It is unlikely that these polygynous husbands are actually running the numbers about whether to intervene on behalf of their children in any explicit way. But the ruthless internal calculus of investment, risk, and benefit at the heart of Dogon family structure ensures that husbands stay on top. Women, potential allomothers — who, in another context, might just resemble kindhearted Nso' "grannies," loving !Kung "aunties," or at least good enough, fair enough polygynous Mormon "other mothers" — instead remain forever cruel sorceresses, evil stepmothers, and wicked co-wives. When it comes to loving children not one's own, it seems, context is just about everything.

JUST LIKE A MOTHER: ATTACHMENT IN CONTEXT

The fact that relatedness matters — a fundamental lesson of sociobiology, human behavioral ecology, and anthropology, amply

demonstrated in a wide range of human and nonhuman populations and dramatically played out among the Yanomamo of the
Amazon, the Kako and Nso' of Cameroon, and the Dogon of Mali —
does not change the fact that many stepmothers and stepchildren
end up doing just fine. Why might this be? Evolutionary biologist
Stephen Emlen, who made a series of predictions about stepfamily
life being more difficult based on an exhaustive review of the animal and human literature on family forms, emphasizes that when
we talk about stepfamily difficulty, "we are talking about probabilities, and any individual problem can be overcome by education and
effort." That is, we can always try to beat the odds, and knowing that
we don't have biology on our side can even help.

From two exceptional cases, however, I learned that some
women just don't seem to have as many problems to overcome — or
at least they don't have the one enormous hurdle in their way that so
many of us do. Barbara Waterman, Ph.D., a northern California psychologist who wrote a book about being a stepmother, and Dana, a
stepmother I interviewed, both feel strongly that their stepchildren
are "their own" — and their stepchildren, even more incredibly,
seem more or less to reciprocate the sentiment. These women and
their husbands' children (or in Dana's case, ex-husband's child)
belong to each other in profound ways, feel very connected, and
even refer to each other as mother and child as opposed to stepmom and stepchild. Thus far in this book, I have been at great pains
to demonstrate all the ways that stepmothering is not mothering.
And indeed it is not. But given the lessons of evolutionary biology,
how do we account for those instances (admittedly rare) where
both stepmother and stepchild feel like mother and child? What
are the circumstances under which a relationship can grow in this
way? Can the rest of us replicate those circumstances, and should
we even try? Are some women exceptions to the evolutionary rule?
Certainly, hearing these two stepmothers' stories, we might feel that
they somehow managed to slip across the divide that separates non-
mothers from mothers and children from the children who insist,
"You're not my mother!"

In her book *The Birth of an Adoptive, Foster or Stepmother: Beyond Biological Mothering Attachments,* Waterman argues that becoming a stepmother can be as profoundly altering an experience as giving birth. In nonbiological mothering, as she calls it, a woman "moves into the motherhood mindset irrespective of whether or not she gives birth to her children and no matter what their ages." Why does it not happen more often, then, that we feel like mothers to our stepchildren? Much of the problem with stepmothering, Waterman suggests, is that stepmothers are "advised to be too diffident, too hesitant to make claims on stepchildren and form bonds with them," and then we heed that advice. Waterman herself certainly felt no such diffidence or hesitation. When she partnered with and then married a man with teenage twin daughters, she gave herself over to the experience entirely, embracing the prospect of being a stepmother with extraordinary enthusiasm and intense commitment:

> *Motherhood completely took me over . . . My brain turned to mush. I devoted my whole being to fathoming my stepdaughters' emotional needs, while I tried to match their feeling states and help them through adolescent doldrums. All relationships, never mind work, took a back [seat] to my mothering attempts. As a new mother I was amazed to discover that the means to a heartfelt attachment with my stepdaughters involved my loving them enough to get lost in them, like a mother who surrenders to the intimacy with her baby.*

Indeed, since coming into the family, Waterman writes, she has done the opposite of the kind of holding back so many of us find not only prudent but necessary. As a full-time stepmother married to a man with full custody, she has taken over "the lion's share of the mothering, including making claims on my stepdaughters with a mother lion's fierceness." It is no slip that she refers to her stepmothering efforts as "mothering," to her stepdaughters as "daughters," and to herself as a "mother" throughout the book. Waterman freely admits that she wants her family "to be just like a nuclear family." Waterman's dedication to the enormous project of building and maintaining a relationship with her stepdaughters — a close, maternal, loving one — is likely to their benefit and is, without question, to Waterman's great credit.

Had I not read Waterman's story first, I might have been very perplexed by the experiences of Dana. Her relationship with Tania, the eighteen-year-old daughter of her ex-husband, was unlike anything my other subjects described. Dana is the owner of a small business near the office I rented for several years, a business I began to frequent once or twice a week because it was convenient, reliable, and immaculate. No surprise there: Dana, I would later learn, is the type of woman who runs a very tight ship. She could seem brusque or preoccupied on busy mornings at her workplace, but she had a way of calling people "Hon" and looking them straight in the eye that was caring and warm, too.

Dana is a direct person, and when she found out I was writing a book about stepmothers, she told me she would love to talk to me about her experiences. A few mornings later, we sat down in my office, and she told me about her life with Tania, a senior in high school, and her young twin sons. My first surprise came when Dana told me, with a laugh, "I call her my daughter, not my stepdaughter. She will not let anyone outside of our family know I am her stepmother. I am her mother. She tells them she came out of my body. Sometimes she even tells people who know she's not my biological daughter, 'No, there was a mistake at the hospital. This is my real mom.' And I say that's not true, and she says, 'It is!'" Dana mirrors this feeling of belonging to each other back to Tania. Of Tania's uninvolved birth mother, who lives hundreds of miles away and with whom Tania speaks very rarely on the phone, Dana told me, "She gave birth to her, and that's it. I'm her mommy."

If being called "Mommy" is something one aspires to and earns from a stepchild, Dana has certainly worked hard for it. She explained to me that she met Tania when the girl was just four years old. Tania's father was Dana's boyfriend of six months at the time. His ex-wife had just had a baby with her new partner, and the first day Dana met Tania, she sensed that the child felt left out and shunted aside. "I decided right then that when she was around me, it was going to be all about her," Dana told me. Although Dana was only twenty-two at the time — an age when many young women might have very little interest in having a boyfriend with a young child, let alone forging a bond with the child — she threw herself fully into the project of connecting with Tania. "I loved it. I loved having her," Dana told me when I asked her whether it was ever hard to be with Tania on the weekends. "I always wanted to be a mom, and here was this little girl who needed me."

Soon Tania was visiting every weekend. "Really, she got more attention from me than her father did," Dana told me with a laugh. They roller-skated and swam together, watched Disney movies and ate popcorn. Dana remembers that one afternoon, as she tried to lie in the sun, Tania lay on top of her, hugging her and refusing to let her father peel her away even half an hour later. It was a telling recollection: Tania got very attached to Dana very quickly, and the feeling was mutual. "When she was five, she asked me, 'Can I call you Mommy?'" Dana said. Sometimes, when it was time for her to go home, Tania would cling to Dana, crying, "I don't want to go!" Soon Dana was asking her boyfriend, with whom things were becoming very serious, whether they might get custody of Tania.

When I asked Dana about her own childhood, it became clear that her experiences at Tania's age had not been easy. Dana's parents divorced when she was three. As the youngest of five kids, she was spared the brunt of her mother's anger and depression over the breakup, but her brothers and sisters were not. Dana recalls her older siblings "having the crap beat out of them." The family was constantly broke. "We moved six times in two years to different schools," she said. "I remember no electricity, no heat, eating peanut butter and jelly sandwiches for every meal. We had it tough. But I don't blame my mom. She was just very depressed about the divorce." Dana's father remarried quickly. "My only memory of my stepmother for the first four or five years is that I hated her," she said. "I hated, hated, hated her. I felt that she took my dad away from my mom." Dana was sexually molested by one of her mother's boyfriends when she was nine. "What can you do about that when you're a kid?" Dana asked me, shaking her head. "You just shut down. That's what I did. You just find a way to switch yourself off to survive it." She told no one, and in spite of, or perhaps because of, all the abuse, Dana became an achiever. She excelled in school and in sports, distinguishing herself in everything she tried. "I pushed myself a lot," she explained. "I lived to please my mother. She was everything to me. I did what I did so my mom could always say she was proud of me. I was the good one."

Dana's own history of abuse may have been Tania's salvation. When she was six, she told Dana that her stepfather had touched her in a way she didn't like. Dana asked a few more questions, put Tania to bed, and flew into a rage. "The anger I felt — I literally was almost blind from it," she said. "I practically couldn't see." But Dana was able to focus her fury, insisting that her boyfriend confront his ex's husband immediately. "Of course, he denied it," Dana told me ruefully. "But I called child protective services, and they visited the next day and scared him. And I also told Tania's mom, if I ever hear about him giving her a bath or touching her in any way ever again, he will be sorry." Fiercely devoted to Tania by now, Dana began a full-court press for custody over the next three years, during which she and her boyfriend married. Tania's mom eventually agreed to a "test drive," saying that the girl was difficult to live with as she approached preadolescence. Dana was ecstatic to have Tania. Although she and her husband broke up, reconciled, and broke up again over the next several years, Dana and Tania were constants in each other's lives. (Dana also eventually adopted twin baby boys.)

Dana explained the relationship with her ex-husband this way: "We split up several times, and I never wanted to go back, but he threatened me with 'You'll never see my daughter again.' I was so afraid of losing her that I kept going back. I didn't want to marry him. I married him because I didn't want to lose my daughter." At the same time her marriage was breaking up, Dana's mother was dying, and she went into a clinical depression. "My entire life had revolved around my mother, and when she died, what was the point . . . of achieving, of being alive?" Perhaps Tania.

Dana went to therapy and focused on helping the girl get what she needed in school. Tania had been diagnosed with dyslexia and a learning disability; Dana didn't buy it. "It just seemed like nobody had focused on what she was capable of. They were look-ing at what she couldn't do. I thought that was stupid." Dana took Tania to be evaluated again and worked with her on her reading. She hired a full-time tutor to work with Tania on summer days when Dana was at work. Slowly, Tania grew more confident academically. One semester, the two of them did a parent-child science project together, and Tania won an award. Dana was immensely pleased and gratified when the praise Tania received seemed to give her the boost she needed. By her senior year in high school, when I interviewed Dana, Tania was an honor student, earning straight A's. "This is the child everyone said had a learning disability," Dana told me with pride. The pride seemed to me entirely warranted: Dana had done all this on her own. Tania's father hadn't been around or sent a penny in years. Her mother lived hundreds of miles away and called only sporadically.

Dana seemed to have "fixed" things in her own life just as she had "fixed" Tania. But I worried about her. The sexual abuse in her past, she told me, often led her to "shut down parts of myself," and having relationships with men was not easy for her. She was a better mother to her stepdaughter than her own mother had been to her, a remarkable achievement, but I sensed that Dana still felt that she was "bad" in some deep way, as if she had earned or somehow been complicit in her mistreatment. Mostly, I worried about what would happen when Tania wanted to be more closely in touch with her birth mother. It was inevitable, wasn't it? A teenage girl could not resist the romance of the story or the fascinating pull of this person — however neglectful — for long. Sure enough, a few days after our interview, Dana called to tell me that Tania and her birth mom had spoken. Mindy, who hadn't seen her daughter in years, was flying in for Tania's high school graduation. "She has every right to come, of course," Dana told me flatly. "But when she called Tania her daughter, when she said, 'I'm so proud my daughter is graduating with honors,' I wanted to tell her off. What has she done? What has she given her? Nothing."

I knew what Dana wasn't saying but wanted to: I'm *her mother.* I'm *the one who's done everything for her.* I *have given her everything.* And she had.

But why? What makes Dana and Barbara Waterman different from most women with stepchildren? It used to be that everyone expected stepmothers to feel and act and be "just like mothers." Experts now know that that is simply asking too much and is generally not a good strategy for any of the people involved. The kids already have a mother, and they're not our kids. Acting otherwise will almost always cause harm, hurt feelings, and confusion all around. Friendship, and in some cases civility, seems to suit not only the vast majority of stepkids but also most stepmothers just fine. Indeed, given what we are up against, that can be difficult enough to achieve.

Are Dana and Barbara better, more loving people than other stepmothers? Are they exceptions to the evolutionary rule, able to do and feel things the rest of us cannot because they are more loving and good? It does look that way at first glance. Listening to Barbara and Dana is likely to make a fair number of us feel guilty that we haven't put ourselves out in the same selfless ways, that we are incapable of such deep feelings toward our husbands' kids. Are Dana and Barbara simply among the group that, as Stephen Emlen suggests, can overcome the challenges of stepparenting with education and effort? This might well be the case, except that they don't seem to be making much of an "effort" at all — they've been crazy about their stepdaughters from the get-go. No, what is most notable about Dana and Barbara is not so much a matter of their hearts or their minds — though those are certainly admirable — but their particular life circumstances. Dana and Barbara may seem like exceptions to the rule, but like William Hamilton's bees and Emlen's white-fronted bee-eaters (see chapter 7), they may actually prove it.

Psychologists and biologists who study attachment — the way we bond with children and they with us — tell us that attachment, rather than being something that happens right away, is a process. Over the course of days, weeks, and even months, mothers and their newborns respond to each other's cues and, if ecological, social, and other circumstances are right, fall in love. This also happens with mothers and their adopted children, who form attachments that are virtually indistinguishable from those between biological mothers and children if the child is very young. "Even when children are older — we don't know the exact cutoff age — outcomes for parents and their adopted children to have loving, bonded relations can be excellent," zoologist and primatologist Dan Wharton of the Chicago Zoological Society told me. We are not mice who will nurse any old mouse pup who ends up in our burrow. But we are also not sheep, who bond with their lambs more or less instantly based on their smell and reject all others out of hand. Human females, it turns out, fall somewhere between these two extremes: we can become fiercely attached to any baby, but even with one we gave birth to ourselves, it takes some time.

Time and particularly timing are everything in cases like Dana's and Barbara's — or almost everything. Dana met Tania when the girl had just turned four, a warm and winning developmental moment when children are generally open to forming meaningful attachments. Further upping the odds in Dana's favor was the fact that Tania's own mother was out of the picture in fundamental ways. Initially preoccupied with her new baby, she moved hundreds of miles away, all but cutting Tania out of her life. Then Tania's father exited the stage. Although these losses were no doubt difficult for the girl, they also paved the way for a relationship between Tania and Dana that was remarkably reciprocal. Tania, unlike many stepchildren, needed and wanted a "mommy." And Dana, it turned out, had "always wanted to be a mom." In fact, she told me subsequently, she had had a miscarriage the year before meeting Tania and struggled with infertility before adopting her boys several years after Tania came into her life. In short, Tania and Dana's meeting was a two-way street. It didn't hurt matters that Dana wanted to, and could, save Tania from the things she herself had suffered — a neglectful mother, an abusive stepfather figure, a stepmother who seemed selfish and uninvolved. Dana came into Tania's life at just the right moment, and Dana's life experiences and motivations seemed custom-made for her to take Tania on with singular dedication.

By contrast, Barbara Waterman's stepdaughters were fifteen years old when she met them — not generally a warm and cuddly age or a receptive-to-adults life stage. In fact, their enthused stepmother came into the picture precisely when it was more or less imperative for them to reject parents and parental figures. At first glance, it seems that the timing, unlike Dana's, could not have been worse. Waterman, a psychologist, was certainly aware of this, and we can presume that she waged her campaign to win the girls over with intelligence and awareness of what she was up against. But Waterman's sensitivity to such issues is likely not the only or even the main reason she succeeded. There were other factors in her favor as well.

First, as Waterman notes, the girls' birth mother was open to help, feeling overwhelmed by the daunting task of dealing with the "mood states" of her two teenage girls on her own. In fact, she quickly agreed to a change in custody and seems to have more or less agreed to share both the hard work and the glory of mothering with Waterman. This is a real departure from the usual state of affairs, where a stepmother is given responsibility without authority and tends to miss out on the goodies, such as Mother's Day and confidences about boys. Second, Waterman also had the support of the girls' father, her husband, who had spent most of his childhood being reared by his father and stepmother. None of this, then, was an unusual state of affairs for him, and we can presume that he more or less let his wife do things her way without much interference, micromanaging, or possessiveness. Presumably, he backed her up when she needed it as well, making it clear to his girls that she was there to stay and that her authority was as genuine as her love. This scenario — two supportive parents — is just as conducive to a good stepmothering experience as two absent parents, perhaps more so.

Both these advantages helped Waterman in her "mothering" attempts. But neither explains her dedication to and her zeal for the task. Waterman says that too many stepmothers heed the advice, promulgated in books and by psychologists, not to act on their desire for closeness with stepchildren or stake claims on their affections. But for most of us, it is less a question of acting on these desires and more an issue of not having them to begin with. Wanting what she wants, and wanting it so badly, is what makes Waterman so extraordinary, and her outcome so good. Apart from the circumstances with the birth parents being right to build connectedness and love, how can we explain Waterman's intense desire for these things? Again in this case, it seems to be an issue of circumstances and timing.

Before meeting the man who would become her husband, Waterman attempted to become pregnant a number of times. She had several miscarriages and, like Dana, struggled with infertility. She also endured the unimaginable disappointment of four "near-miss" adoptions. Each time a child — desperately desired, desperately awaited — came into reach, it disappeared. Waterman had gone to incredible lengths to make her dream of having a baby come true, then endured the evaporation of opportunity after opportunity, until every attempt seemed like a last chance. For Waterman, it was quite nearly too late. And then she found her family: a man and two teenage girls. For many of us, such a prospect might seem harrowing, something to consider very carefully indeed and then enter into with trepidation, if at all. For Waterman, it was a solution, a beautiful answer to the years of questioning, an end to her decade-long search. It is not just important when the "other mother" comes into the child's life, it seems, but also when the child comes into hers. It would be too bald, too unsubtle to say that this situation worked for Waterman because she didn't have a choice, and besides, that is not the point. For she *did* choose her family.

In the end, for Barbara Waterman, Dana, and other women like them, biology matters. Relatedness matters less.

Part IV
Risks and Rewards

CHAPTER NINE
STEPMOTHER SADNESS
AND DEPRESSION

Understanding the Risk Factors

WE HAVE STRUGGLED to normalize it, to sugarcoat it, to sprinkle it with sunshine. For decades, really, there have been efforts — everything from *The Brady Bunch* to updated editions of *Dr. Spock's Baby and Child Care* — to dispel the notion that stepfamilies are different from, or less than or more difficult than, "normal" ones. Certainly, plenty of research shows us that stepfamilies have nothing to feel guilty about or ashamed of. Exhaustive longitudinal studies by experts on remarriage with children prove that the vast majority of kids do well after divorce and remarriage. And as we have seen in chapters 1 and 6, after about five years, remarriages with children are actually stronger, happier, and more likely to last than first marriages. But the fact that a majority of children and partners of remarriage end up mentally healthy and emotionally satisfied does not change the fundamental, secret truth of stepmothering.

Stepmothering is born of grief. It is, at its heart, an unhappy business.

Stepmothering arises from, and cannot be disentangled from, loss. In all senses — etymological, historical, and social — the stepfamily experience is sutured to, inextricable from, the experience of mourning. The Old English form of the word, *steopcild,* also means "orphan"; the *steop* prefix derives from the verb *astiepan/ bestiepan,* "bereave." "The sense is that an orphan is bereaving his lost parents(s)," one etymological Web site explains. Indeed, before the year 800 or so, "stepfather/stepmother" meant "one who becomes a father/mother to an orphan," and the terms "stepmother" and "mother-in-law" were used interchangeably. Distance; not being legitimate; being tacked on or after the fact by paper, rather than sharing blood; coming upon and perhaps even *causing* bereavement and mourning — all these senses are implicit in the term. In fact, the association between the role and loss, even privation, had been set much earlier: the Latin word for "stepson," *privingus,* is derived from the adjective *privus,* "deprived."

But in the twentieth century, as rates of maternal mortality declined and divorce became increasingly common, the sense of being orphaned or of grieving previously implicit in the word "stepchild" was largely lost. As this social and demographic shift has taken hold, we have become (we believe) "enlightened." Many of us — adults and kids alike — scoff at the notion that getting a stepmother is synonymous with suffering. But like a psychological resistance that reveals a patient's vulnerability, the stepmothering stereotypes we push away and deny reveal a profound and discomfiting truth. Despite our insistently upbeat, inclusive take on stepfamilies, the sense of grief associated with them, though covered over, is still there. The words, with their secret history, make it clear that something has been taken away. Death, deprivation, bereavement. Steps — mothers, fathers, and children — are still defined by that distance, that gulf, that space between them. The step.

"I don't like to dwell on it, and I'm not a negative person — I'm really a sappy optimist," a fifty-one-year-old stepmother named Babette told me. "But sometimes, it's really depressing. My son's brothers and sisters — my husband's kids — are so dysfunctional, so screwed up, so angry. So my son doesn't have anybody but us. I get so upset about it." Another stepmother, forty-year-old Dora, expressed it this way:

Sometimes I freak out. What if [my little girls] end up like [their stepsister]? And what if she turns my girls against me? I'm kind of an older mom, and I have these times of overwhelming sadness where I fantasize that I'm going to die before the girls are grown, and she's going to be involved somehow in their growing up and turn them against me. I actually wrote a letter to my girls explaining my side of things, and I was crying when I wrote it. I carry these feelings around with me, in the back of my mind.

Other women told me of the sadness of being worn down, day after day, by being disliked by their stepchildren, and of having no control over how they are seen. *I'm nice,* at least a dozen women with step-kids told me in so many words. *I really am!* For some women, there is the unutterable sadness of not being part of a "normal" family, of feeling responsible for or battered by tensions that are absent in first families, which we may fantasize about as the way things might have been, a loss that can feel unbearable. More than one woman told me that she had taken on her husband's grief for him: "[His children] ostracize him, and he doesn't deserve it," a stepmother named Gabby said. "When they don't call him on Father's Day, I want to die from the look of sadness on his face." As for the woman whose husband decides that he is not up for having more children after all, despite promising as much, sadness and anger may engulf her, leaving her with a sense that there is nothing else left.

Of course, all stepmothering scenarios are not so dire as these, and some days Babette, Dora, and Gabby feel just fine. They may even have wonderful, conflict-free weeks and months at a time with their husbands' kids. But I did not interview a single woman who reported a completely happy or even mostly stress-free stepmothering experience. Once we acknowledge our unhappiness, where can we go with it? How can we overcome our tendency to dismiss or overlook it without being consumed by it? And when will we cease comparing it to what a child or a father has lost?

It is frequently said that depression — the intense, all-encompassing grief that drains the world of color and texture and dimension, reducing everything to a kind of dead emotional flatness — may actually be anger at someone or something else, anger that we are afraid to express, turning it on ourselves instead. Conveniently and efficiently, depression is both an expression of rage and a punishment for having felt it in the first place. It is the proof, to ourselves and the rest of the world, that we have not hurt the other person, that we would never do such a thing: *You see*, the depressed person says, I *am the one who suffers.* We are strangely reassured, then, by our own depression, that we are not the kind of people who would harm others.

Especially his children. Depression among women with stepchildren is surprisingly common. It is well-known and amply documented that, in general, women suffer depression far more frequently than men. About twice as many women as men will become depressed during their lives. Whether this is due to biology (women synthesize serotonin half as quickly as men); hormones (their radical monthly fluctuation can have a dramatic effect on serotonin levels and mood); social inequalities (being disenfranchised leads to feelings of hopelessness, anger, and depression); or personal, emotional, or family history (in the broadest sense, it seems, depression is "hereditary," though there are conflicting opinions as to whether genes, socialization, or some combination of the two determine whether a depressed person's offspring will also be depressed), it is clear that when women enter the crucible of remarried relationships, we have already been primed for damage by the second X chromosome alone. And so while researchers have long focused on self-reported dissatisfaction, unhappiness, adjustment issues, and depression in children of remarriages, a few have turned their attention to stepmothers over the years. Remarriage experts Marilyn Ihinger-Tallman and Kay Pasley, as well as a number of other researchers and psychologists, report that stepmothers are dramatically more likely to experience depression than mothers. More specifically, clinical psychologist and stepfamily researcher E. Mavis Hetherington found that women who brought their own children to a remarriage in which their husband also had children reported significantly less life satisfaction and more depression than did non-stepmothers. Why might this be true? What makes stepmothers depressed? What puts them at risk?

Researchers who have taken on this question have discovered what so many of us have long suspected or, in some unfortunate cases, experienced firsthand: stepmothering is something of a "perfect storm" for depression. Marrying a man with children creates and sets in motion a number of potent, interlocking risk factors that can fuel and intensify one another, resulting in ideal conditions for this most destructive emotional experience.

WHAT PUTS US AT RISK FOR DEPRESSION?
Risk Factor 1: Isolation and Alienation

"In my experience, I have noticed that, compared to the population at large, stepmothers are more likely to feel — and become — isolated, lonely, and self-doubting," Manhattan psychoanalyst Stephanie Newman told me. I flashed back to my pregnancy and the other women in my prenatal yoga class. "Oh, built-in babysitters," they would coo if it came up in the conversation that I had teenage stepdaughters. They meant well, but their painfully naive take on my situation, and what felt to me like their insistence that I should be as upbeat as they were about it, left me with the sense that I was excluded from their world and a kind of bitter, shut-out sadness known as alienation. It seemed to me that I was the only person in my orbit who wasn't just starting a family with my husband. I already had one, sort of, and the girls weren't too thrilled that I was having a baby.

Although I knew how I was supposed to feel, the truth is that I was angry that they were so unhappy about what was, for me, such a happy thing, for pouting and retreating to their rooms for hours whenever they saw me folding baby clothes or caught sight of a book of baby names. I understood that this was difficult for them, a huge and frightening change. But I resented them, too, for acting as though I had done something terrible to them. I also couldn't help noticing that they weren't mad at Daddy about this. Once again, I was the bad guy. This realization, and my anger about it, compounded even further my sense of estrangement from the girls, my husband, and the world. And the more I perceived myself as having little in common with my pregnant peers — women in first marriages; women who were feathering their nests without the intrusion of resentful stepkinder and enraged exes; women who didn't have screeching arguments with their husbands about his teenage children's TV habits, temper tantrums, and hygiene — the more I stayed away from them and everybody else, and the fewer friends I had. Simply put, being a stepmother made me feel — and made me — cut off, different, apart. The eminent couples researcher Sue Johnson, author of *Hold Me Tight,* likens being alienated to "numbing out" and told me that it happens "when the sense of not belonging is so painful that the woman gives up or turns to desperate enraged blaming, feeling abandoned."

Other women with stepchildren report feeling similarly "marooned" in their family situations. Kendra, whom we met in chapter 6, told me, "I don't know anybody in a situation like mine. Nobody. I know a few women with stepkids, but they have a weekends-only situation. So I don't have anybody to compare notes with or anything. And when I describe my situation to my friends who have kids, they're very sympathetic and say, 'That sounds really hard; you can always come to my place and talk and take a break,' which is really nice. But it's not the same. They really don't have any idea what my life is like." The more lonely and isolated we feel, the more it fuels our impulse to retreat into ourselves. Our network of friends and acquaintances shrinks, and our daily interactions in the world dwindle. More and more, we are in our own heads. Particularly dangerous is the sense of being cut off from our husbands over stepfamily issues. This happens when conversations go nowhere and arguments go round and round, bottoming out in recriminations. After years of research, Johnson told me with all confidence, "Emotional connection between human beings is like oxygen, something incredibly basic that people need. It's wired into our brain by evolution, and isolation is actually dangerous for us." And so the foundation for depression is built.

Risk Factor 2: Rumination

It's not just the isolation that is so destructive to women with step-children; it's also the kind of thinking it encourages, says Yale psychologist Susan Nolen-Hoeksema, Ph.D., who studies women and depression. "When she's isolated and has no compadres, a woman is prone to thinking it's all about what *she's* doing wrong," Nolen-Hoeksema has observed. From there it's a short leap to what she calls "ruminative thinking," which she defines as "a cycle of rethinking the past, worrying excessively about the future, not taking action, going over and over the same issues, letting concern spread to other issues, until there's an avalanche of concern and a feeling of being overwhelmed."

Nolen-Hoeksema elaborates: "A nasty comment your step-child makes about how you've redecorated a room reminds you of a nasty remark she once made about a dinner you made, which then leads you to remember her father refusing to acknowledge her being rude to you once, which then leads you to think, 'He always takes her side' and rehearse, in your mind, all the times you believe he did so." Women are far more prone to ruminative thinking than men, Nolen-Hoeksema has discovered, and in fact this snowball effect was amazingly common among the women I spoke to. (A perfect example is the story about phone messages in chapter 4.) According to Nolen-Hoeksema's years of research, ruminative thinking contributes to depression and anxiety, as well as to such self-destructive behaviors as binge eating and binge drinking.

What we might call the Bermuda triangle of stepmotherhood — isolation, which leads to feelings of alienation and also to ruminative thinking — is utterly overwhelming, a place where we risk being swallowed up, our former selves lost without a trace. Sally exemplifies this tendency to ruminate. She told me what happened one day when her stepson and his wife did not show up for a family event. "I just couldn't stop thinking about it" she said. "They had done much worse things, but this one set me off. I brooded and brooded, and the more I thought about it, the more angry and kind of obsessed I got. I just went around and around, like I couldn't stop." When we fixate or ruminate in this way, we lose hours and days of our lives and parts of ourselves. "It's exhausting to obsess like I did, and like I sometimes still do, about his kids and the stuff they do," Sally concluded. "It detracts so much from my life when I do it."

Risk Factor 3: Relational Tendencies

Sally is not alone. Revisiting our feelings of anger, sadness, and disappointment over and over can be something of an occupational hazard for women with stepchildren. Laynie, a physician, told me that on particularly bad days with her partner's son (now her stepson), whom she describes as "difficult, difficult, difficult, so mean and rejecting and hostile sometimes," she used to stand in the shower "and wash my hair really hard, and while scrubbing and scrubbing, I'd think, 'Is it worth it to marry this guy? Because this kid comes along with him!' Over and over and over while scrubbing away."

As discussed in chapter 4, women are relaters par excellence. Liking and being liked are generally of paramount importance to us, a kind of interpersonal bull's-eye that makes us feel happy and successful. Predictably, then, the unremitting hostility and rejection that may come from our stepchildren can feel devastating. Failing to connect, failing to fix is something women take to heart. With our self-esteem thus undermined, we're increasingly prone to anxiety, stress, and feelings of worthlessness. Extended periods of experiencing such feelings can lead to — you guessed it — depression. Indeed, as sociologist and family expert Virginia Rutter puts it succinctly, "Women get depressed when stepfamily life goes badly, and they blame themselves."

As if feeling responsible for the failure or success of our unblended families isn't enough of a setup, Susan Nolen-Hoeksema adds that when a relationship is not going well, it activates and fuels our tendency to ruminate, which in turn fuels our dissatisfaction, in a cycle that can feed itself forever. We process and interpret and reinterpret. When things went poorly with my husband and stepdaughters, for example — which they did virtually nonstop for a couple of years — I took it to heart and took it personally. Sometimes, sitting in my office mulling over yet another terse exchange with my husband about yet another incident of his daughters' sullenness and general hostility, and his failure to support me, it seemed to me that in marrying a man with children, I had joined a cult. I felt as if I had renounced the normal world, giving up everything I had ever been and valued in order to embrace a new, draining cause — a cause that others didn't understand and that became the central focus of my life. For relational beings, this sense of apartness can be devastating.

Because women are more relational than men, psychologist Anne Bernstein told me, we tend to see problems sooner than our husbands do, feel them more acutely, and consider them more important to address and more urgent to resolve. This can lead to dynamics that stress our marriages to the breaking point. Not sensing the problem himself, or considering it a more trivial matter than we do, our husbands tell us to drop it or accuse *us* of being the problem. The predictable result: we feel betrayed, abandoned, and enraged by their indifference.

Bernstein explained that there are other dynamics created by our relational tendencies as well, such as "conflicts by proxy," whereby women married to men with children take on their husbands' emotional work, literally fighting their battles for them, acting on and acting out their unvoiced issues (see chapter 6). Bernstein told me that because men with children who remarry often tend to respond to conflict with paralysis (see chapter 5), are generally slow to know their own feelings, and are unaccustomed to emotional expression, their wives may find themselves in a relational back-and-forth: he says it's no big deal; we insist that it is, in fact, a huge deal. If our husbands then accuse us of overreacting and being irrational, this fuels further conflict.

The stepfamily is a tinderbox of sorts: our own relational tendencies, in combination with less emotionally savvy husbands and resentful stepchildren, can easily result in overwhelming conflagrations that reignite again and again. We may find ourselves trying to put them out for weeks, months, even years or decades, without truly understanding the dynamics that fan and fuel them. This work, predictably thankless and exhausting, sets the stage for a slide into depression.

Risk Factor 4: Overcompensation and the Need to "Fix It"

South Dakota State University sociologist Cindi Penor-Ceglian, Ph.D., has observed that "we are immersed in a society that promotes the idea that stepmothers mistreat their stepchildren." This central idea takes as its premise, and suggests by extension, that stepmothers are rotten, suspect, inherently bad, and this suggestion affects our psyches and our behavior. The lack of control over how we are perceived and what society thinks of us can be frustrating, painful, and destructive. We hear that we are wicked, and we are prone to believe it, especially when the rigors of taking on life with a man with children bring out, as they sometimes inevitably will, the worst in us.

In our can-do culture, which so values personal achievement and pumps us up with the notion that, with therapy, discipline, and drive, we can achieve anything, we are more than ever prone to believe that our reputations as stepmonsters are of our own making and that we can unmake them at will with perseverance, love, good intentions, and effort. With the specter of the wicked stepmother floating above our heads, we are under enormous pressure to prove — to the world and to ourselves — that we are not corrupt or sadistic, that we are, in fact, good, even perfect and beyond reproach. A fifty-eight-year-old stepmother named Belinda calls this the "Cinderella-in-reverse syndrome" — the stepmother's drive to be whiter than white, better than best, and her tendency to overcompensate at her own expense. "Maybe I have a good relationship with my stepdaughters because I was always the one sticking up for them if their dad was being strict," Belinda told me. "I have always been the one saying 'Yes, I'll tell your father you shouldn't be grounded' or 'Get the more expensive wedding dress. That's okay — I want you to have it.' My stepdaughters used to always say, 'Daddy's so much nicer now that he's married to Belinda!'"

Whenever my husband tells the story of the first Christmas I spent with him and his daughters, I see how clearly I felt the unspoken but overwhelming imperative to prove that I was the opposite of an evil stepmother. In his version of events, I planned and ordered and wrapped gifts for his girls; slaved heroically over the menu; and basically did everything I could to give two demonstrably unappreciative teenage girls a perfect holiday on a platter. "It looks like a gift shop in here," my older stepdaughter pronounced flatly as she looked at all the presents — each one wrapped in leopard-print paper that I thought she would love and tied with a red ribbon — letting me know that she felt there was something not legitimate, something fake, about what I was doing. "It's okay, but it's not *that* good," my younger stepdaughter snapped when her father remarked on her third helping of dessert. I now know that to my stepdaughters, liking or appreciating what I had done for them that day would have felt a lot like betraying their mom. And while I felt unappreciated by them that day, I certainly cannot blame them; they hadn't asked me to give them a second over-the-top Christmas, one that they could not help but read as an attempt to compete with their mother. I did not, I realize now, make such an effort for their sakes alone. I also did it for myself, and for my husband, to prove that I was nice and generous, warm and giving. The crackling hearth, the popcorn strings on the tree, and the roasted pears in the oven — the Christmasy spirit I was trying so hard to engineer — would testify, I hoped, to the fact that I was the opposite of a selfish, possessive, uncaring stepmonster.

Other women attempt to prove their worthiness and goodness in different ways, largely unaware that they are doing so. One woman, forty-three-year-old Anne Marie, reported helping her stepchild with hours of homework every night and sometimes at the last minute in the morning before school. "It was crazy," Anne Marie, the mother of two toddlers and the stepmother of a nine-year-old, told me. "It got to the point where I had no time to relax and unwind before my next stressful day at work. My life was just consumed with his needs. I let that happen, of course. It was like I felt I *had* to put myself last where he was concerned. I didn't matter."

Why do we do it? Why do we try so hard? Pioneering stepfamily researcher Lucile Duberman, Ph.D., summed it up tidily when she observed in 1975, "A stepmother must be exceptional in order to be considered adequate." And try to be exceptional we do — at a very high price. In the mid-1980s, Canadian psychiatrists Kati Morrison and Airdrie Thompson-Guppy realized that something unusual, and very specific, was going on with a subset of the women who sought treatment at local mental health clinics. Twenty-two women, all of them stepmothers, came in presenting what the researchers described as "a clinical picture similar to depressive illness." But when the doctors looked more closely, they realized that this was depression with a difference. The symptoms these women suffered from included "preoccupation with position in the family, feelings of anxiety, rejection, ineffectiveness, guilt, hostility, exhaustion and loss of self-esteem." Looking at what was underlying these symptoms, Morrison and Thompson-Guppy realized that these women were actually experiencing a special kind of burnout: they had "overcompensated in their role by providing total care of their stepchildren, in order to prove that they were not wicked stepmothers." And now their psychological distress was coming to the surface. The researchers found that these symptoms were "remarkably uniform," so much so that they proposed the problems they were struggling with be thought of as a new syndrome, one they called "Cinderella's Stepmother Syndrome." Stepmothers who suffer from it have more contact with stepchildren than stepfathers do; are expected to, and expect themselves to, assume a greater responsibility for rearing the stepchildren than stepfathers do; and show as much warmth to children as biological mothers do.

Building on Morrison and Guppy's research, subsequent experts also found that stepmothers overcompensate for the "wicked" stereotype. In one study, stepmothers reported responding as positively to their stepchildren as the biological mothers did, and less negatively as well on a number of measures of parental control and warmth. Sociologist and stepfamily expert Constance Ahrons notes that stepmothers also seek far more advice and read far more books about how to be a good stepparent than stepfathers do. Working so hard and trying for so long will likely intensify the feelings of failure and rejection women experience when they discover, over and over, that they can't "fix" their stepfamilies.

Factor 5: Double Standards That Disempower

There is a fundamental inequity that many of the women with stepchildren I spoke with mentioned: Stepchildren are allowed, even encouraged (subtly and sometimes explicitly) to dislike and resent us. We are given no such permission or understanding. It is not at all rare to hear adults venting about "my awful stepmother." Compare this to the number of women who feel comfortable admitting that they find a stepchild of any age anything short of perfect. Stepchildren have every social support as they express their deepest anger and most unprocessed resentment; meanwhile, all eyes are trained on the stepmother, waiting, suspicious.

Once, at a dinner party, at the urging of my good friend, the hostess, I did an imitation of my stepdaughter ranting about how her life was a vale of tears; how she was persecuted by her teachers, her principal, her peers, her parents, her stepmother. It was one of those moments when you presume that all the parents of preteen girls in the room, likely to be putting up with the same kind of behavior every day, will laugh with recognition and bond. Which we did. Except for one. "Oh, that's really *nice*," a woman in her forties hissed at me, turning on her heel and walking away.

Later, I tracked her down to apologize for having offended her and to find out what, precisely, had made her so upset. She told me that her father had divorced her mother and remarried when she was a teenager. As we talked, we realized that we had children the same age. But she was a stepdaughter herself, a stepdaughter first and foremost, and I was a stepmother. Perhaps in her mind, I was even *her* stepmother. And so, absurdly but inevitably, a line was draw in the sand. She was wary; the exchange did not segue into friendly chatter about kids and schools as it likely would have otherwise; the ice was not broken. I apologized — for what, I don't know. Had I made her father leave her mother? Had my husband left his wife for me? No, and no again. And if my husband had, so what? What on earth, I wondered with a certain outraged bewilderment, did my situation with my teenage stepdaughter have to do with this woman's experience with her stepmother? We were in our respective corners, the stepmother and the stepchild. Even though we were strangers and I was some ten years younger than she, the dynamic had been reactivated. She was not going to warm up to me, or acknowledge that I had some nice qualities, or even speak to me: *Stepmonster.*

Risk Factor 6: Punching Bag Syndrome

The struggle to be perfect (or even just good) and loved (or even just liked), women with stepchildren know, is more than merely thankless. It is sometimes downright masochistic. "Tell me something I don't know," more than one woman with stepkids snorted when I mentioned studies validating her feeling that her stepkids blamed her for everything. Our sense that we get blamed for things that aren't our fault is amply documented by stepfamily researchers and experts, who confirm that much of a child's resentment and anger at Dad is likely to be projected onto Stepmom. Why might this be? Why blame Stepmom for Dad leaving Mom (which stepkids tend to do even if he was divorced for years before he even met her)? Why the anger at Stepmom when Dad sets limits about behavior or says no to a loan? We may, in fact, have advocated for new rules and the like, and his kids may resent us for doing so. But they also tend to let Dad off the hook. Anne Bernstein says this happens because stepmothers are, in some way, more expendable, less loved, and so less scary to confront. She writes:

> *Step[mothers] can be a free-fire zone in families, detouring parent-child conflicts that may be scarier to deal with. One 13-year-old boy clearly stated that he enjoyed getting his stepmother worked up; it was obviously safer to provoke her than the father who was . . . more loved. Even as adults, stepchildren may focus on the stepparent as*

the cause of either childhood or continued unhappiness, diverting their gaze from their parents.

One man I interviewed — whose parents divorced and then both remarried when he was in his late teens — epitomizes the tendency to blame one's stepmother. Tommy is a mild person, a successful commercial artist who is wry, self-deprecating, thoughtful, and sensitive in his assessments of his family story. After telling me that he's never had any problems with his stepfather, he referred to his stepmother as "a fucking witch." A few minutes later, he admitted that in some ways, she is "sweet, very, very sweet, and incredibly vulnerable. She is someone who never made much of her life, and she's probably actually depressed. She never worked or had a career or anything . . . and I have no respect for her for that. It's like she just wants to be kept." He was sure that his stepmother was behind his father's lack of financial generosity. "Sometimes," he said, "I would ask my father for something — a plane ticket, money for the doctor, whatever, and when we spoke about it later, he'd say, 'Your stepmother's not into it.'"

Did he think this was an excuse his father used, that his father hid behind his wife in order to avoid saying no himself? I asked. Tommy paused, then said, "Well, I think he won't stand up to her." I considered this sentence, and all it implied, and said nothing. "Maybe that's just me giving him a pass and blaming her," he mused. A few minutes later, he told me that his stepmother often called spontaneously and left messages to say that she missed him and loved him, inviting him to come visit his father and her in Arizona. "Anybody else who heard that would think she's nice and normal," he said, shaking his head, "but I know what she's *really* like." For the next hour, Tommy spoke about how angry he was at his father. At one point, he circled back to the past, when he was a teenager, and mentioned how miserable he had found the twice-weekly "family dinners" with his father and stepmother, "because they were always tense and fighting."

From my vantage point, I could vividly imagine what it might be like to have an unenthusiastic, resentful teenager show up for dinner a couple of times a week. Did Tommy consider whether his stepmother and father had been tense because *he* was around — that there may have been disagreement between his father and stepmother about how Tommy was being raised or how he should act in their house? Tommy seemed genuinely surprised by my question. "No no no," he told me emphatically. "They didn't fight about me. They just . . . fought all the time." I didn't understand how he could be so sure, and I did not ask. What I noticed was the alacrity with which he dismissed a notion that had never even occurred to him yet seemed obvious to me, a stepmother myself.

After the interview, Tommy e-mailed me an apology "for going on and on like that." When I called to reassure him that I had found his thoughts very interesting and helpful, he told me, "The real anger I have is at him, I think, and she's just baggage around him, sort of like a layer." Tommy's stepmother is lucky that her stepson can acknowledge his father's failings rather than continue to hold her responsible for all of them. Many stepchildren never recognize that, using their stepmother as a screen for their projected anger forever. But the fact that someone as mature and intelligent as Tommy had no idea that his own behavior might have caused friction between his father and stepmother was sobering to me.

Risk Factor 7: Unsupportive Husbands

A woman's husband can make all the difference in her adjustment to a remarriage with children and to the smooth functioning of the family (see chapters 5 and 6). One study, however, found that nearly half of the remarried men with children interviewed expected their wives to be "more maternal" than they were with their children. Such expectations can clash with women's agendas and desires, especially when we are repeatedly rebuffed or disappointed in our attempts to build a bridge to his kids. And unfortunately, our husbands may make matters worse by telling us to "ignore it" or "just let it go — what's the big deal?" when we complain about a problem with his kids, point out something questionable about his behavior, or simply try to vent. This adds to the already stressful mix a feeling of being belittled or dismissed, and even of mattering less. At the extreme end of the spectrum, many of us may find that we have lost our voice. Peggy, a fifty-eight-year-old musician, told me about a "family" trip:

> We took my stepdaughter's daughter on a trip with us. On the plane, she behaved atrociously. It was so embarrassing — she screeched and demanded and sulked and threw a tantrum. She was six at the time but acting like a two-year-old. You could just tell she was doing it because she knew she could and was testing to see how bad she could be. My husband seemed at a loss. We hadn't been married for long, but I couldn't help myself. I very firmly told her to knock it off, told her that she was going to get in big trouble, that I was going to cancel the trip if she couldn't behave. Lo and behold, she stopped. The trip was okay — she behaved better . . . and I swear she loves it when I'm firm with her. Anyway, when [that weekend away] was over, I rolled my eyes and said something about how bratty she had been. My husband got livid, just furious. He said, "I can say that about her. She's my daughter's daughter. I can criticize my daughter and the way she's raised her child, but you shouldn't! You can't say mean things about her like that!" Boy, did I learn my lesson. I have never said a word against any of my three stepchildren or stepgrand-children since. Not one word of criticism of any of them since that day. I bite my tongue. Don't ever complain to your husband about his kids or criticize his kids to him. Just don't.

Abandoning her own internal compass, her sense of what is right to expect from her husband's child (or grandchild in this case) and what she can and should feel comfortable saying about it, Peggy goes mute. But *not* expressing ourselves is hard work. Peggy's husband's expectation that she not be critical, which in turn becomes her own, comes at a cost to their marriage and to her emotional well-being. Any feeling that we cannot air has to go somewhere, and too often when we hold it in or tamp it down, it grows aggressively beneath the surface, blooming into a dense thicket of resentment, fear, rage, and even depression. His children (and in some cases, their children, too) and his expectation that we should love them can widen the gulf between our husbands and us.

Risk Factor 8: Professional Bias and Bad Advice

Lack of support from our husbands takes many forms, one of which is withdrawal. When our husbands won't discuss problems with us, we are left looking for advice and support elsewhere. Unfortunately, friends and family can be utterly clueless, if well-intentioned, when it comes to dealing with the structural and emotional complexity of stepfamilies. Indeed, partnering with a man who has kids usually sets off an avalanche of unsolicited advice — much of it emphatically delivered and quite often contradictory, not to mention useless. Sifting through it all, we can't figure out who or how we should be. But from the cacophony of righteous voices, we definitely get the sense that we had better do it perfectly, or there will be hell to pay.

Act like a parent. / Don't act like a parent; act like an aunt.

Keep on trying to connect with your stepkids, no matter how badly they treat you. / Don't extend yourself emotionally.

Keep trying; keep reaching out. Love conquers all. / Stop pandering; your stepkids won't respect you.

You'll get back what you give. Keep giving. / Don't let them treat you like a doormat.

She's tried so hard with her stepkids. That's why they all get along. [Subtext: You should do the same thing.] / Just check out.

Among the best advice: "This is hard. Find a shrink to help you." Turning to a professional certainly makes sense, but therapy is not necessarily a sure solution. Those "experts" we turn to might not be fully aware of stepfamily dynamics and the challenges of stepmothers in particular. Even a therapist who says she is experienced in "couples work" may never have worked with a *remarried* couple with children, and a "family therapist" is not necessarily experienced in working with stepfamilies. This is no great surprise. Despite the growing number of remarriages with children, the field of stepfamily studies, just three decades or so old, is so new that it might still be considered an emerging practice area.

Complicating the issue of finding a helpful therapist even further is the reality that in its earliest years, the field of stepfamily studies was itself biased. Research was initially dominated by what is now called the "deficit-comparison approach." Comparing stepfamilies to first families, psychologists and researchers focused on things such as lower levels of cohesion and higher levels of conflict and generally found stepfamilies wanting. The problem with such an approach, as Iowa State University sociologist and stepfamily expert Susan Stewart, Ph.D., points out, is that "the group that comes out 'worse' in these analyses is assumed to be inherently deficient" rather than just qualitatively different. Too often, these problem-oriented studies became self-fulfilling prophecies that exaggerated differences in outcomes between types of families at the same time they perpetuated the stigma.

Although most researchers have moved beyond such an approach, it seems that this perspective continues to affect the thinking of more than a few practitioners. A University of Missouri study that investigated the attitudes of 285 therapists toward stepparents and stepchildren found that many viewed nuclear and stepfamilies differently. Adults described as stepparents were seen as less effective and less well-adjusted than adults believed to be from intact nuclear families.

Another bias persists in the research being done on stepfamilies: it is stepfather-centric, focusing overwhelmingly on stepfather versus stepmother families. Since some 86 percent of minor-age stepchildren live predominantly with their mothers and stepfathers, and since we tend to equate families with households (as we can accurately and easily do with first families), stepmothers, with their "part-time" status, might seem less important to study than stepfathers. But this thinking is doubly misguided. First, residency is relatively fluid and dynamic in stepfamilies, with kids tending to move back and forth between households, sometimes for months or years at a time. So "part-time" stepmothers often wind up being full-time, residential stepmothers (albeit unofficially, since such arrangements are rarely registered in court). Second, a number of studies have shown that being a part-time stepmother is considerably more difficult than being a full-time one and likely more difficult overall than being a stepfather. In spite of these realities, women with stepchildren remain something of a blind spot in stepfamily studies.

In many cases, this results in professionals who fail to recognize quickly the external realities — such as loyalty binds and resentment from stepchildren, coupled with cultural expectations that stepmothers should "mother" their stepchildren — that tend to confound most of our attempts at stepmothering. Ignorant of all the typical stepfamily traps, such therapists may leap to suggest that a stepmother's problems are internal (related to her own attachment style, family history, or other problems) rather than typical issues in a remarriage with children.

Stepfamily researcher Elizabeth Church has noted that a number of her subjects had a hard time getting help from psychologists, psychiatrists, and others in the "helping professions," even some who claimed they had experience and training dealing with stepfamilies. One couple she spoke with, whom she calls Martha and Wilf, told her that the family therapist they consulted initially told them that they had traumatized his kids with their marriage. Feeling implicated and guilty, they did not return for more "help." Meetings with subsequent therapists did not go much better. Several told Martha that she should try to be more of a "mother" to her stepchildren, who resented her enormously. For example, one stepdaughter took Martha's makeup and clothing without asking and then failed to return them. When Martha asked for help in dealing with the situation, the therapist told her that "mothers and daughters always do that kind of thing" and suggested that this type of "sharing" would help them to feel more like "one big happy family." Clearly, either the therapist was not hearing that Martha found her stepdaughter's pilfering distressing, or she considered such a response "abnormal." The problem, Church points out, is that by "assuming that stepfamilies are just like nondivorced families headed by two biological parents, these therapists may offer inappropriate, even harmful, guidance." For example, they may recommend that the woman act "more like a mother," or, just as harmfully, they may fail to point out to the couple (because they themselves do not know) that a great deal of conflict is common in the beginning of a remarriage with children. Indeed, knowledgeable experts agree that one of the most important things a therapist can do for remarried couples with kids from previous unions is to help these couples understand that many of the things they're struggling with and feeling like failures about are normal. This is an empowering and profoundly reassuring insight, one that usually brings tremendous relief and helps free couples from recrimination, anger, and depression.

Two of the most difficult truths about stepmothering are that nothing is simple and nothing is what we expected it to be. Women who marry men with children get a lot that we didn't bargain for. We also sacrifice quite a bit: we give up the fantasy of the white picket fence and 2.3 kids; we forfeit the possibility of being the first and only in our husbands' lives; and we will never have our husbands all to ourselves. These are among the things that stepmothers forgo relative to our husbands and our stepchildren. But there is something we lose that has little to do with them, that detracts only and utterly from us. Perhaps most powerfully and most painfully, what we almost inevitably are forced to give up when we become stepmothers is the fantasy of our own goodness and inherent likability. We are, sometimes for the first time in our lives, disliked, rejected, resented, and misunderstood, yes. That pain comes from the responses of others to us, and it can make us reel. But a deeper pain comes from the response we have to ourselves as "I will love my stepkids like my own" morphs into the secret, ugly knowledge that we cannot. One woman wrote the following frighteningly frank letter to an advice columnist about her stepmothering experience:

> *I am ashamed to say this but I can't stand sharing my home with my two young stepchildren. My husband won full custody of them three years ago [and] . . . I live for summer vacation when they go to their mother's and visit us every other weekend. When they are around it is like having permanent, irritating houseguests . . . I feel like a stereotypical wicked stepmother when I complain about my stepchildren because they are good kids . . . [but] I don't love them now and I don't think I ever will. I used to think that something was wrong with me because I could not feel love for them. When I was pregnant with my daughter I hoped that her birth would throw some internal switch . . . and loving her would help me to love her half-siblings too. But that never happened. I am madly in love with my own child but still cannot feel anything for my stepchildren. In fact, most of the time I wish they would just go away so that I could live my life in peace with my husband and daughter. I fear that this will harm them or cause problems for them later in life but I also feel powerless to change it. The truth is that right now I really don't want to. I just want them to go away.*

This woman's plea for help and understanding is so dangerously honest and direct, so uncensored, that we may wince when reading it. I can imagine stepchildren recoiling with indignation, anger, and righteousness. "She's the grownup," they assert, "so she needs to get over it!" A mother who has no stepchildren herself, or whose husband has remarried, exclaims, "What is wrong with her? We're talking about *children*. This is unforgivable. She is *sick*." A husband feels outraged at the idea that the woman he has married does not love or perhaps even like his kids; he might never forgive her for it.

Indeed, this woman *did* choose to marry a man with children, and we may quite naturally wonder whether she couldn't have seen at least some of this coming. But the truth is that when we choose a man with children, we are choosing *him* and very likely in the thrall of what nearly every one of us believes will happen: we will win his kids over, they will win us over, and there will be instant love all around. Then reality sets in: stepchildren can be irritating and rejecting; they can be downright hostile. Even when they are not, even when they are "good kids," as this woman says her stepkids are, they are not our own, and their demands, their needs, may fray us until we feel ready to break. Every woman with stepchildren I spoke to expressed, to some extent, a feeling of being overwhelmed by the fact of her step-children at times, of needing to withdraw, or occasionally of even wishing them away — just for a moment — so that life would be a little more peaceful. What stepmother has not felt the urge to banish her stepchildren, for five minutes or forever? The letter writer above may be at the extreme end of the spectrum — from overwhelmed to wishing them gone for good — but who among us has not thought it, whispered it, secretly wished it? We protest too much when we act as if she is entirely Other.

Stepmothering forces us, almost to a woman, to mourn the loss of a perfect, idealized self — a self who would never tell a child to shut up or get the hell out, a self who would never feel jealousy, resentment, or dislike for a child, let alone her own husband's child. That "awful woman," the one who wrote the letter, is not us, we tell ourselves. And yet she is. When we become stepmothers, and as we live it, we are changed. As we learn that stepfamily life is difficult, as we struggle to fix it, as we experience rejection and hostility and failure along the way, we discover, often with great and overpower-ing sadness, parts of ourselves that we did not know were there.

The good news is that a number of psychologists and psycho-therapists have given much thought to how to help women with stepchildren. The National Stepfamily Resource Center can help you find the practitioners who are truly experts in stepfamily and stepmother matters. In addition, you might get a referral from another stepmother, if you are lucky enough to know any, who may also be able to lead you to a formal or informal stepmother support group in your area. Always interview a potential therapist before signing up for help. Asking "Do you work with remarried couples?" and "Do you work with women with stepchildren?" may not be enough. You need to ask more specific questions, such as whether he or she trained at an institute that specializes in stepfamily issues or is affiliated with an organization such as the National Stepfamily Resource Center. Also ask how many remarried couples or stepfamilies he or she has actually treated.

You'll know that a stepfamily expert really is one if his or her first step in working with you is "psychoeducation" — talking about what's normal in a stepfamily and explaining that conflict and difficulty are par for the course. "Learning that stepfamilies do fight and that there are insider/outsider positions in a stepfamily or that it's normal to dislike your stepchildren, for example, can make something that feels like a terrible personal failure feel normal," Patricia Papernow of the National Stepfamily Resource Center told me. The next step in couples or stepfamily counseling, she and others recommend, is learning simple interpersonal skills, such as effective ways to get your message across to your partner and to build middle ground together (as discussed in chapter 6). The third and final step is to tackle the intrapsychic issues. "The old bruises from your family of origin can come into play in a stepfamily setting," Papernow explained. For example, being a stepmother can be particularly difficult for a woman who never felt special in her own family or who grew up feeling like an outsider. Experts are quick to point out, however, that this third phase of stepfamily therapy should *never* come first. "When you start out at this level, the level of exploring each person's background and how it's affecting the family process, it can feel like villainizing the individual in a very tough position. [It's] almost like saying all the difficulty is her fault, and that is just so damaging," Papernow said. "You've got to start out by helping these women understand that difficulty is the rule here, not the exception, and that it can get better. Then you go on to the other levels."

CHAPTER TEN
WOMEN WITH ADULT STEPCHILDREN

Lessons from "Lifers"

THE UNSPOKEN BUT POWERFUL consensus in our society regarding stepchildren seems to be "When they graduate from high school, you're done." Research on stepfamilies concentrates on those with younger children; books address issues such as how to support, understand, and discipline stepchildren (which presumes they are of an age at which you can do so); and when things get rough, friends are likely to counsel, "Hang in there — just three more years until he goes to college!" To paraphrase stepfamily researcher Susan Stewart, a review of stepfamily literature and social attitudes leads one to conclude that stepfamily life ends when the children turn eighteen.

Nothing could be further from the truth. In Western countries, the population is aging, and older parents with adult children are increasingly likely to re-partner or remarry after a death or divorce. In addition, stepfamilies that formed in the 1970s and 1980s, when we saw an upswing in the number of divorces, are themselves aging. All this means more adult stepchildren — and more stepmothers of adult stepchildren — than ever before. Additionally, adolescence has now been stretched out into the thirties, as twentysomethings take longer to establish their careers, make homes of their own, and marry and start families. This is combined with the recent trend toward "more involved parenting for longer," in which expectations have shifted toward more financial and emotional relatedness between adult children and their parents than ever before. The demographic shift toward an older population, the protracted nature of adolescence, and "more parenting for more years" ensure that the issues with stepchildren tend to remain complex, and often become even more complex — rather than simply abating or "fixing themselves" — with the passage of time. One otherwise remarkably upbeat woman, echoing the sentiments of several of the women in their fifties and sixties I interviewed, described her experience with her adult stepchildren with a weary smile: "I had hoped that when they moved out and moved on, when they had busy lives of their own, things would be less stressful. But so far, there's no end in sight."

"DAD'S WIFE, OR WHATEVER SHE IS": ISSUES FOR ADULT STEPCHILDREN

Many adults disavow the significance of getting a stepmother in their late teens, twenties, thirties, forties, and even fifties. "My dad married her when I was already out of the house, so it's not really relevant, the whole stepmother thing, to me" and "My siblings and I are adults, so it's pretty much a nonissue" were the frequent mantras of the adult stepchildren I spoke to. In spite of this posture of disengagement, however, they often went on to catalog the ways in which they found their stepmothers lacking, giving very specific and detailed reasons for their disappointment with their fathers' choice of a partner. This happened both in long-term stepfamilies and in ones that had been formed relatively recently. What puzzled me most was that these complaints about stepmothers sounded on the surface rather petty, the types of things a grownup of goodwill might easily accommodate:

She has terrible taste.

She's so chilly as a person.

She doesn't work and never has, and I have no respect for that. She doesn't really have a life.

I can't relate to her politics at all.

She gets so uptight when I visit her with my children. Children make a mess, and you can tell it really gets to her.

She's basically just phony.

In a number of instances, I was taken by surprise by how "stuck" many of the otherwise emotionally mature and high-functioning adults I interviewed seemed and the vehemence with which they sometimes expressed their disapproval of their fathers' union with, as one woman in her thirties put it, "Dad's wife, or whatever she is." I wanted to understand just what makes an adult child unable to feel close to a stepmother, and vice versa. Why do antagonisms persist between basically well-adjusted adults — adults who just so happen to be stepchildren and stepmothers and who are generally likable in their own right? And what is a stepmother of an adult stepchild to do? What are her particular challenges and options?

Getting a realistic lay of the land seems to be the first step. Moving beyond the assumption and the hope that "things will necessarily be better now, and if they're not, we're somehow failing," can be tremendously liberating. As one woman told me, "Years into it, the good news is, we're more comfortable together, just from the hours logged in each other's company. That feels familiar and good. The bad news is that things morph, and there are still things about my stepkids and the way my husband relates to them that drive me crazy. I have news for you — new stuff pops up as life changes, as they get older and you get older. Overall, I'd say things are easier for me than in the first years, but still not easy by any means!"

The issue of nomenclature — "Dad's wife, or whatever she is" — provides perhaps the most important clue to deciphering stepmother– adult stepchild tensions. Nomenclature is a very real conundrum for adult stepchildren, expressing as it does a larger, underlying structural problem, one that defines, to a great extent, the relationship between adult stepchildren and their stepmothers. As many experts note, at this life stage a person is less in need of a parent figure, or even an additional adult

support figure, than ever before. The developmental imperative is to separate — to get a life and a career, to marry and
have a family of his or her own. A stepparent — whether she
is new or long-term — may be more purely "extra" than ever
before, and more likely to be perceived as an extra burden. As
one stepdaughter in her thirties told me, "My stepmother's okay,
but there's just so much to do, and there's only so much time. I
can't always chat with her on the phone when I call for my dad.
Then she gets annoyed. I just don't need that, to get dragged
back into old patterns." Viewed from the stepmother's perspective, the young adult's gradual separation from the family — or
failure to achieve it — means even more role ambiguity as she
tries to get a toehold in her husband's family. Who am I? Who
are they? What are we to each other? How should I be toward
them? These become even more profound questions for women
with adult stepchildren. As Olivia, age fifty-eight, told me:

> It's not like a mothering thing, given how late I came into their lives.
> I hope they get, I think they get, how nice it is for their father to have
> a partner. I don't really need them to cherish me or anything. I don't
> expect it. I just would hope for civility and acceptance from them.
> I guess that's the goal. We're pretty much there . . . I was actually
> friends with one of my husband's daughters before he and I got
> together. She's basically my age. I met him at a party at her house!
> There's not a mother-daughter thing going on for us. I'm not sure
> what it is, honestly. Over the years, it's basically become a friendship
> again.

Sally, age sixty-five, put it this way: "I guess I would say that after
twenty-five years of marriage to their dad, I've become sort of
detached. They have their busy lives; I have mine. My expectations
are lower. That's not necessarily bad. They still do stuff that drives
me nuts, but now it's more like I'm watching it happen rather than
playing a big part in it."

Role ambiguity and adult stepchildren's continuing ambivalence, the sense — even if it is unacknowledged — that accepting us would be a betrayal of Mother, that Father loving us is a betrayal of both Mother and them, can make matters more complicated still. In her essay "Step Shock," from *My Father Married Your Mother: Writers Talk About Stepparents, Stepchildren, and Everyone in Between,* Candy Cooper describes the day of her father's remarriage:

> *My new stepmother, a year older than my relatively new husband, looked radiant, and everyone celebrated in high spirits in the days that followed. I nursed a fever in my darkened hotel room. The hotel doctor prescribed antibiotics for an eye infection, but I suspected something else — step fever, a plague of unfinished grief. I grew vigilant, seeking signs of my father's happiness. My new stepmother's considerable effort to include us all, her love and devotion to children, her attentiveness to my father's ills — these registered, but faintly. As for his happiness, there could be no right amount: if too little was a bad sign, too much meant betrayal.*

Cooper's case is specific — the grief of a child who, having lost her mother, now fears an additional loss, nearly unbearable to contemplate, the loss of a unique closeness, of clear and mutual emotional primacy, with her father. After a review of the literature, sociologist Susan Stewart concluded than the issues of adult stepchildren are basically no different, and no less potent, that those of younger stepchildren. These issues include feeling emotionally distressed by a parent's decision to remarry; feeling rejected, betrayed, or angry toward a parent or stepparent; experiencing a loss of self-esteem; struggling to accept a stepparent who is the same age; disliking seeing the couple hold hands, embrace, or flirt; and having trouble coping with parental pressure to develop a close relationship with a stepparent.

That an adult stepchild can feel off-kilter and unhealed for years after his or her father's remarriage was brought home to me with particular force by Annie, whom we met in chapter 3. As she sobbed in my office while describing her father's wedding a year after her mother's death, I was unable to maintain my usual stance of "supportive neutrality" and joined her in crying. What I glean from Cooper, and learned from Annie that day as well, was that her father's happiness felt like a negation not only of the primacy of her dead mother but also of herself and her own primacy:

> *He waited just over a year to remarry. It was like the bare minimum, and only because my sister insisted it was inappropriate to marry any sooner. It felt like he was just walking away. Anyway, there was my stepmother wearing white at her third wedding, fourteen months after my mother's death. It made you think. I cried through the whole ceremony. It's been nine years, but it's still very vivid for me . . . the feeling that he should have waited, should have had the decency to wait longer.*

For a stepmother, what would seem like a natural resistance in a young child can be more jarring and difficult to accept in an adult. Kind and empathic as we may be, few of us can imagine it would feel good to have an adult stepchild with whom we had put in our best effort sob throughout our wedding to his or her father.

Annie went on to tell me, "When someone calls my father and my stepmother 'your parents' — like recently the car service called, and the dispatcher said, 'We just picked your parents up at the airport' — I feel like I've been stabbed." She is unlikely to tell her stepmother this, and more likely to simply withdraw from her or reject her overtures. This leaves them both, nearly ten years after the wedding, in a standoff of mutual wariness, suspicion, and misunderstanding. As Annie told me later in our interview, when I asked what would happen if, hypothetically, one of them were to reach out to the other at this late stage, "What would my stepmother do if I invited her out to lunch? [laughs] Good question. She'd probably show up and wonder what I was up to. And if she invited me out to lunch, I'd figure it was because she had an agenda. Like she wanted to tell me I had to give her the key to their house back or something!"

A father remarrying after a divorce can also activate surprisingly intense feelings of grief, ambivalence, and pain in some adult children. British psychologist Sarah Corrie, one of a handful of researchers who has written on the specific psychological issues of adult stepchildren, points out that they may have insecure attachment styles and other continuing unresolved problems related to their parents' divorce. These can include "maladaptive notions of the relationship between self, others and the stability of relationships in general." Or, in the words of New York City psychoanalyst Stephanie Newman, "Children of divorce, whether they're young or grown, may not have a lot of faith in relationships in general. That can mean not only less respect for Dad and Stepmom's marriage, but less incentive to have any relationship with her at all. Some adult children of divorce may just feel like, *What's the point?*"

Even when the adult child has "worked through" the biological parents' divorce — by accepting its permanence and mourning the loss of lingering fantasies about an idealized family life — Corrie emphasizes that there may still be difficulties. Specifically, she underscores one of the biggest challenges for a woman marrying a man with adult children. In cases of divorce, the bond between an adult child and his or her parent can be very intense and close indeed. Sometimes they can even feel like peers or spouses. Corrie writes:

> *In my experience, the breakdown of a family of origin can foster the development of a[n especially] close bond between a parent and adult child. This can be seen as reflecting a state of mutual adulthood that provides more opportunities for giving and receiving support in more reciprocal ways than were possible [previously]. The arrival of a stepparent can, therefore, be perceived as disrupting this bond, precipitating feelings of anger, jealousy, or competition. If unresolved in the longer term, these feelings are likely to represent a threat to self-esteem and sense of security.*

Astonishingly, what Corrie has found in her clinical work, and what she describes here, is the previously unconsidered possibility that adult children are *more* likely to have a problem with "getting a stepmother" or "having a stepmother" than younger children. The closeness of an adult child and a parent is very special, she suggests, and may eclipse even the closeness of a younger child and a parent. And so, contrary to what common sense may tell us, a stepmother is likely more threatening if she makes her first appearance later in the child's life. Gabby, whom we first met in chapter 1, married Pryce when his kids were young adults — and practically her peers. Pryce and his ex-wife had separated after years of irresolvable problems, but Gabby, rather predictably, took the fall in both the ex's eyes and in the eyes of her adult stepchildren. It didn't make things easier, she told me, that Pryce's children were close to her in age.

> *It just made it all seem kind of . . . cliché to them, I think. Dad's with someone nearly our age. Ewww. That kind of thing. But mostly the problem was that they got so much bitterness from their mother, and they felt compelled to take that on as their own. We weren't invited to things — I wasn't invited to things — because "it will upset Mom" . . . I think they should have been and still should be grateful to me. When I got together with their father, he was killing himself. He was smoking three packs a day and drinking nonstop. And I helped pull him out of that, and made him get treated for his depression. And look at him now.*

Gabby and Pryce have a fifteen-year-old daughter. Gabby described their relationship with Pryce's two adult sons, one of whom visits a couple of times a year, as "a little strained but getting better." But they have not heard from Pryce's adult daughter, Janine, in nearly five years. She always seemed, Gabby told me, to be looking for excuses to feel hurt by her father and to be fantasizing about ways she was excluded or the least favored child.

It was so important to me that all his kids be part of the wedding.
And after that, we always made a point to see them . . . I felt so close
to her then. But there was always this tension, especially after I had
Suki not long after she had [her child]. She seemed to have a chip on
her shoulder. She seemed to be looking for proof that Bryce loved her
less. There was an incident with Pryce, who is rushed on the phone
with everyone. He got off the phone quickly, and she told her brother
that she was just hurt to the quick by that. Shortly after that, she got
angry that her brother spontaneously spent the night after coming to
visit while Suki was a toddler. She felt she had never spent the night
with us, so why should he, is how the story came back to us. I don't
know the real truth, because she has not spoken to us since.

Stepdaughters, we know from the research, can feel extraordinarily competitive with their stepmothers and tremendously threatened by them (see chapters 3 and 4). Add to the mix the likelihood that young women often develop an extremely close bond with their fathers before their remarriage; the confusion of getting a stepmother close to one's own age; the feeling that liking Stepmom would kill Mom; and feeling overshadowed by Stepmother giving birth shortly after you do. These realities would present challenges for even a healthy adult child, challenges she could overcome. But for a child who is overidentified with her mother and who still nurses wounds to her self-worth stemming from her parents' divorce, as far in the past as it may be, they are a recipe for interpersonal disaster. And unfortunately, an adult stepdaughter who cannot accommodate change or assimilate disequilibrium has likely been honing her defenses for years. She is able to rationalize her anger in ways that no young child can and has a uniquely adult weapon in her arsenal — the ability to simply walk away forever.

Developmentalists have noted that a person's twenties — Janine's age when Gabby came into her life — are characterized by a tension between wanting to be both separate, or independent, and together, or cooperative, with our families of origin. Until adult stepchildren have resolved this typical developmental conundrum of balancing intimacy and isolation, the stepmother is a convenient target of their frustration. Sarah Corrie describes a patient named Louise, whose envy, insecurity, and misplaced sense of loyalty to her mother led her to reject her young stepmother's overtures of friendship and communication repeatedly. But Louise could only hold her stepmother at bay; her stepmother was not going away. Confronted with this reality and feeling on some level vanquished, Louise slumped into a depression. Corrie could have been describing any number of adult stepchildren I interviewed when she wrote, "For Louise, it felt as though she had been replaced by her stepmother in her father's affections. The arrival of a stepmother had reactivated fears about her acceptability and worth, rather than caused them." Louise's problems, Corrie notes, were largely internal issues of self-esteem that she externalized onto her stepmother. The stepmother then became a "bad object," whose actions, Louise asserted, made her "feel awful." When her stepmother initiated contact, for example, Louise felt invaded. When her stepmother kept her distance, Louise felt ignored and cut off from her father. Louise's view of her mother as an innocent victim in the divorce exacerbated her sense that it was "wrong" to have a relationship with her stepmother.

Corrie notes a very particular difficulty women might have with their adult stepchildren: figuring out whether and how to talk to them about problems in the relationship and in general. Adult children are likely to push away the feelings of ambivalence about Daddy remarrying, considering them weak and "immature," and so these feelings remain unresolved. Yet a parent or stepparent who initiates a conversation with an adult child on the topic is likely to be rebuffed, as the adult child may, in Corrie's words, "find high levels of nurturance and parental or stepparental support intrusive and inappropriate." The stepmother's conundrum at this developmental stage is the same as it is at any other, only more so. If she makes an effort, it may well be read as pushy and presumptuous, as

Louise described her stepmother. If she fails to make an effort, she risks that this will be interpreted as proof that she doesn't care or is "cold."

Adult stepchildren, however, due to their more evolved self-knowledge and ability to articulate what might be complex emotional states, can provide wonderful insight into the workings of not only their own but also the younger stepchild's mind. In his essay "On Having a Stepmother Who Loves Opera," for example, author Andrew Solomon describes meeting his widowed father's first serious girlfriend.

> *We arranged an evening when I sat next to her. I can say now, almost fifteen years later, that Bobye is one of the nicest people in New York, but when I sat next to her that night I took offense at everything she said, and when I got home I wrote my father a letter saying that Bobye was a terrible person. My father called back and we both cried . . . It wasn't easy for anyone. She was both a person in her own right and a stage in my grief, and it was not always possible to reconcile these functions.*

Viewed by Solomon as both "a person in her own right and a stage in my grief," Bobye might consider herself lucky. Many adult stepchildren would not be able to acknowledge or glimpse her personhood, viewing the world instead through the prism of their turbulent response to change. And so a person becomes a problem: "one of the nicest people in New York" morphs into the enemy.

In spite of Solomon's clear ambivalence about his father finding a partner, when he and his brother met the next serious girlfriend many months later, they made it their business to keep this woman, Sarah B., on their father's radar. Solomon found himself "smitten" with Sarah B., who was witty, intelligent, and emotionally magnanimous. But eventually, when things took a serious turn and he was asked by Sarah B., with whom he had become quite close, which of several dates would suit him for a wedding, Solomon felt betrayed and enraged. "Very much to my own surprise I was apoplectic; it seemed like a complete disruption of a delicate ecosystem and jarred on my inner life and my sense of what rooted me to the earth," he writes. "The idea that my father should marry again seemed to trivialize the institution he had shared with my mother." Here again is the sense of betrayal — of oneself and of one's mother — that Candy Cooper and Annie both described.

And then we get to the heart of the matter, or perhaps *another* heart of the matter: the fearful question of power and hierarchy that seems to dog everyone who becomes a stepchild, regardless of his or her age. "Then too, I disliked the fact that my father [who had said he would never remarry] had reversed himself," Solomon writes. "My father does not usually reverse himself with me, and the fact that he would do so with someone else made me jealous. He hadn't consulted with my brother and me before he made this momentous decision."

Many stepmothers will nod in recognition at this expectation of the stepchild that he or she "should" have a say in when — and even whether — Dad remarries. It harks back to the letter Solomon wrote to his father about Bobye — the presumption that he had a "right" to determine whether and with whom his father would become involved. My husband reminds me that after his older daughter, then fifteen, had met me a second time, she said, "She's nice, but I don't want you to marry her!" My husband let her know that he cared about her feelings and knew it was hard for her to see him with someone other than her mother. But he also let her know that she didn't have a vote about his getting married again — that it was his decision — drawing a clear map of just who was in charge of what here. It is not so easy to draw such a line with an adult child, who is out of the realm of discipline and who is in a relationship with the father because he or she chooses to be, something like a peer, rather than because he or she has to be, as is the case with a young child. And as in Cooper's and Solomon's cases, it is likely harder when the marriage ended due to the mother's death. Then, the mother is a ghostly, idealized presence, furthering the sense that the entrance of a new person — and accepting her — inevitably means a slipping away, even a repudiation, of Mom.

But what else does the adult stepchild fear? Perhaps, Solomon suggests, the loss of control of a beloved parent, as well as a kind of exclusion that activates primal terrors about isolation, loss, and losing.

> *The relationship between my father and Sarah B., which had been my pet project, was now taken quite out of my reach and became very much their own. The wedding went ahead . . . It was a very difficult time and helped propel me into a depression. I felt a fathomless sea of anxieties opening out. If Sarah B. and I differ, then when will he do what I want, and when will he do what she wants? With my mother it was never an issue — he did what she wanted, because they were seamless that way, but what she wanted was generally what was best for me. It is my underlying fear that my father will be weak and subject to Sarah B.'s influence and that I will somehow alienate her and in so doing lose him. I claim historical precedence, and she claims current primacy.*

What crystallizes in this complex passage — and impresses as much as its raw honestly — is the insight that Sarah B. was *not* his mother, that she was, in fact, very much like Bobye, a person in possession of a will separate from his. The possibility that she might somehow overthrow or seek to banish him — like a classic wicked stepmother — recasts the remainder of his life (at least in the moments when he succumbs to this thinking) as a struggle in which he is a powerless child again, vulnerable to someone who is Not My Mother. Sarah B., we learn, was a warm person, extraordinary and loving, tending to Solomon's great-aunt's faded carpets and hangnails when no one else even noticed them. But the fear that she might be wicked, a fear that has wrapped inside of it the recognition that "Daddy may love her as much as or better than he loves me," continues to menace. Solomon knowingly refers to it as his "deep paranoia." For it is deeply regressive, primitive, and difficult to shake.

Auburn University stepfamily expert Francesca Adler-Baeder told me that "children, especially when they're young, need to be connected to their parents." In the studies of stepfamily experts Emily Visher, Ph.D., and John Visher, M.D., she explained, children "were experiencing and describing stepparents as threats to their basic human need. Even as adults, we might revert back to when we most felt that vulnerability and need for emotional attachment. Sometimes that's why the stepparent feels like a threat over the long term."

Even while adult children disavow the significance of getting a stepmother, they may in fact have significant emotional hurdles to cross. This means that ultimately, the anger, jealousy, and feeling of displacement may be reworked into a sense that the stepmother "wrecked things." "Feeling rejected or left out by a father is likely to reexpress itself as a tendency to find fault with *her*," Stephanie Newman told me. Clearly, this relationship that so many adults dismiss with a wave of their hands and an "I was grown when they married" will not be so easy to categorize as "unproblematic" or "a nonissue" for their fathers' wives. Whether we marry their fathers when the kids are in their twenties, thirties, or beyond, or married into a family with stepkids years ago and have watched his kids grow up, we will likely face myriad issues and challenges as we move through later life stages as women with stepchildren. Sally seemed to struggle with them all.

ON BEING A STEPMOTHER THIRTY YEARS IN: SALLY

I first met Sally almost twenty years ago. She is the kind of person about whom people would say, "I wish I had a mom like her," and I was no exception. Sally married Dan twenty-five years ago but has been with him for thirty. Her relationship with his two children, now adults in their forties, has spanned not only three decades but also a number of life transitions (hers, his, and theirs). Sally has two grown children of her own. Now successful adults with young kids, her son and daughter lived with Dan and her in San Francisco during high school and live close to them still. Dan's kids, very close in age to Sally's, also lived in San Francisco, with their mother, during high school. Now that Dan's children are grown, they live on the East and West coasts. Sally recently retired from her job as a family therapist in northern California, where, interestingly enough, she ran a support group for stepfamilies for several years. A realist, she recently described herself as "someone who used to try very, very hard with my stepkids, but I feel a little more detached now." She also said, "Every friend I have who is a stepmom has a pretty low bar for happiness . . . In fact, I wouldn't even call [the objective] happiness. I'd call it peace." Having several grandchildren has forced her to prioritize: "When you have kids, stepkids, stepgrandkids, and grandkids, you can only be in so many places at one time!" Of her relatively new, more detached, and peaceful outlook on stepmothering — achieved after years of struggle — she recently told me, "It's like giving up control. Then you're more like an outsider, looking into another world."

Sally settles into the couch in my office with a cup of tea, having complimented me on what I am wearing. This is typical Sally — even when it's supposed to be all about her, even when she is jet-lagged and doing me an enormous favor just by showing up, she nonetheless cannot help being interested in others and putting them first. Her generosity and maternal warmth do not jibe with the fact that she worries, several times during our initial interview, about being "selfish" and "feeling mean" regarding her stepchildren.

I feel the stepmother herself is forbidden territory! People just don't want to hear about it. A few times, I've been really blunt and honest with people about how hard it's been and how I'm not so enthused about being a stepmother. And they look at me like, What's your problem? When you asked to talk to me, I kept thinking, No way does she want to talk to me. I'm just not making that much of an effort with my stepkids at the moment! I have often felt guilty that

I don't like them so much and that right now I don't have a lot of energy for them. You would think that given my work, I'd have it all figured out. But often therapy for me was a way of learning from other people! . . . I used to try very hard to be a great stepmother, but now . . . What I know is that being a parent is hard on a marriage, but being a stepparent is even harder. On top of that, being a grandmother and a stepgrandmother — it's a lot! I think at least one of my stepkids wishes I would be more "grandmotherly," more involved.

Role Strain

Sally is typical of many women with stepchildren at this life stage, according to Francesca Adler-Baeder. She has come to the point where there are relationships not only with children and stepchildren but also with daughters- and sons-in-law, stepdaughters- and stepsons-in-law, and grandchildren and stepgrandchildren. Factor in the parents of the kids-in-law and stepkids-in-law, and you need a flow chart to keep everything straight. Adler-Baeder explained:

At this point, women sometimes just have to be pragmatic and prioritize. There are so many relationships. Not only are they spread thin, but then there are extra expectations, not only about how a mother and stepmother should be but also [about] what a stepgrandmother and grandmother should do. Sometimes at this point, they choose to go back to putting their energy into their marriage and their biological grandkids. It's a pretty neutral decision, and one that makes sense in my opinion, when you consider that these kids have biological grandparents of their own to love them. But stepkids might make attributions — might interpret her redirection of her energies as a loaded decision, or as unfair in some way.

The act of withdrawing can be read, as Sally rightfully observed, as cold. ("At least one of my stepkids wishes I would be more 'grandmotherly,' more involved.")

Making matters more complicated, role strain is likely dogging the woman's adult stepchildren as well. Indeed, adult stepchildren may find themselves shuttling among four households (his mother, his father and stepmother, her father, her mother and stepfather, for example) in an effort to keep the peace and please everyone who wants a "family holiday." Anyone in such a predicament — traveling long distances with young children rather than staying home and relaxing — is likely to feel frazzled and resentful. This may explain why an adult stepchild's feeling that a stepmother's focus on her own kids and grandkids is wrong or unfair tends to come to a head around holidays, which are often a kind of stepfamily flash point. Sally told me about a recent holiday experience with the whole extended clan:

> *[My husband's son] Isaac decided to come to town for Christmas with his wife and kids and his mother-in-law. So my son and his wife, who were hosting, graciously agreed. I was busy helping with preparation and serving and the little kids. I thought everything was fine. But Isaac called Dan afterward and said they had all felt "dissed" and ignored. Dan was shocked — everything had seemed fine! Isaac said, "You also skipped [my daughter's] gymnastics meet. I expect this treatment from Sally, but not from you." I was really surprised. I feel I've really done a lot, really invested a lot of effort with him over the years . . . so this was so disappointing.*

The annual gymnastics meet, which Sally and Dan usually attend, is held seven hours from where they live, and that year they had told Isaac they simply weren't up for it, especially as they would be making the same trip two months later and could see everyone then. Practicality aside, it seems the decision struck a deeper chord with Isaac, reactivating very old feelings about being excluded, overlooked, and generally "second-best." Later, over spring break, Dan's daughter Nora, her husband, and their four energetic children, all under age ten, joined Sally and Dan at their vacation house in the

Napa Valley. There Nora voiced what her older brother had likely been feeling a month before. As Sally described it:

> *The kids come in like a tornado. They're nice kids, but Nora and her husband don't have a lot of rules, and it was starting to tip into chaos. So when they started wrestling in the living room and almost knocked over the coffee table, I said, "This isn't the playground. No wrestling please." The kids took it fine, but Nora gave me this look. Later, when the two-year-old was walking around with a butter knife, I said, "Can I give her a toy instead?" And again [Nora] was so irritated. She said, "Do you want us to leave? Because we can just leave!" I said, "I don't want you to leave!" And she said, "You know, this brings up issues for me. Like how your kids were always favored when we were younger." I said, "Look, I love you, and I want you to stay. I was just trying to keep the kids a little calmer, that's all. Can we just let it go?" [Sally sighs]. But I really felt like, Oh, for crying out loud! See, my stepkids are a little odd in their own way.*

Stepmother Depletion

It is not hard to see how, thirty years along, a woman's reserves of patience for such ongoing "issues," as Nora called them — not to mention for feeling blamed and set up — might be drained. Another woman might have snapped, "That's silly; get over it!" — exactly the thing a parent often does when "confronted" by an adult child over some perceived slight or parental failing in the distant past. But like most stepmothers, Sally censors herself much more with her stepchildren than she does with her own children. "With my own kids," she told me, "we can argue. We fight. But we get it out there." There is no such release valve in her relationships with Nora and Isaac. Bending over backward not to offend them for so many years only exacerbates feelings of stress and resentment.

The result of all this is what we might call "stepmother depletion," and I noticed it, to some degree, in virtually all the women I interviewed who had been in long-term stepfamily situations.

Stepmother depletion is sometimes made worse by the addition of stepdaughters-in-law and stepsons-in-law, which often adds an additional layer of interpersonal complexity to an already complicated picture. "I just don't have the patience for it all that I used to," said Gigi, who has two adult stepsons, one of whom is married with children of his own. She described weekends at her house in the country as stressful, even after years of "practice," since the introduction of her stepson's wife into the picture.

> She's entitled. She thinks people are supposed to take care of things for her. So she and my stepson will leave their wet towels on the bathroom floor when they're at my place. They don't strip the bed when they leave, or even ask if they should, or any of those courtesies that you and I would if we stayed at someone's place. Basically, they park the kids with us and sit in the hammock while I work. I used to cook elaborate meals for them every time they showed up, and they never once offered to clean up afterward. Now I order in. My feeling is I'm not the upstairs maid. My husband will see the closed bathroom door and say, "Why's it closed? Is someone in there?" and I'll say, "No, they left their towels on the floor, and I didn't feel like looking at it," and walk away. It's a power struggle, and I just won't get into it anymore. Then I'd be the bad guy, and I won't give them that power.

Gigi has a new strategy, one that seems to work on a practical level. But her feelings of being overlooked and taken advantage of persist and are magnified by the fact that this treatment is coming from adults who don't seem to have done the amount of growing up one might reasonably expect.

When prompted by me, Sally tried to remember precisely when she decided that she was "done," as she put it — "You know, done putting in a big effort, done sending presents and not getting a thank-you, done trying to be super-stepmom and super-stepgrandma." Initially, she thought it might have been after Isaac's angry rant about the holiday and gymnastics meet. But when we met later, she shared a realization:

Now I remember what it was, when it was. My daughter and son-in-law struggled with infertility for many years. Dan and I helped them out as much as we could financially and emotionally. They wanted a child very badly, and we wanted it for them, too. Finally, my daughter became pregnant. We had a shower at our place, and neither of my stepkids made it to the shower. My daughter put on a good face, but she was actually very hurt. My stepdaughter-in-law did show up, four hours late, and she said, "I left the present at home on the kitchen table." And I think that's when I pulled back. Dan and I had been schlepping seven hours to baton-twirling competitions and birthday parties for twelve years and . . . [when they didn't reciprocate] I just felt they felt my daughter and her husband didn't matter. And after that shower, my stepkids didn't come to see the baby for a long, long time either. They didn't come to the christening.

I just finally kind of stopped being so interested in them and their lives, I think. At one point, Dan told me something about Isaac, and I didn't respond. I just nodded, and Dan said, "You don't like him, do you?" He didn't say it in an accusing way; he just wanted to know. And I said, "It's not that. It's just that I feel kind of done. I'll go there, I'll do things, but I don't want to put out so much anymore." He understood. But it still feels mean sometimes.

Like a lot of the women I spoke with, Sally feels burned by the failure of her stepkids to "try as hard" as she has, to make a polite and grown-up effort. She also feels justified to hold them personally responsible for it now that they are adults. The dashing of this hope for a more reciprocal relationship could be especially hard to tolerate for Gigi, Sally, and other women with adult stepchildren because they have likely already endured the difficult teenage years and the self-absorbed twenties — and been the target of any residual or unresolved anger their stepchildren feel toward their fathers. The lack of ease in relationships with stepchildren in their thirties and forties — an ease these stepmothers had understandably looked forward to — can come as a particular, and exasperating, disappointment. Perhaps this is why so many women with adult stepchildren told me of feeling "used up."

Complex Stepfamilies, Complex Feelings

As for Sally's stepchildren Nora and Isaac, what they both underscored with their complaints was, among other things, an ongoing difficulty particular to their specific stepfamily constellation. Sally and Dan's stepfamily is "complex" — meaning that she and he both brought children to the union. In these types of stepfamilies, researchers and stepfamily members themselves note, suspicions and accusations of favoritism are common. University of Virginia psychologist E. Mavis Hetherington has observed that "complex stepfamilies have more troubled family relationships, and more problem behavior in children." Why might this be? Hetherington explains that, just like machines, "stepfamilies are subject to the complexity principle: the more working parts the greater the risk of a breakdown." Trouble may appear in the form of alliances, scapegoating, and divisive loyalty issues, Hetherington warns.

Gwen, who is seventy-five years old and the mother of three, had a philosophical take on the matter. She told me of her own experience as a stepdaughter: "I came to love my stepmom, and I know she really cared about me. She was a wonderful woman, and because of her, I got to be part of a household full of warmth and laughter. But I don't know that she loved me like she loved her own girls. How could she?" Gwen does not feel angry or resentful, she told me, but she described her experience as a stepchild among biological children as "a certain kind of longing. I just felt it."

Dan's children never lived with Sally and Dan, unlike her own kids, who did for several years. Moreover, Sally described Dan's relationship with her kids as "very unproblematic compared to his relationship with his biological kids. There was none of the stress and strain. He didn't have a lot of expectations of my kids or put a lot of pressure on them, and they just got along. They still do. They're very close." This is typical of many longer-term stepfather-stepchild relationships, which researchers have discovered tend to be characterized by exponentially lower levels of conflict than stepmother-stepchild relationships, as well as much higher levels of reported "closeness." Most of the adult stepchildren I interviewed, in fact, described loving, positive relationships with their stepfathers. This extra source of support can be wonderful for children of any age. But it can be an additional emotional challenge for the father's own children — a challenge they may not necessarily work out over time.

Clearly, seeing not only Sally but also their father interacting comfortably with Sally's adult kids and grandkids activated a "longing" in Nora and Isaac not unlike the one Gwen described. And that longing continues to be reexpressed as resentment and anger toward Sally, the person they hold responsible for "depriving" them of what her own kids have. Rather than receding, these resentments can harden and flare over the years, seeming increasingly unjust once stepchildren have children of their own, whom they also perceive as less favored or getting less because of their stepmother and her children and grandchildren being in the picture as well. For Nora and Isaac, having a mother they lived with and a father who remained committed to a relationship with them throughout their childhood, teens, and twenties may not have been enough. The existence of a stepmother with children of her own, with whom their father chose to live and came to build a close, very loving bond, is something that Nora and Isaac have yet to assimilate.

Haunted Houses: The Half-Life of a Difficult Adolescence

Coming from a complex stepfamily inevitably complicates matters. But a stepmother's resentment about unreciprocal behavior can have roots not so much in the structure of the family as in the past. A feeling that a grown stepchild takes but doesn't give often harks back to one of the most difficult times in a stepchild's development, a time when the child was most selfish and ungiving: adolescence. One stepmother described her adolescent stepchildren, with accurate and bleak humor, as "black holes of taking and hating." When Sally talked about her stepkids not reciprocating and being "takers, not givers," for example, she seemed especially to be referring to Isaac, who was an exceptionally difficult adolescent. He dealt drugs, dropped out of school, and was involved in a drunk-driving incident in which a peer of his died. Isaac also consistently stole from Sally — money from her wallet, odds and ends from the household, and even her jewelry. Another woman I interviewed had a teenage stepdaughter whose favorite greeting was "Fuck you. I don't have to listen to anything you say. Get out of my way."

It is not hard to see why sometimes, as stepfamily researchers Marilyn Coleman and Larry Ganong observe, a stepmother may not be able to simply forgive and forget a stepchild's adolescence, a period when she was likely to have been singled out for very poor treatment indeed. Stepmothers are human, and we have our limits and our feelings. As Coleman and Ganong write, "When stepchildren decide to ignore, disregard, or actively dislike the stepparent, there is little [she] can do. Sometimes, over time, stepchildren change their minds about a stepparent [only to find it] is too little, too late. Stepparents, to protect their own ego and dignity, may have withdrawn. Children may have forgotten how ugly they were to their stepparents [or] they may have discounted the impact their behavior had."

Similarly, in a study of twenty-five women's long-term relationships with adult stepchildren, researchers and experts on aging Barbara Vinick, Ph.D., and Susan Lanspery, Ph.D., found that 44 percent of the women whose husbands had divorced their previous wives rated their relationships with their stepchildren as "not close." Women who had married widowers, however, *all* rated their relationships with their stepkids as "close" or "very close." Our first instinct here might be to attribute this discrepancy solely to the presence of the mother. We know that when she's in the picture, there is likely more conflict all around, and hence relations between stepchildren and stepmothers are more strained and less close (see chapter 6). However, Vinick and Lanspery note that the most significant factor in better versus worse outcomes may well be that "the stepmothers of the children of divorce had to contend far more often with the turbulence of the teenage years. All of the widowers' children were in their twenties and thirties at the time of their fathers' remarriage, more often settled in their own lives."

Even the most committed wife and stepmother may be unable to get past a difficult adolescence, furthering the sense, even when it is in the distant past, that she is "done." The adult stepchild in this case may be left wondering why Dad's wife won't give him or her a chance. But as Sally told me, "I'm at peace with being more detached from my stepkids now. Sometimes I feel guilty about not having them around more, not making more of an effort. But on the other hand, I'm learning that the less I put in and expect, the less I resent. I think it's better for everyone that I've just stepped back like I have."

RETHINKING "HAPPILY EVER AFTER": OUTCOMES WITH ADULT STEPCHILDREN

There are a number of "happy outcomes" for women with adult stepchildren if we make our definition of happiness more encompassing and realistic. For Sally, it means taking a more distant approach and finally finding peace in stepping away, focusing on her marriage and her own kids and grandkids with less guilt.

For Nan and Belinda, two other women with adult stepchildren I interviewed, it means throwing themselves wholeheartedly into the family systems of their stepchildren, their stepchildren's spouses, and their stepgrandchildren. This may be easier for women who have no children of their own — Nan and Belinda don't — and who grew up as only children with a yen to be part of something bigger, noisier, and with lots of moving parts — as Nan and Belinda both did. Belinda, who described her own upbringing as "lonely — I was an only child and both my parents were only children, too" — said she was delighted at being included in planning her stepdaughter's wedding. "I had been prepared to take a much smaller role and was so happy to be the one shopping for her dress with her," she told me. She also described gratifying trips to Europe with her husband and her grown stepdaughters and their husbands. This was the reward, she said, for enduring years of teen-girl drama during which, she joked, "I sometimes wanted to smack them!" Belinda told me that she is eager for her stepdaughters to have children "so I can do the grandma thing. I'm ready!"

Nan, a sixty-three-year-old former paralegal, laughed when she said, "I grew up in such a quiet, strict house, and I married into a pretty unruly clan" of five stepchildren and, now, fifteen stepgrand-children. Over our lunch meeting, she asked me if I wanted to see her family, then showed me a photo of all her husband's kids and grand-kids, and even his ex-wife. "Going with the flow," as Nan described her step-mothering philosophy twenty-five years into it, involves big holidays with everyone, again including her husband's ex, at the same table. She explained that this tradition began after her own parents refused to speak to her once she married a divorced man with children, saying it was "wrong" and against their religious values. "It never occurred to me," she said, "that my husband wouldn't spend the holidays with his ex-wife and kids." (Another woman might, in fact, be astonished by the idea that he *would,* and she would be just as "right" as Nan is.) In dealing with so many relationships that others might find challenging, it doesn't hurt that Nan considers herself, her husband, and her husband's ex all to be "products of that whole seventies hippie thing, anti-authority, into doing things in new ways and charting new territory. Our lives were sort of an experiment." It wasn't always easy, of course. Nan described early years in which her husband's ex was very hurt that he had re-partnered. She also described her younger self as "clueless when it came to having step-kids." Although Nan used the word "overwhelmed" a lot to describe her experience as a stepmother — "There are so many of them!" she said with a laugh, explaining that "I was just twenty-eight, and some of his kids were just eight years younger than me, plus I didn't know a single other stepmother" — she does not seem to regret that she and her husband did not have a child of their own.

> *This might sound awful, but he had his hands full with the five he had, and I didn't always agree with the way he raised them, and*

271

we had words about it more than once. I would have wanted more structure for his kids, but my husband doesn't really have the discipline gene. It's not him! I just thought that since we could barely handle his five, we shouldn't have one ourselves. And I'm not going to sit around and regret it or mull it over. You just have to make a decision and move on. I have fifteen — fifteen! — beautiful grandchildren, and I'm happy with things the way they are.

When I asked Nan to summarize her experience as a stepmother, there was a very long pause. Then she said of her stepchildren, "I'm glad they were all here." Nan's easygoing personality, her tendency not to ruminate or resent, her bohemian spirit, and her particular family history have all made her choice to "embrace the noise and chaos," as she put it, easier and more gratifying for her than it might be for someone else. Indeed, a woman's personality and her own family history may play a large role in determining just how willing and able she is to keep making an effort as the stepkids grow up, marry, and have kids of their own.

And then there is the added factor of what we might simply call chemistry. A few women just get along with their stepkids — or perhaps better with one of them than with the other(s). Other women find themselves in more fraught relationships. Several of the women I interviewed told me that it was less a matter of divorce and remarriage and more a matter of difference. "If we met at a party, if we were total strangers, we wouldn't have much to talk about" and "We really aren't each other's cup of tea," more than one woman said of an adult stepchild. A good part of step-relations may be simply the luck of the draw — how our personalities and outlooks fit together with those of our husbands' kids.

This comes as no surprise to Dan Wharton of the Chicago Zoological Society, who has been a keen observer of some of our closest relatives — gorillas — for many years. Because gorilla society is made up of groups of a single male and a number of unrelated females with whom he sires offspring, it is not difficult to see a stepmother analogy in the offing — and perhaps a lesson for us.

"Among gorillas, the relationship between females and the offspring of their husband with another female is really a matter of individual chemistry," Wharton told me. "The individual animals will define the relationship based on their own temperaments. Some will have closer bonds, while others will be more conflictual." The lesson: "Better to let the relationship evolve based on chemistry than step into mothering territory," Wharton said, and to recognize, as dispassionately as possible, that "there may not be potential for much beyond civility or, on the other hand, to become great friends."

There is no one "right" outcome for long-term stepfamilies or for the families of men who remarry later in life when their kids are adults. Not everyone wants to embrace, or is capable of embracing, the challenge of this stage, or this type, of stepfamily life in the same way Nan and Belinda have. Some of us will jump into it or continue to put lots of energy into relationships with adult stepchildren. Others, like Sally and Gigi, will reassess and retreat.

Women's pairings with men with children are both inevitable and improbable. Statistically, such partnerships are likely to happen, but they are also likely to be tremendously difficult and may well fail. The women who have negotiated the chasm between these two poles of stepmother experience know that the mantra "A stepmother can never stop trying" is unrealistic, more likely to breed resentment and skewed expectations than to create the "happiness" we tend to want to stick, like a punctuation mark, at the end of the story. But long-term stepmothers — some of whom refer to themselves, with a laugh, as "lifers" — also know this profound and surprising and simple truth about being married to a man with children: that it can be done.

Lessons from the Wicked One

Lifers seem to sense — seem to have learned, from years of hard-won experience — that the wicked stepmother has much to teach us about who we are and, counterintuitively perhaps, that she has a lesson or two to impart about surviving stepmotherhood with our self-respect intact. The happiest, most successful women with stepchildren, it seems, have first of all accepted the ugly truth that we will, some days, be ugly — jealous, resentful, and angry. Slowly, the women who succeed at marriage to a man with children learn that these charged feelings are not only terribly taboo; they are also grounded in reality. Jealousy, as stepfamily expert Elizabeth Church writes, comes from feeling powerless, and stepmothers are certainly often that. Resentment indicates that we are feeling unappreciated and that our overtures of kindness are going unreciprocated — another common and maddening reality of stepmother-stepchild relations. Anger may be a sign that our unrealistic expectations of stepfamily harmony have been dashed. Or it may be a healthy response to feeling spurned and unsupported for years on end, and it may eventually motivate us — and our husbands — to take constructive action.

Like the classic wicked stepmother, the happiest lifers no longer seem hobbled by the need to be liked by their stepkids. If things work out, that's fine. And if they don't, well, the lifers shrug as if to say, *It's okay to stop trying if you know you gave it your best. Some battles just can't be won and aren't worth my energy.* Nor do successful lifers seem gagged by the fear that stepkids, husbands, friends, or the world at large will think of them as stepmonsters if they speak up about wanting respect and civil treatment, or to be treated as a person rather than an obstacle in front of Dad or a maid. Such fears and the need for approval are likely the biggest obstacles a stepmother must overcome in her quest to put her own happiness on a par with that of the rest of the family. It may be difficult or frightening at first to assert ourselves, feeling like outsiders in the family hierarchy as we likely do, but the alternative is worse. Again and again, women with stepkids showed me that it is a quick slide from "I bite my tongue when his kids say something rude or mean to me because I don't want to get into an argument with them" to "I'm afraid to lay down the law in my own home." Next stop is "I nag my husband to get his kids to act better and be nicer to me, and then he and I have a huge fight." Then on to "I hate being a stepmother" and, finally, "I just can't do this anymore."

It might just be that some of the strategies of the classic wicked stepmother — toned down but essentially gleaned straight from her ostensibly evil behavior — can pull us back from the brink and even make marriage to a man with children pleasurable. Every day, for example, the wicked stepmother looks at her reflection and asks, "Mirror, mirror on the wall, who's the fairest of them all?" The real life lesson here is not to be a homicidal, envious narcissist, of course, but to put yourself first. Stepmothers, as we have seen from the studies of their rates of burnout and depression, constantly lose sight of their own needs — arguably even of themselves — as they deal with, blame themselves for, and attempt to fix stepfamily dynamics. Giving yourself a little love will counterbalance the powerful but unreasonable cultural imperative that you must put his kids first. And a little vanity is the best antidote to the typical step-dilemma of becoming so consumed with the unhappiness that sometimes surrounds you that you forget you are an attractive woman, an appealing wife, and a compelling, sexy person — that is, that you have an identity apart from being a stepmom. As a stepmother of two teens told me, "Love thyself, because your stepkids won't."

The wicked stepmother does more than gaze at herself in the mirror, of course. She schemes, pulls strings, and consolidates her power. Real stepmothers have no need for any of that. Mostly. But it does pay for a woman with stepchildren to be canny, to observe, and to be strategic in her dealings with her husband and his kids. For example, there are worse things than helping your husband see that you are on the receiving end of quite a lot of bad treatment from his kids (whom he may naturally but unrealistically idealize until you help him see the truth about their behavior) and that it hurts you. It helps to remember that men generally have an easier time dealing with a wife who is sad or pained than one who is aggrieved and angry. Learning to show what is underneath your alienating fury — vulnerability and sadness — will not hurt your efforts. And as for power, don't forget that you are, in fact, the queen of your household. Pandering and kowtowing to stepchildren of any age who do not respect you as one of the two people who rule your roost will not get them to like you, and it will not make them easier for you to like either. Lifers know that everyone wins when you can find it within yourself to say "Please don't be rude to me in my home."

The classic wicked stepmother is, of course, cold and unfeeling. She is emotionally stingy. And she may just have a point — sort of. After all, for a lot of good reasons, your stepkids are extremely unlikely to appreciate, let alone thank you for, your efforts with them. In all likelihood, neither will they gratify your desire to be loved. Your response should be never to give too much. Don't give stepkids the opportunity to break anything of value to you, including your heart. Lowering your expectations of them and maintaining your focus on your own life — a toned-down version of being cold — will create a pressure-free environment in which a friendship might eventually take hold and even flourish.

Perhaps most notoriously, the wicked stepmother loves her own children best and doesn't hesitate to put them first. The lesson here is not to be spiteful or petty, of course, or to overtly play favorites. But lifers and experts concur: don't try to pretend that you love his kids and your kids the same, and don't buy into the destructive belief that you should. His kids aren't yours, you likely didn't know them when they were beguiling babies or toddlers, and they are probably not making an effort to be lovable now. No guilt and no self-flagellating, then, when those without a clue observe, "You probably love them like they're your own," and it makes you want to roll your eyes. The expectations of the uninformed — especially regarding "maternal" behavior — are a particular burden for stepmothers. But others' hopes needn't become your obligation. Knowing the difference between what you can realistically achieve and what others think you *ought* to be able to do is the equivalent of a lifeline for women with stepkids. "I'm not a miracle worker," a stepmother named Laynie told me. "I'm a mom who's got a daughter and a job and a stepson who's very rejecting, and getting through the day without yelling at him is a tall order some days." The idea of the "good enough stepmother" — rather than the perfect stepmother, who is, after all, just a reaction against the classic wicked stepmonster, her other face — is one that women with stepchildren who feel satisfied with their lives and their marriages seem to embrace.

In this book, I have aimed to illuminate the universal qualities — and the variety — of the stepmother experience. By airing the most taboo feelings that women with stepchildren have — rage, jealousy, resentment — as well as less dramatic ones — exhaustion, disappointment, depression — and by examining stepmothering through the lens of disciplines such as anthropology, literary criticism, and evolutionary biology, I hoped to bring the depth and breadth of stepmother reality to life. Our culture's passionate and peculiar relationship to stepmothers — we expect them to be despicable, and yet we want them to love children who are not their own as if they were; we see them at once as everyday, regular women and as frightful, larger-than-life signifiers of evil (or just pathology); we portray them as utterly selfish and narcissistic even as we expect them to be selfless "stepmartyrs" — has distorted our sense not only of who women with stepchildren really are but also of what they should be able to accomplish and how they ought to feel.

Pulled from pole to pole in this way, portrayed through contradictions that cannot hold, it is hard for the woman with stepchildren to know herself. Obliged to prove she is not, in fact, wicked, she may have difficulty asserting her basic right to be and feel. But women with stepchildren do have definite emotional needs, a particular historical legacy, and very specific cultural baggage to bear. Putting actual stepmothers on center stage for once, exploring their reality in depth, and urging them to focus on themselves and their own lives seems a modest undertaking. In the end, it was ultimately a very personal one for me: I researched and wrote the book that I wished I could find, the book that I desperately needed myself. If it makes another woman with stepchildren feel better understood, less alone, and more normal; if it deepens one stepchild's sense of who Dad's wife really is; if it helps one man finally see what his partner is up against and how much she has accomplished, *Stepmonster* will have done a great deal.

ACKNOWLEDGMENTS

Women with stepchildren are used to being judged. And so I feel not only gratitude but also admiration for the interview subjects who told me their stories, disclosing details and sharing confidences that immeasurably enhanced my understanding of the topic. I thank these women whom I cannot mention by name, but whose insights and experiences shaped this book in the realest sense.

In the course of my research, I learned firsthand that concepts such as family and kinship are at once genetic facts and something more metaphorical and malleable. I thank my husband's daughters, Alexandra and Katharine, for giving me something so interesting to think about over the past decades and for being good sports about all the changes their father's remarriage has brought to their lives. A number of friends have been as supportive a family as one could ask for over the last few years of thinking and writing. Many thanks to Lucy Barnes, Sally Foster, Mary Ghiorsi, Elizabeth Kandall-Slone, Wellington Love, Rebecca Mannis, Stephanie Newman, Jeff Nunokawa, and Ellie Steinman for listening, asking questions, and taking an interest.

This book and my youngest son shared a due date. This could have been an unhappy coincidence indeed. But I gave birth to an accommodating baby, who allowed me to dote on my book as well as on him. His older brother spent more than one evening drawing and playing on my office sofa as I worked. Thank you, Lyle and Eliot. A number of the book's "stepmothers" were, like stepmothers everywhere, patient and understanding in the face of bad behavior and less-than-ideal circumstances when the book was delayed. For their forbearance — and their insight and uncanny sense of how best to tell a story — I thank Jane Rosenman and Deanne Urmy. I also thank Jackie Cantor for encouraging me, early on, to pursue the idea of telling the truth about stepmothering in a different way, and Miriam Altshuler for her open mind and advocacy.

Several women showed extraordinary dedication to my children over the past few years, and without their help I could never have dreamed of sitting down to work. Thank you to Sarah Swatez, Gina Edward, Amelia Swan, Clementine Swan, Ellen Murphy, and Karen Hemmings for making it possible for me to be a mother and a writer.

A number of experts were remarkably generous with their ideas and time. In particular, Steven Josephson patiently answered my questions about anthropology and evolutionary biology, while Dan Wharton kindly shared his time, expertise, and ideas about primate families. Many thanks to Kermyt Anderson, Martin Daly, and Richard Prum for helping me bring their perspectives to bear on stepparenting. Thanks also Francesca Adler-Baeder, Stephanie Newman, and Patricia Papernow, as well as the many other psychologists and researchers who shared their time and insights. Alexia Paul helped shape the manuscript, and Brent Bagwell tended to details I could not. Rachel Moser and Julie Segal not only unearthed facts and analyzed trends for a previous project but also enriched this one.

My greatest debt is to my husband, Joel. From the outset, he supported me in every way, including cooking, child care, cleaning, and cheerleading. He helped me refine concepts and hone ideas. He was put under the microscope and put to the test, and this book is for him.

NOTES

INTRODUCTION

1   *Experts estimate:* Larry L. Bumpass, R. Kelly Raley, and James A. Sweet, "The Changing Character of Stepfamilies: Implications of Cohabitation and Non-marital Childbearing," *Demography* 32 (1995): 425–36; E. Mavis Hetherington, personal conversation, quoted by Dr. Ron L. Deal, "The Stepcouple Divorce Rate May Be Higher Than We Thought," Successful Stepfamilies, http://www .successfulstepfamilies.com/view/176.

In fact, divorce rates: Alan Booth and John N. Edwards, "Starting Over: Why Remarriages Are More Unstable," *Journal of Family Issues* 13, no. 2 (1992): 179–94. See also Melvyn A. Berke and Joanne B. Grant, *Games Divorced People Play* (Englewood Cliffs, NJ: Prentice Hall, 1981); E. Mavis Hetherington and John Kelly, *For Better or for Worse: Divorce Reconsidered* (New York: Norton, 2002), p. 178.

experts recommend delaying marriage: Hetherington and Kelly, *For Better or for Worse,* pp. 197–99, 201. See also University of Florida, Institute of Food and Agricultural Sciences, "Stepping Stones for Stepfamilies — Lesson 3: Building Step Relationships," http://edis.ifas.ufl.edu/FY034; Lawrence Ganong and Marilyn Coleman, "Adolescent Stepchild and Stepparent Relationships," in *Stepparenting: Issues in Theory, Research, and Practice,* ed. Kay Pasley and Marilyn Ihinger-Tallman, pp. 87–105 (Westport, CT: Praeger, 1995); Patricia Lutz, "The Stepfamily: An Adolescent Perspective," *Family Relations* 32 (1980): 367–75; C. S.

Chillman, "Remarriage and Stepfamilies: Research Results and Implications," in *Contemporary Families and Alternative Lifestyles: Handbook on Research and Theory*, ed. Eleanor D. Macklin and Roger H. Rubin, pp. 147–63 (Beverly Hills, CA: Sage, 1983); E. Brand and W. Glenn Clingempeel, "Interdependence of Marital and Stepparent-Stepchild Relationships and Children's Psychological Adjustment," *Family Relations* 36 (1987): 140–45. *Some research suggests that women:* P. K. Prilick, *The Art of Stepmothering*, cited in Ann L. Orchard and Kenneth B. Solberg, "Expectations of the Stepmother's Role," *Journal of Divorce and Remarriage* 31, nos. 1/2 (1991): 107–23; Anne C. Bernstein, *Yours, Mine, and Ours: How Families Change When Remarried Parents Have a Child Together* (New York: Norton, 1991), p. 49; Jamie Kelem Keshet, "Gender and Biological Models of Role Division in Stepmother Families," *Journal of Feminist Family Therapy* 1 (1989): 29–50; Jamie Kelem Keshet, *Love and Power in the Stepfamily* (New York: McGraw-Hill, 1987), pp. 7–10, 73–82; Marilyn Coleman and Lawrence Ganong, "Stepfamilies from the Stepfamily's Perspective," *Marriage and Family Review* 26, nos. 1/2 (1997): 107–21.

3   *E. Mavis Hetherington, Ph.D.:* Hetherington and Kelly, *For Better or for Worse*, pp. 192–93.

4   *It is no shock:* Constance R. Ahrons and L. Wallisch, "Parenting in the Binuclear Family: Relationships Between Biological and Stepparents," in *Remarriage and Stepparenting: Current Research and Theory*, ed. Kay Pasley and Marilyn Ihinger-Tallman, pp. 225–56 (New York: Guilford, 1987); F. Furstenberg and C. Nord, "Parenting Apart: Patterns of Childrearing After Marital Disruption," *Journal of Marriage and the Family* 47 (1985): 893–905; I. Levine, "The Stepparent Role from a Gender Perspective," *Marriage and Family Review* 26 (1997): 177–90; W. MacDonald and A. DeMaris, "Parenting Stepchildren and Biological Children," *Journal of Family Issues* 23 (1996): 5–25; Laurence E. Sauer and Mark A. Fine, "Parent-Child Relationships in Stepparent Families," *Journal of Family Psychology* 1 (1988): 434–51; Lynn White, D.

Brinkerhoff, and A. Booth, "The Effect of Marital Disruption on Child's Attachment to Parents," *Journal of Family Issues* 6 (1985): 5–22.

5   *Remarriage experts Kay Pasley:* Kay Pasley and Marilyn Ihinger-Tallman, eds., *Remarriage and Stepparenting: Current Research and Theory* (New York: Guilford, 1987), pp. 94–95; Francesca Adler-Baeder and Brian Higginbotham, "Implications of Remarriage and Stepfamily Formation for Marriage Education," *Family Relations* 53 (2004): 448–58.

   Stepfamily researchers such as: James H. Bray and John Kelly, *Stepfamilies: Love, Marriage, and Parenting in the First Decade* (New York: Random House/Broadway Books, 1998), p. 28.

8   *Stepfamily developmental expert:* Patricia Papernow, "The Stepfamily Cycle: An Experiential Model of Stepfamily Development," *Family Relations* 33 (1984): 355–63.

1. A WALL OF ONE'S OWN: BECOMING A STEPMOTHER

19   *"setting up housekeeping":* Mary Peterson, "With Evelyn," in *Mercy Flights* (Columbia: University of Missouri Press, 1985), p. 34.

20   *"These children have become":* Patricia Papernow, interview, March 2008.

24   *Prominent stepfamily researchers:* Marilyn Coleman and Lawrence Ganong, "Stepfamilies from the Stepfamily's Perspective," *Marriage and Family Review* 26, nos. 1/2 (1997): 107–21.

25   *British psychotherapist Sarah Corrie:* Sarah Corrie, "Working Therapeutically with Adult Stepchildren: Identifying the Needs of a Neglected Client Group," *Journal of Divorce and Remarriage* 37, nos. 1/2 (2002): 135–50.

26   *Research confirms that:* Linda Nielsen, "Stepmothers: Why So Much Stress? A Review of the Research," *Journal of Divorce and Remarriage* 30, nos. 1/2 (1999): 115–48.

27   *"affinity-seeking behaviors":* Lawrence Ganong, Marilyn Coleman, M. Fine, and P. Martin, "Stepparents' Affinity-Seeking and

Affinity-Maintaining Strategies with Stepchildren," *Journal of Family Issues* 20 (1999): 299–327.

28   *The husband who is older:* Jamie Kelem Keshet, *Love and Power in the Stepfamily* (New York: McGraw-Hill, 1987), p. 42.

29   *as research indicates:* See Elizabeth A. Church, *Understanding Stepmothers: Women Share Their Struggles, Successes, and Insights* (Toronto: HarperCollins, 2004), p. ix; Elizabeth A. Church, "Who Are the People in Your Family? Stepmothers' Diverse Notions of Kinship," *Journal of Divorce and Remarriage* 31, nos. 1/2 (1999): 83–105; Susan D. Stewart, *Brave New Stepfamilies: Diverse Paths Toward Stepfamily Living* (London: Sage, 2007), pp. 11, 118–20.

30   *Although the divorce rate:* J. Lawton, Stepfamily Project, University of Queensland, cited in Virginia Rutter, "Lessons from Stepfamilies," *Psychology Today,* May 1, 1994, p. 5.

32   *When psychologists Ann Orchard:* Ann L. Orchard and Kenneth B. Solberg, "Expectations of the Stepmother's Role," *Journal of Divorce and Remarriage* 31, nos. 1/2 (1991): 116.
      Another study, of thirty-two: Pauline I. Erera-Weatherley, "On Becoming a Stepparent: Factors Associated with the Adoption of Alternative Stepparenting Styles," *Journal of Divorce and Remarriage* 25, nos. 3/4 (1996): 155–74.

33   *"I feel like I'm alone":* Ibid., p. 161.
      end up calling the shots: James H. Bray and John Kelly, *Stepfamilies: Love, Marriage, and Parenting in the First Decade* (New York: Random House/Broadway Books, 1998), pp. 28, 42.
      "We developed friendly contact": Ibid.
      Although "friend" seems to be: Ibid., p. 163; Church, "Who Are the People in Your Family?"

2. "SHE'S SUCH A WITCH!": FAIRY TALE HISTORY AND THE STEPMOTHERING SCRIPT

37   *Researchers have amply documented:* Laura V. Salwen, "The Myth of the Wicked Stepmother," *Women and Therapy* 10 (1990): 117–25; Marilyn Coleman and Lawrence Ganong, "Stepparent: A Pejorative Term?" *Psychological Reports* 52 (1997): 919–22; Stephen

Claxton-Oldfield, "Deconstructing the Myth of the Wicked Stepparent," *Marriage and Family Review* 30 (2000): 51–58; Emily B. Visher, *Stepfamilies: Myths and Realities* (Secaucus, NJ: Citadel, 1979); Esther Wald, *The Remarried Family: Challenge and Promise* (New York: Family Services Association of America, 1981); Janet Strayer, "Trapped in the Mirror: Psychosocial Reflections on Mid-Life and the Queen in *Snow White*," *Human Development* 39 (1996): 155–72; Marianne Dainton, "Myths and Misconceptions of the Stepmother Identity," *Family Relations* 42 (1992): 93–98.

38   *"We generally tend"*: Linda Nielsen, "Stepmothers: Why So Much Stress? A Review of the Research," *Journal of Divorce and Remarriage* 30, nos. ½ (1999): 121.

       Psychologist Anne C. Jones: Anne C. Jones, "Transforming the Story: Narrative Applications to a Stepmother Support Group," *Families in Society* 85 (January 2004): 129. See also Roni Berger, *Stepfamilies: A Multidimensional Perspective* (New York: Haworth, 1998).

39   *In the late 1800s:* Andrew J. Cherlin, *Public and Private Families* (Boston: McGraw-Hill, 1999); Elizabeth A. Church, *Understanding Stepmothers: Women Share Their Struggles, Successes, and Insights* (Toronto: HarperCollins, 2004), p. 4; Wald, *The Remarried Family.*

       In his recent memoir: Sean Wilsey, *Oh the Glory of It All* (New York: Penguin, 2005).

40   *Criminologist and historian:* Joseph Laythe, "The Wicked Stepmother? The Edna Mumbulo Case of 1930," *Journal of Criminal Justice and Popular Culture* 9 (2002): 33–54.

44   *And how could people:* Anna Haebich, "Murdering Stepmothers: The Trial and Execution of Martha Rendell," *Journal of Australian Studies* (December 1, 1998): 1–16. See also Michel Foucault, "Truth and Power," in *Power/Knowledge: Selected Interviews and Other Writings, 1972–1977*, ed. C. Gordon (New York: Pantheon, 1980).

45   *"organized the known facts":* Laythe, "The Wicked Stepmother?" p. 33.

       centuries old fairy tales: Maria M. Tatar, ed., *The Annotated Brothers Grimm* (New York: Norton, 2004).

47 *the evil schemer:* Sandra Gilbert and Susan Gubar, *The Madwoman in the Attic: The Woman Writer and the Nineteenth-Century Literary Imagination* (New Haven, CT: Yale University Press, 2000).

49 *Based on a late-eighteenth-century:* Tatar, *The Annotated Brothers Grimm,* pp. 208–23.

51 *In not crying:* Haebich, "Murdering Stepmothers," p. 7.

52 *"a figure of gripping":* Tatar, *The Annotated Brothers Grimm,* p. 243. *Classicist Patricia Watson:* Patricia Watson, *Ancient Stepmothers: Myth, Misogyny, and Reality* (Leiden: Brill Academic Publishers, 1997), pp. 2–5.

53 *"And do not remarry":* Euripides, *Alcestis* 305–10, quoted in Watson, *Ancient Stepmothers,* p. 7.
    "A boy was [honoring]": Garland of Philip, quoted in Watson, *Ancient Stepmothers,* p. 13.
    "an abominable woman": Seneca, quoted in Watson, *Ancient Stepmothers,* p. 99.

54 *Sally Bjornsen's* The Single: Sally Bjornsen, *The Single Girl's Guide to Marrying a Man, His Kids, and His Ex-Wife: Becoming a Stepmother with Humor and Grace* (New York: New American Library, 2005).
    stepfamily expert Elizabeth Church: Church, *Understanding Stepmothers,* pp. 6–7.

55 *"Instead of Cinderella":* Ibid., p. 7.

56 *Between the myth:* Cindi Penor-Ceglian and Scott Gardner, "Attachment Style and the Wicked Stepmother Spiral," *Journal of Divorce and Remarriage* 34 (2000): 114. See also Dainton, "Myths and Misconceptions," pp. 93–98; Elizabeth Einstein and Linda Albert, "The Instant Love Expectation: Downhill Slide to Trouble," in *Strengthening Your Stepfamily* (Circle Pines, MN: American Guidance Association Press, 1986).

3. "You're Not My Mother!": And Five Other Universal Step-Dilemmas

59 *A number of studies:* See, for example, C. J. Pill, "Stepfamilies: Redefining the Family," *Family Relations* 39 (1990): 186–93;

James H. Bray and John Kelly, *Stepfamilies: Love, Marriage, and Parenting in the First Decade* (New York: Random House/ Broadway Books, 1998).

60 *The ties do not bind:* Lawrence Ganong and Marilyn Coleman, "Adolescent Stepchild and Stepparent Relationships," in *Stepparenting: Issues in Theory, Research, and Practice,* ed. Kay Pasley and Marilyn Ihinger-Tallman, pp. 87–105 (Westport, CT: Greenwood, 1995); Lawrence Ganong and Marilyn Coleman, "Stepchildren's Perceptions of Their Parents," *Journal of Genetic Psychology* 148 (1986): 5–17; E. Mavis Hetherington and W. Glenn Clingempeel, "Coping with Marital Transitions: A Family Systems Perspective," *Monographs of the Society for Research in Childhood Development* 57 (1992); Charles Hobart, "Experiences of Remarried Families," *Journal of Divorce* 13 (1989): 121–44.

"stepfamily architecture": Patricia Papernow, "Meeting the Challenge of Stepfamily Architecture" (handout).

Yet only 20 percent: E. Mavis Hetherington and John Kelly, *For Better or for Worse: Divorce Reconsidered* (New York: Norton, 2002), p. 232.

in her comprehensive study: Constance R. Ahrons, *We're Still Family: What Grown Children Have to Say About Their Parents' Divorce* (New York: Harper-Collins, 2004), p. 134.

66 *stepfamily therapist Jamie Kelem Keshet:* Jamie Kelem Keshet, "Gender and Biological Models of Role Division in Stepmother Families," *Journal of Feminist Family Therapy* 1 (1989): 29–50.

69 *it is difficult to imagine:* Hetherington and Kelly, *For Better or for Worse,* p. 191; Melvyn A. Berke and Joanne B. Grant, *Games Divorced People Play* (Englewood Cliffs, NJ: Prentice Hall, 1981); Ganong and Coleman, "Adolescent Stepchild and Stepparent Relationships"; Ganong and Coleman, "Stepchildren's Perceptions"; Patricia Lutz, "The Stepfamily: An Adolescent Perspective," *Family Relations* 32 (1980): 367–75; C. S. Chillman, "Remarriage and Stepfamilies: Research Results and Implications," in *Contemporary Families and Alternative Lifestyles:*

Handbook on Research and Theory, ed. Eleanor D. Macklin and Roger H. Rubin, pp. 147–63 (Beverly Hills, CA: Sage, 1983); E. Brand and W. Glenn Clingempeel, "Interdependence of Marital and Stepparent-Stepchild Relationships and Children's Psychological Adjustment," *Family Relations* 36 (1987): 140–45. *Researchers suggest:* Linda Nielsen, "Stepmothers: Why So Much Stress? A Review of the Research," *Journal of Divorce and Remarriage* 30, nos. 1/2 (1999):

115–48; Aaron Ebata, Anne C. Petersen, and J. Conger, "The Development of Psychopathology in Adolescence," in *Risk and Protective Factors in the Development of Psychopathology,* ed. J. Rolf, pp. 308–34 (New York: Cambridge University Press, 1990); Lee Robins and Michael Rutter, *Straight and Devious Pathways from Childhood to Adulthood* (New York: Cambridge University Press, 1990).

"more likely to say": Nielsen, "Stepmothers: Why So Much Stress?" p. 138.

Such self-esteem issues: Nan Bauer Maglin and Nancy Schniedewind, eds., *Women in Stepfamilies: Voices of Anger and Love* (Philadelphia: Temple University Press, 1989); Elizabeth Verner, "Marital Satisfaction in Remarriage," *Journal of Marriage and the Family* 51 (1989): 713–25.

sociologists have pointed out: Stephen Mintz, *Huck's Raft: A History of American Childhood* (Cambridge, MA: Belknap Press, 2006).

E. Mavis Hetherington recommends: Hetherington and Kelly, *For Better or for Worse,* p. 201.

70   *Most important, advises psychologist:* Lauren Ayers, *Teenage Girls: A Parent's Survival Manual* (New York: Crossroad, 1996).

71   *teens of divorce:* Hetherington and Kelly, *For Better or for Worse,* p. 7.

74   *Many couples in this situation:* David Jacobson, "Financial Management in Stepfamily Households," *Journal of Divorce and Remarriage* 19 (2001): 221–38; Susan D. Stewart, *Brave New Stepfamilies: Diverse Paths Toward Stepfamily Living* (London: Sage, 2007), pp. 44–46.

when a woman without: Jean M. Lown and Elizabeth M. Dolan, "Remarried Families' Economic Behavior," *Journal of Divorce and Remarriage* 22 (1994): 103–19.

75 *most adult children presume:* Grace Gabe and Jean Lipman-Blumen, *Step Wars: Overcoming the Perils and Making Peace in Adult Stepfamilies* (New York: St. Martin's, 2004), p. 222.

79 *sociologist Linda Nielsen notes:* Nielsen, "Stepmothers: Why So Much Stress?" p. 135.

"Things didn't improve": Kenneth Cissna, Dennis Cox, and Arthur Bochner, "Relationships Within the Stepfamily," in *The Psychosocial Interior of the Family,* ed. G. Handel and G. Whitchurch (New York: Aldine, 1994), p. 265.

4. "You're Not My Child!": Anger, Jealousy, and Resentment

83 *"A large body":* Virginia Rutter, "Lessons from Stepfamilies," *Psychology Today,* May 1, 1994, p. 8. See also Judith Jordan, "The Relational Self: A Model of Women's Development," in *Daughtering and Mothering,* ed. J. Van Mens-Verhulst, K. Schreus, and L Woertman, pp. 135–43 (London: Routledge, 1993); Judith Jordan, Alexandra Kaplan, Jean Baker Miller, Irene Stiver, and Janet Surrey, *Women's Growth in Connection* (New York: Guilford, 1991); Nancy Chodorow, *The Reproduction of Mothering: Psychoanalysis and the Sociology of Gender* (Berkeley: University of California Press, 1978).

"Women are raised": Elizabeth Carter, quoted in Rutter, "Lessons from Stepfamilies," p. 8.

84 *stepmothers are more self-critical:* James H. Bray and John Kelly, *Stepfamilies: Love, Marriage, and Parenting in the First Decade* (New York: Random House/Broadway Books, 1998), p. 156.

Studies show that: Marilyn Coleman and Lawrence Ganong, "Stepfamilies from the Stepfamily's Perspective," *Marriage and Family Review* 26, nos. 1/2 (1997): 114–15; Patricia Papernow, *Becoming a Stepfamily: Patterns of Development in Remarried Families* (Cleveland: Analytic Press, 1993); Linda Nielsen,

"Stepmothers: Why So Much Stress? A Review of the Research," *Journal of Divorce and Remarriage* 30, nos. 1/2 (1999): 115; E. Mavis Hetherington and W. Glenn Clingempeel, "Coping with Marital Transitions: A Family Systems Perspective," *Monographs of the Society for Research in Childhood Development* 57 (1992).

87   *"When a stepmother feels":* Jamie Kelem Keshet, *Love and Power in the Stepfamily* (New York: McGraw-Hill, 1987), p. 38.

88   *Ayelet Waldman nails:* Ayelet Waldman, *Love and Other Impossible Pursuits* (New York: Anchor, 2007), pp. 224–29.

92   *Psychoanalyst Melanie Klein:* Melanie Klein, "Envy and Gratitude," in *Envy and Gratitude and Other Works* (1957; repr., New York: Delacorte, 1975).

93   *Borrowing from:* Elizabeth A. Church, "The Poisoned Apple: Stepmothers' Experience of Envy and Jealousy," *Journal of Feminist Family Therapy* 11 (1999), pp. 1–18.
       "Many stepmothers felt": Ibid., p. 4.
       "It is important": Ibid., p. 5.

97   *Elizabeth Church points out:* Ibid., p. 8.

99   *To disengage . . . requires:* StepTogether.org, "Disengaging," http://www.steptogether.org/disengaging.html.

5. HIM: UNDERSTANDING YOUR HUSBAND

104   *"I'm sitting there":* Posting, Urban Baby message board, UrbanBaby.com, 2007.

106   *"This is one":* Stephanie Rosenbloom, "My Father, American Inventor," *New York Times,* August 16, 2007.

108   *constant contact between kids:* Peter Crabb, quoted in Jane Gross, "A Long-Distance Tether to Home," *New York Times,* November 5, 1999.

110   *the research on men:* Leslie Buckle, Gordon G. Gallup Jr., and Zachary A. Rodd, "Marriage as a Reproductive Contract: Patterns of Marriage, Divorce, and Remarriage," *Ethology and Sociobiology* 17 (1996): 363–77.

A 2002 Penn State study: Zhenmei Zhang and Mark D. Hayward, "Childlessness and the Psychological Well-Being of Older Persons," *Journal of Gerontology* 56 (February 2001): S311–20.

A study . . . of cortisol: L. Meyers, "Relationship Conflicts Stress Men More Than Women," *Monitor on Psychology* 37 (2006): 14.

men in stepfamilies: Kirby Deater-Deckard, Kevin Pickering, Judith Dunn, and Jean Golding, "Family Structure and Depressive Symptoms in Men Preceding and Following the Birth of a Child," *American Journal of Psychiatry* 155 (June 1998): 818–23.

111 *the standard of living:* Lenore Weitzman, *The Divorce Revolution: The Unexpected Social and Economic Consequences for Women and Children in America* (New York: Simon & Schuster, 1987).

112 *divorced fathers suffer:* William S. Comanor, ed., *The Law and Economics of Child Support Payments* (Northampton, MA: Edward Elgar, 2004).

Linda Nielsen of Wake Forest: Linda Nielsen, "College Daughters' Relationships with Their Fathers: A 15-Year Study," *College Student Journal* 41 (March 2007): 1–10.

6. YOUR MARRIAGE

124 *Approximately half:* Francesca Adler-Baeder and Brian Higginbotham, "Implications of Remarriage and Stepfamily Formation for Marriage Education," *Family Relations* 53 (2004): 448–58; Andrew J. Cherlin, *Marriage, Divorce, Remarriage* (Cambridge: Harvard University Press, 1981); U.S. Census Bureau, 1998 census, table 157.

Remarriage with children also has: Susan D. Stewart, *Brave New Stepfamilies: Diverse Paths Toward Stepfamily Living* (London: Sage, 2007), p. 9; Kay Pasley and Marilyn Ihinger-Tallman, "Divorce and Remarriage in the American Family: A Historical Review," in *Remarriage and Stepparenting: Current Research and Theory,* ed. Kay Pasley and Marilyn Ihinger-Tallman (New York: Guilford, 1987).

A 1689 census: John Demos, *A Little Commonwealth: Family Life in Plymouth Colony* (New York: Oxford University Press, 1999), p. 196; Stewart, *Brave New Stepfamilies,* p. 9.

Psychotherapist and marriage researcher: Susan Gamache, "Stepfamily Life and Then Some," *Family Connections,* Summer 1999, pp. 1–5.

Owing to the production-centered: Stewart, *Brave New Stepfamilies,* p. 5; Gamache, "Stepfamily Life"; Pasley and Ihinger-Tallman, "Divorce and Remarriage," p. 33.

today 90 percent: Larry L. Bumpass, R. Kelly Raley, and James A. Sweet, "The Changing Character of Stepfamilies: Implications of Cohabitation and Non-marital Childbearing," *Demography* 32 (1995): 425–36.

125 *To complicate matters:* Andrew J. Cherlin, "The Deinstitutionalization of American Marriage," *Journal of Marriage and the Family* 66 (2004): 848–61. *This means dealing with:* Stewart, *Brave New Stepfamilies,* p. 42.

thought to be about 60 percent: Andrew J. Cherlin and Frank Furstenberg Jr., "Stepfamilies in the United States: A Reconsideration," *Annual Review of Sociology* 20 (1994): 359–81.

E. Mavis Hetherington suggests: E. Mavis Hetherington and John Kelly, *For Better or for Worse: Divorce Reconsidered* (New York: Norton, 2002); E. Mavis Hetherington, personal conversation, quoted by Dr. Ron L. Deal, "The Step-couple Divorce Rate May Be Higher Than We Thought," Successful Stepfamilies, http://www.successfulstepfamilies.com/view/176.

126 *50 percent higher:* Hetherington and Kelly, *For Better or for Worse,* p. 178. *a mere 5 percent:* Ibid., p. 182.

although children typically: Kay Pasley and Marilyn Ihinger-Tallman, *Remarriage* (Beverly Hills, CA: Sage, 1987), pp. 93–95.

"The parent feels": Patricia Papernow, "Stepfamily Role Development: From Outsider to Intimate," in *Relative Strangers: Studies of the Stepfamily Processes,* ed. William R. Beer (Totowa, NJ: Rowman and Littlefield, 1992), p. 59.

127 *Such men tend:* Maria Schmeeckle, "Gender Dynamics in Stepfamilies: Adult Stepchildren's Views," *Journal of Marriage and the Family* 69 (2007): 174–89; Adler-Baeder and Higginbotham, "Implications of Remarriage."

129 *This perception becomes:* Cherie Burns, *Stepmotherhood: How to Survive Without Feeling Frustrated, Left Out, or Wicked* (New York: Random House, 2001), p. 35.

stepfamily experts such as: Emily B. Visher and John S. Visher, *Stepfamilies: Myths and Realities* (Secaucus, NJ: Citadel, 1979); Bray and Kelly, *Stepfamilies. "Marital satisfaction almost always":* Bray and Kelly, *Stepfamilies,* p. 24.

130 *putting the marriage first:* Ann Sale Dahl, K. Cowgill, and R. Asmundsson, "Life in Remarriage Families," *Social Work* 32 (1987): 40–45; Emily Visher, John Visher, and Kay Pasley, "Remarriage Families and Stepparenting," in *Normal Family Processes: Growing Diversity and Complexity,* ed. Froma Walsh, pp. 153–75 (New York: Guilford, 2003); Patricia Papernow, *Becoming a Stepfamily: Patterns of Development in Remarried Families* (Cleveland: Analytic Press, 1993).

131 *"involves wresting the sanctuary":* Papernow, "Stepfamily Role Development," p. 54.

And nothing makes: Burns, *Stepmotherhood,* p. 35.

132 *roughly one-quarter of couples:* Anne C. Bernstein, *Yours, Mine, and Ours: How Families Change When Remarried Parents Have a Child Together* (New York: Norton, 1991), p. 319.

133 *ex-wives feel more threatened:* Ibid., p. 151.

134 *such a fundamental difference:* Ibid., pp. 25–28.

139 *the first twenty-four months:* Bray and Kelly, *Stepfamilies,* p. 23.

the settling-in period: Papernow, *Becoming a Stepfamily;* Patricia Papernow, "The Stepfamily Cycle: An Experiential Model of Stepfamily Development," *Family Relations* 33 (1984): 355–63.

not fighting, or fighting the wrong way: Tara Parker-Pope, "Marital Spats, Taken to Heart," *New York Times,* October 2, 2007.

141 *marriage, like childhood:* Michael Vincent Miller, *Intimate Terrorism: The Crisis of Love in an Age of Disillusion* (New York: Norton, 1996).

All heterosexual couples: Anne C. Bernstein, "Remarriage: Redesigning Couplehood," in *Couples on the Fault Line: New Directions for Therapists,* ed. Peggy Papp, pp. 306–33 (New York: Guilford, 2000).

the pursuer/distancer dynamic: Hetherington and Kelly, *For Better or for Worse,* pp. 26–27; John Gottman, *Why Marriages Succeed or Fail and How You Can Make Yours Last* (New York: Fireside, 1994), pp. 137–62.

"Now the woman has": Anne Bernstein, phone interview, February 2008.

143 *Remarrieds with children:* Anne C. Bernstein, "Between You and Me: Untangling Conflict in Stepfamilies." SAA's Counseling Corner, Stepfamily Association of America, Spring 1993, http://www.stepfamilies.info/education/Articles/counseling/conflict.php.

144 *If you ease up:* Bernstein, interview.

One way to break: Patricia Papernow, phone interview, February 2008.

146 *John Gottman has studied:* John Gottman and Nan Silver, *The Seven Principles for Making Marriage Work* (New York: Norton, 1999), pp. 25–46.

147 *Family therapist James Bray has noted:* Bray and Kelly, *Stepfamilies,* pp. 28–29.

149 *Cherie Burns recommends:* Burns, *Stepmotherhood,* p. 31.

150 *"the biological force field":* Bray and Kelly, *Stepfamilies,* p. 146.

In these cases: Jamie Kelem Keshet, *Love and Power in the Stepfamily* (New York: McGraw-Hill, 1987), pp. 7–10.

"middle ground": Sonia Nevis, "Diagnosis: The Struggle for a Meaningful Paradigm," in *Gestalt Therapy: Perspectives and Applications,* ed. Edwin C. Nevis (New York: Routledge, 1997), pp. 57–78. See also Dahl, Cowgill, and Asmundsson, "Life in Remarriage Families."

151 *"paths of easy connection":* Papernow, interview.

"much of what": Ibid.

152 *"If the husband"*: Ibid.

sometimes surrendering: Papernow, "The Stepfamily Cycle."

153 *These sentiments echo:* Hetherington and Kelly, *For Better or for Worse;* Constance R. Ahrons and Roy H. Rodgers, *Divorced Families: A Multidisciplinary Developmental View* (New York: Norton, 1987); Constance R. Ahrons, *The Good Divorce: Keeping Your Family Together When Your Marriage Falls Apart* (New York: HarperCollins, 1994).

mothers are generally thought: Bernstein, *Yours, Mine, and Ours,* p. 150; Hetherington and Kelly, *For Better or for Worse,* p. 189.

resentment is more sustained: Hetherington and Kelly, *For Better or for Worse,* p. 58; Ahrons, *The Good Divorce,* pp. 218–19.

154 *the same tendency:* Hetherington and Kelly, *For Better or for Worse,* p. 57.

ex-husbands . . . are more likely: E. Mavis Hetherington and M. Stanley-Hagan, "The Effects of Divorce on Fathers and Their Children," in *The Role of the Father in Child Development,* ed. Michael E. Lamb, pp. 191–211 (New York: Wiley, 1997); Hetherington and Kelly, *For Better or for Worse,* pp. 57–59.

"Letting go": Anne C. Bernstein, "Revisioning, Restructuring, and Reconciliation: Clinical Practice with Complex Post-Divorce Families," *Family Process* 46, no. 1 (March 2007): 67–78.

155 *"accusatory suffering":* Arthur and Elizabeth Seagull, quoted in Shirley Glass, "Infidelity," *Clinical Update* (American Association of Family and Marital Therapy) 2, no. 1 (2000): 1–18.

children with single mothers: Linda Nielsen, "Stepmothers: Why So Much Stress? A Review of the Research," *Journal of Divorce and Remarriage* 30, nos. 1/2 (1999): 115–48.

Sociologist Linda Nielsen: Nielsen, "Stepmothers."

Researchers suggest: Ahrons, *The Good Divorce;* Patricia Bell-Scott, ed., *Double Stitch: Black Women Write About Mothers and Daughters* (New York: Harper Perennial, 1991); David Blankenhorn,

Fatherless America: Confronting Our Most Urgent Social Problem (New York: Basic Books, 1994); Lyn Mikel Brown and Carol Gilligan, *Meeting at the Crossroads: Women's Psychology and Girls' Development* (Cambridge: Harvard University Press, 1992); Patricia Hill Collins, "The Meaning of Motherhood in Black Culture and Black Mother-Daughter Relationships," in *Double Stitch: Black Women Write About Mothers and Daughters,* ed. Patricia Bell-Scott (New York: Harper Perennial, 1991); Elizabeth Debold, Marie C. Wilson, and Idelisse Malave, *Mother Daughter Revolution: From Good Girls to Great Women* (New York: Addison-Wesley, 1992); Sharon Hays, *The Cultural Contradictions of Motherhood* (New Haven, CT: Yale University Press, 1996); Hetherington and Stanley-Hagan, "The Effects of Divorce."

White women of means: Stephanie Coontz, *The Way We Really Are: Coming to Terms with America's Changing Families* (New York: Basic Books, 1997), pp. 119–21.

156 *very educated white single mothers:* Margaret Crosbie-Burnett, "The Interface Between Stepparent Families and Schools: Research, Theory, Policy, and Practice," in *Remarriage and Stepparenting: Current Research and Theory,* ed. Kay Pasley and Marilyn Ihinger-Tallman, pp. 199–216 (New York: Guilford, 1987). *The parenting style:* Nielsen, "Stepmothers: Why So Much Stress?"; Ahrons, *The Good Divorce;* Sarah McLanahan and Gary Sandefur, *Growing Up with a Single Parent: What Hurts, What Helps* (Cambridge: Harvard University Press, 1994).

if an ex-wife: Nielsen, "Stepmothers: Why So Much Stress?"

Although most researchers: Ibid.; Lucile Duberman, "Step-Kin Relations," *Journal of Marriage and the Family* 35 (1973): 283–92; Lucile Duberman, *The Reconstituted Family: A Study of Remarried Couples and Their Children* (Chicago: Nelson Hall, 1975); Thomas S. Parish and Bruno M. Kappes, "Impact of Father Loss on the Family," *Social Behavior and Personality* 8 (1980): 107–12; Jacqueline Lesley Burgoyne and David Clark, *Making a Go of It: A Study of Stepfamilies in Sheffield* (London: Routledge, 1984); Elsa Ferri, *Stepchildren: A National Study* (Windsor, Eng.: Routledge, 1984).

157 *"good fences"*: Bernstein, "Revisioning."
"the good divorce": Ahrons, *The Good Divorce.*

159 *But research also shows:* Adler-Baeder and Higginbotham, "Implications of Remarriage."

160 *Hetherington found minimal:* Hetherington and Kelly, *For Better or for Worse*, p. 139.

7. SOCIOBIOLOGY: WHAT THE BIRDS, THE BEES, AND THE WHITE-FRONTED BEE-EATERS CAN TEACH US ABOUT STEPMOTHERING

167 *"the first reproductive ecologist"*: Sarah Blaffer Hrdy, *Mother Nature: Maternal Instincts and How They Shape the Human Species* (New York: Random House/Ballantine, 1999), p. 29.

168 *"they managed their"*: Ibid., p. 30.
"greater goodists": Helena Cronin, *The Ant and the Peacock: Altruism and Natural Selection from Darwin to Today* (Cambridge: Cambridge University Press, 1991).

169 *"highly discerning mothers"*: Ibid., p. 31.

170 *"where only one"*: Ibid., p. 61.

171 *"underlies the evolution"*: Ibid., p. 63
later studies of humans: Richard Alexander, *Darwin and Human Affairs* (Seattle: University of Washington Press, 1979); Kermyt G. Anderson, Hilliard Kaplan, David Lam, and Jane Lancaster, "Paternal Care by Genetic Fathers and Stepfathers. II: Reports by Xhosa High School Students," *Evolution and Human Behavior* 20, no. 6 (November 1999): 433–51; Kermyt G. Anderson, Hilliard Kaplan, and Jane Lancaster, "Men's Financial Expenditures on Genetic Children and Stepchildren from Current and Former Relationships" (Population Studies Center Research Report No. 01-484, Ann Arbor, MI, 2001); Mark V.

Flinn, "Step and Genetic Parent/Offspring Relationships in a Caribbean Village," *Ethology and Sociobiology* 9, no. 6 (1988): 335–69; Douglas W. Mock and Geoffrey Parker, *The Evolution of Sibling Rivalry* (Oxford: Oxford University Press, 1997); Mary Jane West-Eberhard, "Foundress Associations in Polistine Wasps: Dominance Hierarchies and the Evolution of Social Behavior," *Science* 157 (1967): 1584–85.

"in humans we can": Hrdy, *Mother Nature*, p. 63.

172   *And so it is inevitable:* Sarah Blaffer Hrdy, "Fitness Tradeoffs in the History and Evolution of Delegated Mothering with Special Reference to Wet-Nursing, Abandonment, and Infanticide," *Ethology and Sociobiology* 13 (1992): 427.

anything that a parent: Robert Trivers, "Parental Investment and Sexual Selection," in *Sexual Selection and the Descent of Man, 1871–1971*, ed. B. Campbell (Chicago: Aldine, 1972), p. 173.

173   *"Parent and offspring":* Robert Trivers, "Parent-Offspring Conflict," *American Zoologist* 14 (1974): 249.

"Weaning conflicts": Hrdy, "Fitness Tradeoffs," p. 429.

When !Kung mothers: Marjorie Shostak, *Nisa: The Life and Words of a !Kung Woman* (Cambridge: Harvard University Press, 1981), p. 46.

175   *"Animals that live":* Stephen Emlen, quoted in Will Hively, "Family Man," *Discover,* October 1997, http://discovermagazine.com/1997/oct/familyman1237/?s earchitem=stephen%20emlen.

"The reason I went": Ibid.

176   *Such behaviors have been:* Craig Packer, "Reciprocal Altruism in *Papio Anubis*," *Nature* 265 (February 1977): 441–43; Robert M. Seyfarth and Dorothy L. Cheney, "Grooming, Alliances, and Reciprocal Altruism in Vervet Monkeys," *Nature* 308 (April 1984): 541–43; Dan Wharton, phone interview, February 2008.

"If a nest": Emlen, quoted in Hively, "Family Man."

177   *"a swirling soap opera":* Hively, "Family Man."

178   *"The kids from":* Emlen, quoted in Hively, "Family Man."

"Sometimes, there is": Ibid.

179 *"Both genetics and environment":* Stephen Emlen, quoted in David Kaplan and Molly Vanduser, "Evolution and Stepfamilies: An Interview with Dr. Stephen T. Emlen," *Family Journal: Counseling and Therapy for Couples and Families* 7, no. 4 (October 1999): 410. *A particularly elegant study:* William Jankowiak and Monique Diderich, "Sibling Solidarity in a Polygamous Community in the USA: Unpacking Inclusive Fitness," *Evolution and Human Behavior* 2, nos. 1/2 (March 2000): 125–39.

181 *"there is a pronounced":* Ibid., p. 135.

182 *a 1981 national survey:* Andrew J. Cherlin and Frank Furstenberg Jr., "Stepfamilies in the United States: A Reconsideration," *Annual Review of Sociology* 20 (1994): 359–81.

The simple fact: Francesca Adler-Baeder, phone interview, February 2007; James H. Bray and John Kelly, *Stepfamilies: Love, Marriage, and Parenting in the First Decade* (New York: Random House/Broadway Books, 1998), p. 35; Lawrence Ganong, Marilyn Coleman, M. Fine, and P. Martin, "Stepparents' Affinity-Seeking and Affinity-Maintaining Strategies with Stepchildren," *Journal of Family Issues* 20 (1999): 299–327; Marilyn Coleman, Lawrence Ganong, and M. Fine, "Reinvestigating Remarriage: Another Decade of Progress," *Journal of Marriage and the Family* 62 (2000): 1288–1307; E. Mavis Hetherington and W. Glenn Clingempeel, "Coping with Marital Transitions: A Family Systems Perspective," *Monographs of the Society for Research in Childhood Development* 57 (1992).

there is little empirical evidence: Melady Preece, "Exploring the StepGap: How Parents' Ways of Coping with Daily Family Stressors Impact Stepparent-Stepchild Relationship Quality in Stepfamilies" (University of British Columbia Publications, 1996), http://www.psych.ubc/ca/~mpreece.compdoc.pdf.

183 *A number of researchers:* Charles Hobart, "The Family System in Remarriage: An Exploratory Study," *Journal of Marriage and the Family* 50 (1988): 649–61; Charles Hobart, "Conflict in Remarriages," *Journal of Divorce and Remarriage* 15 (1991):

69–86; Bray and Kelly, *Stepfamilies;* Leslie A. Baxter, Dawn O. Braithwaite, and John H. Nicholson, "Turning Points in the Development of Blended Families," *Journal of Personal and Social Relationships* 16 (1999): 291–314; Patricia Papernow, *Becoming a Stepfamily: Patterns of Development in Remarried Families* (Cleveland: Analytic Press, 1993); Terry Waldren, "Cohesion and Adaptability in Post-Divorce Remarried and First Married Families: Relation-ships with Family Stress and Coping Styles," *Journal of Divorce and Remarriage* 14, no. 1 (1990): 13–28.

184 *ornithologist Harry Power asserted:* Martin Daly and Margo Wilson, *The Truth About Cinderella: A Darwinian View of Parental Love* (New Haven, CT: Yale University Press, 1998), p. 19.

186 *Summarizing Rohwer's work:* Ibid., pp. 63, 64.

187 *a co-residing stepparent:* Ibid., p. 32.

They had conscientiously tested: Martin Daly and Margo Wilson, "Is the Cinderella Effect Controversial?" in *Foundations of Evolutionary Psychology,* ed. Charles Crawford and Dennis Krebs (New York: Psychology Press, 2008).

189 *"indiscriminate allocation":* Daly and Wilson, *The Truth About Cinderella,* p. 38.

"If the psychological underpinnings": Daly and Wilson, "Is the Cinderella Effect Controversial?" p. 383.

In fact, research has shown: Hrdy, *Mother Nature,* pp. 130–34.

190 *First of all:* Martin Daly and Margo Wilson, *Homicide* (New Brunswick, NJ: Transaction, 1988), pp. 85–93.

191 *this was likely more:* Paula K. Ivey, "Cooperative Reproduction in Ituri Forest Hunter-Gatherers: Who Cares for Efe Infants?" *Current Anthropology* 41, no. 5 (December 2000): 856–66; Sarah Blaffer Hrdy, "The Past, Present, and Future of the Human Family," Tanner Series Lecture on Human Values, University of Utah, Salt Lake City, February 27 and 28, 2001.

unrelated males have evolved: Hrdy, *Mother Nature,* p. 237.

Such indifference: Ibid.

"non-adaptive byproducts": Martin Daly and Margo Wilson, personal communication, March 2008.

For Daly and Wilson: Daly and Wilson, *The Truth About Cinderella,* p. 30.

192 *Still, they insist:* Ibid., p. 65.

"Might it not": Ibid., p. 59.

the American Humane Association: Ibid., p. 61.

195 *"It is easy":* Ibid., p. 62.

Since the beginning of time: Hrdy, *Mother Nature,* pp. 288–317.

8. STEPMOTHERS WORLDWIDE: ANTHROPOLOGY, ATTACHMENT, CONTEXT

196 *"The uniqueness of":* Marjorie Shostak, *Nisa: The Life and Words of a !Kung Woman* (Cambridge: Harvard University Press, 1981), p. 3.

197 *"My milk is":* Ibid., p. 46.

"When I was growing up": Ibid., p. 56.

the Efe Pygmies: Paula K. Ivey, "Cooperative Reproduction in Ituri Forest Hunter-Gatherers: Who Cares for Efe Infants?" *Current Anthropology* 41, no. 5 (December 2000): 856–66.

Thanks to such allomothers: See Monique Borgerhoff Mulder and Maryanna Milton, "Factors Affecting Infant Care in the Kipsigis," *Journal of Anthropological Research* 41, no. 3 (1985): 255–60; Riley B. Bove, Claudia R. Valeggia, and Peter T. Ellison, "Girl Helpers and Time Allocation of Nursing Women Among the Toba of Argentina," *Human Nature* 1, nos. 3/4 (2002): 457–72; Patricia Draper and Henry Harpending, "Parental Investment and the Child's Environment," in *Parenting Across the Lifespan: Biosocial Dimensions,* ed. Jane B. Lancaster, Jeanne Altman, Alice S. Rossi, and Lonnie R. Sherrod, pp. 207–35 (New York: Aldine, 1987); Karen L. Kramer, *Maya Children: Helpers at the Farm* (Cambridge: Harvard University Press, 2005); Karen L. Kramer, "Children's Help and the Pace of Reproduction: Cooperative Breeding in Humans," *Evolutionary Anthropology* 14, no. 6 (2005): 225–37; Paul W. Turke, "Helpers at the Nest: Childcare Networks on Ifaluk," in *Human Reproductive Behavior:*

A Darwinian Perspective, ed. Laure Betzig, Monique Borgerhoff Mulder, and Paul Turke, pp. 173–89 (Cambridge: Cambridge University Press, 1988).

there is ample evidence: Sarah Blaffer Hrdy, "On Why It Takes a Village: Cooperative Breeders, Infant Needs, and the Future," *Tanner Lectures on Human Values,* vol. 23 (Salt Lake City: University of Utah Press, 2002), pp. 57–110; Sarah Blaffer Hrdy, "Comes the Child Before the Man: How Cooperative Breeding and Prolonged Post-Weaning Dependency Shaped Human Potential," in *Hunter-Gatherer Childhoods,* ed. Barry S. Hewlett and Michael E. Lamb, pp. 65–91 (New Brunswick, NJ: Transaction, 2005); Sarah Blaffer Hrdy, *Mother Nature: Maternal Instincts and How They Shape the Human Species* (New York: Random House/Ballantine, 1999); Ivey, "Cooperative Reproduction"; Kramer, *Maya Children;* Kramer, "Children's Help"; Stephen T. Emlen, "The Evolution of Cooperative Breeding in Birds and Mammals," in *Behavioural Ecology: An Evolutionary Approach,* ed. John R. Krebs and Nick B. Davies (London: Blackwell, 1984).

198 *"My father told":* Shostak, *Nisa,* p. 155.

199 *"A co-wife is":* Ibid., p. 154.
"[My younger brother and I]": Ibid., pp. 248–49.
"Even the woman": Ibid., pp. 249–50.

200 *"My mother just":* Ibid., p. 250.
"It grew and grew": Ibid., pp. 168, 203.

201 *"Why don't you":* Ibid., pp. 282–83.
"seldom does a child": Barry Hewlett, "Demography and Childcare in Preindustrial Societies," *Journal of Anthropological Research* 47, no. 1 (Spring 1991): 19.
Of the ten Ache children: Ibid., pp. 19–23.

202 *A number of anthropologists:* Kermyt G. Anderson, "Relatedness and Investment in Children in South Africa," *Human Nature* 16, no. 1 (2005): 3–25; Kermyt G. Anderson, Hilliard Kaplan, and Jane Lancaster, "Men's Financial Expenditures on Genetic Children and Stepchildren from Current and Former

Relationships" (Population Studies Center Research Report No. 01-484, Ann Arbor, MI, 2001); Kermyt G. Anderson, Hilliard Kaplan, David Lam, and Jane Lancaster, "Paternal Care by Genetic Fathers and Stepfathers. II: Reports by Xhosa High School Students," *Evolution and Human Behavior* 20, no. 6 (November 1999): 433–51; Mark V. Flinn, "Step and Genetic Parent/Offspring Relationships in a Caribbean Village," *Ethology and Sociobiology* 9, no. 6 (1988): 335–69; Jane Lancaster and Hilliard Kaplan, "Parenting Other Men's Children: Costs, Benefits, and Consequences," in *Adaptation and Human Behavior: An Anthropological Perspective,* ed. Lee Cronk, Napoleon Chagnon, and William Irons, pp. 179–203 (New York: Aldine, 2000); Frank Marlowe, "Showoffs or Providers? The Parenting Effort of Hadza Men," *Evolution and Human Behavior* 20 (1999): 391–404.

203 *biological anthropologist Edward Hagen:* Edward Hagen, Raymond B. Hames, Nathan M. Craig, Matthew T. Lauer, and Michael E. Price, "Parental Investment and Child Health in a Yanomamo Village Suffering Short-Term Food Stress," *Journal of Biosocial Sciences* 33 (2001): 503–28.

205 *the offspring of one's offspring:* Steven Josephson, "Does Polygyny Reduce Fertility?" *American Journal of Human Biology* 14, no. 2 (February 2002): 222–32. *People in the United States:* Steven Josephson, personal communication, March 2008.

206 *nearly a third:* Catrien Notermans, "Fosterage in Cameroon: A Different Social Construction of Motherhood," in *Cross Cultural Approaches to Adoption,* ed. Fiona Bowie (London: Routledge, 2004), p. 1.

"If you have": Patricia Draper and Anne Buchanan, "'If You Have a Child You Have a Life': Demographic and Cultural Perspectives on Fathering in Old Age in !Kung Society," in *Father-Child Relations: Cultural and Biosocial Contexts,* ed. Barry S. Hewlett, pp. 131–52 (New York: Aldine, 1992).

in Africa they are associated: Notermans, "Fosterage in Cameroon," p. 2.

"not wanting a child": Hrdy, *Mother Nature*, p. 374.

"A child has": Heidi Verhoef, "'A Child Has Many Mothers': Views of Child Fostering in Northwestern Cameroon," *Childhood* 12 (2005): 369–90.

"Being outside": Ibid., p. 370.

207 *These foster mothers also expressed:* Ibid., p. 382.

208 *anthropologist Caroline Bledsoe:* Hrdy, *Mother Nature*, pp. 373–74. Hrdy is citing Caroline Bledsoe, "The 'Trickle-Down' Model Within Households: Foster Children and the Phenomenon of Scrounging," in *Health Transition: Methods and Measures,* ed. J. Cleland and A. G. Hill, pp. 115–31 (Canberra: Australian National University, 1991); Caroline Bledsoe, "'No Success Without Struggle': Social Mobility and Hardship for Foster Children in Sierra Leone," *Man* 25, no. 1 (1990): 70–88.

209 *A twenty-two-year-old:* Notermans, "Fosterage in Cameroon," pp. 4–5.

210 *Anthropologist Beverly Strassman:* Beverly I. Strassman, "Polygyny, Family Structure, and Child Mortality: A Prospective Study Among the Dogon of Mali," in *Adaptation and Human Behavior: An Anthropological Perspective,* ed. Lee Cronk, Napoleon Chagnon, and William Irons, pp. 49–67 (New York: Aldine, 2000).

213 *"we are talking":* Stephen Emlen, quoted in David Kaplan and Molly Vanduser, "Evolution and Stepfamilies: An Interview with Dr. Stephen T. Emlen," *Family Journal: Counseling and Therapy for Couples and Families* 7, no. 4 (October 1999): 409.

214 *Waterman argues that:* Barbara Waterman, *The Birth of an Adoptive, Foster or Stepmother: Beyond Biological Mothering Attachments* (London: Jessica Kingsley, 2004), pp. 11–13, 81. *Indeed, since coming:* Ibid., pp. 52–53.

9. STEPMOTHER SADNESS AND DEPRESSION: UNDERSTANDING THE RISK FACTORS

225 *Exhaustive longitudinal studies:* Constance R. Ahrons, *The Good Divorce: Keeping Your Family Together When Your Marriage Falls*

Apart (New York: Harper-Collins, 1994); E. Mavis Hetherington and John Kelly, *For Better or for Worse: Divorce Reconsidered* (New York: Norton, 2002).

after about five years: Virginia Rutter, "Lessons from Stepfamilies," *Psychology Today,* May 1, 1994, p. 6.

"The sense is": Take Our Word for It, http://www.takeourword-forit.com/Issue009.html.

before the year 800: Ibid.

226 *the Latin word for "stepson":* Watson, *Ancient Stepmothers: Myth, Misogyny and Reality,* p. 3.

228 *women suffer depression:* Andrew Solomon, *The Noonday Demon: An Atlas of Depression* (New York: Scribner, 2001), p. 173.

depression is "hereditary": Ibid., p. 174.

stepmothers are dramatically: Kay Pasley and Marilyn Ihinger-Tallman, eds., *Remarriage and Stepparenting: Current Research and Theory* (New York: Guilford, 1987), p. 101. See also Laurence E. Sauer and Mark A. Fine, "Parent-Child Relationships in Stepparent Families," *Journal of Family Psychology* 1 (1998): 434–51.

women who brought: Hetherington and Kelly, *For Better or for Worse,* pp. 196–97.

230 *"When she's isolated":* Susan Nolen-Hoeksema, phone interview, spring 2006. See also Susan Nolen-Hoeksema, *Women Who Think Too Much: How to Break Free of Overthinking and Reclaim Your Life* (New York: Henry Holt, 2003).

231 *"A nasty comment":* Nolen-Hoeksema, interview.

232 *"Women get depressed":* Rutter, "Lessons from Stepfamilies," p. 8. See also Judith Jordan, "The Relational Self: A Model of Women's Development," in *Daughtering and Mothering,* ed. J. Van Mens-Verhulst, K. Schreus, and L. Woertman, pp. 135–44 (London: Routledge, 1993). See also Judith Jordan, Alexandra Kaplan, Jean Baker Miller, Irene Stiver, and Janet Surrey, *Women's Growth in Connection* (New York: Guilford, 1991); Nancy Chodorow, *The Reproduction of Mothering: Psychoanalysis and the Sociology of Gender* (Berkeley: University of California Press, 1978).

233 *"we are immersed"*: Cindi Penor-Ceglian and Scott Gardner, "Attachment Style and the Wicked Stepmother Spiral," *Journal of Divorce and Remarriage* 34 (2000): 111–26.

235 *"A stepmother must be"*: Lucile Duberman, *The Reconstituted Family: A Study of Remarried Couples and Their Children* (Chicago: Nelson Hall, 1975), p. 50.

In the mid-1980s: Kati Morrison and Airdrie Thompson-Guppy, "Cinderella's Stepmother Syndrome," *Canadian Journal of Psychiatry* 30 (1985): 521–29.

236 *stepmothers reported responding:* Mark A. Fine, P. Voydanoff, and B. W. Donnelly, "Relations Between Parental Control and Warmth and Child Well-Being in Stepfamilies," *Journal of Family Psychology* 7 (1993): 222–32.

stepmothers also seek: Ahrons, *The Good Divorce*, p. 233; See also Linda Nielsen, "Stepmothers: Why So Much Stress? A Review of the Research," *Journal of Divorce and Remarriage* 30, nos. 1/2 (1999): 134.

237 *Our sense that:* Elizabeth A. Church, *Understanding Stepmothers: Women Share Their Struggles, Successes, and Insights* (Toronto: HarperCollins, 2004), p. 84; Hetherington and Kelly, *For Better or for Worse*, p. 193; Anne C. Bernstein, "Between You and Me: Untangling Conflict in Stepfamilies," SAA's Counseling Corner, Stepfamily Association of America, spring 1993, http://www.stepfamilies.info/education/Articles/counseling/conflict.php; Melvyn A. Berke and Joanne B. Grant, *Games Divorced People Play* (Englewood Cliffs, NJ: Prentice Hall, 1981).

238 *"Step[mothers] can be"*: Bernstein, "Between You and Me," p. 2.

239 *nearly half of the remarried men:* Ann L. Orchard and Kenneth B. Solberg, "Expectations of the Stepmother's Role," *Journal of Divorce and Remarriage* 31, nos. 1/2 (1991): 120.

242 *"the group that comes"*: Susan D. Stewart, *Brave New Stepfamilies: Diverse Paths Toward Stepfamily Living* (London: Sage, 2007), p. 30. *Too often, these problem-oriented:* Ibid. See also Marilyn Coleman and Lawrence Ganong, "Remarriage and Family Research

in the 80s: New Interest in an Old Family Form," *Journal of Marriage and the Family* 52 (1990): 925–40.

A University of Missouri study: S. H. Bryan, Lawrence Ganong, Marilyn Coleman, and Linda R. Bryan, "Counselors' Perceptions of Stepparents and Stepchildren," *Journal of Counseling Psychology* 32, no. 2 (April 1985): 279–82.

Since some 86 percent: Mary Ann Mason, "The Modern American Stepfamily: Problems and Possibilities," in *All Our Families: New Policies for a New Century,* ed. Mary Ann Mason, Arlene Skolnick, and Stephen D. Sugarman, pp. 96–116 (New York: Oxford University Press, 1998).

243 *residency is relatively fluid:* James H. Bray and John Kelly, *Stepfamilies: Love, Marriage, and Parenting in the First Decade* (New York: Random House/Broadway Books, 1998); Marilyn Coleman, Lawrence Ganong, and M. Fine, "Reinvestigating Remarriage: Another Decade of Progress," *Journal of Marriage and the Family* 62 (2000): 1288–1307.

a number of studies have shown: Alan Booth and Judith F. Dunn, eds., *Stepfamilies: Who Benefits? Who Does Not?* (Hillsdale, NJ: Erlbaum, 1994); Andrew J. Cherlin and Frank Furstenberg Jr., "Stepfamilies in the United States: A Reconsideration," *Annual Review of Sociology* 20 (1994): 359–81; Mark A. Fine and Andrew I. Schwebel, "Stepparent Stress," *Journal of Divorce and Remarriage* 17 (1992): 1–15; Nan Bauer Maglin and Nancy Schniedewind, eds., *Women in Stepfamilies: Voices of Anger and Love* (Philadelphia: Temple University Press, 1989); Charles Hobart, "The Family System in Remarriage: An Exploratory Study," *Journal of Marriage and the Family* 50 (1988): 649–61; Charles Hobart, "Conflict in Remarriages," *Journal of Divorce and Remarriage* 15 (1991): 69–86; Patricia Papernow, *Becoming a Stepfamily: Patterns of Development in Remarried Families* (Cleveland: Analytic Press, 1993); Donna S. Quick, Patrick C. McKenry, and Barbara M. Newman, "Stepmothers and Their Adolescent Stepchildren," in *Remarriage and Stepparenting: Current Research and Theory,* ed. Kay Pasley and Marilyn

Ihinger-Tallman, pp. 105–27 (Westport, CT: Praeger, 1995); Sarah Turner, "My Wife-in-Law and Me: Reflections on a Joint-Custody Stepparenting Relationship," in *Women in Stepfamilies: Voices of Anger and Love,* ed. Nan Bauer Maglin and Nancy Schniedewind, pp. 310–30 (Philadelphia: Temple University Press, 1989); Lynn White, "Stepfamilies over the Life Course," in *Stepfamilies: Who Benefits? Who Does Not?* ed. Alan Booth and Judith F. Dunn, pp. 109–37 (Hillsdale, NJ: Erlbaum, 1994); D. Whitsett and H. Land, "The Development of a Role Strain Index for Stepparents," *Families in Society* 73 (January 1992): 14–22.

Stepfamily researcher Elizabeth Church: Church, *Understanding Stepmothers,* pp. 275–79.

245 *"I am ashamed":* Letter, *Salon,* December 1, 2005.

10. WOMEN WITH ADULT STEPCHILDREN: LESSONS FROM "LIFERS"

248 *To paraphrase:* Susan D. Stewart, *Brave New Stepfamilies: Diverse Paths Toward Stepfamily Living* (London: Sage, 2007), p. 190.

older parents with adult children: Ibid., p. 202.

adolescence has now been: Ibid., p. 193.

the recent trend: See, for example, Jane Gross, "A Long-Distance Tether to Home," *New York Times,* November 5, 1999; Stephen Mintz, *Huck's Raft: A History of American Childhood* (Cambridge: Belknap Press, 2006).

252 *"My new stepmother":* Candy Cooper, "Step Shock," in *My Father Married Your Mother: Writers Talk About Stepparents, Stepchildren, and Everyone in Between,* ed. Anne Burt (New York: Norton, 2006), p. 239.

the issues of adult stepchildren: Stewart, *Brave New Stepfamilies,* p. 195.

254 *"maladaptive notions":* Sarah Corrie, "Working Therapeutically with Adult Stepchildren: Identifying the Needs of a Neglected

Client Group," *Journal of Divorce and Remarriage* 37, nos. 1/2 (2002): 141.

"*In my experience*": Ibid., p. 137.

256 "*For Louise, it felt*": Ibid., p. 144.

257 "*find high levels*": Ibid., p. 138.

"*We arranged an evening*": Andrew Solomon, "On Having a Stepmother Who Loves Opera," in *My Father Married Your Mother: Writers Talk About Stepparents, Stepchildren, and Everyone in Between,* ed. Anne Burt (New York: Norton, 2006), p. 51.

258 "*Very much to my*": Ibid., p. 56.

"*Then too, I disliked*": Ibid.

259 "*The relationship between*": Ibid., p. 57.

267 "*complex stepfamilies have more*": E. Mavis Hetherington and John Kelly, *For Better or for Worse: Divorce Reconsidered* (New York: Norton, 2002), p. 196.

268 *This is typical:* Paul Schrodt, "Sex Differences in Stepchildren's Reports of Stepfamily Functioning," *Communication Reports* 21, no. 1 (January 2008): 46–58.

269 "*When stepchildren decide*": Marilyn Coleman and Lawrence Ganong, "Stepfamilies from the Stepfamily's Perspective," *Marriage and Family Review* 26, nos. 1/2 (1997): 119.

270 "*the stepmothers of the children*": Barbara Vinick and Susan Lanspery, "Cinderella's Sequel: Stepmothers' Long-Term Relationships with Adult Stepchildren," *Journal of Comparative Family Studies* 31 (June 2000): p. 381.

BIBLIOGRAPHY

Abraham, Laurie. "Can This Marriage Be Saved? A Year in the Life of a Couples-Therapy Group." *New York Times Magazine,* August 12, 2007.

Adler-Baeder, Francesca. "Development of the Remarriage Belief Inventory for Researchers and Educators." *Journal of Extension* 43 (June 2005): 1–7, http://www. joe.org/joe/2005june/iw2. shtml.

———. "What Do We Know About the Physical Abuse of Stepchildren? A Review of the Literature." *Journal of Divorce and Remarriage* 44 (2006): 67–81.

Adler-Baeder, Francesca, and Brian Higginbotham. "Implications of Remarriage and Stepfamily Formation for Marriage Education." *Family Relations* 53 (2004): 448–58.

Ahrons, Constance R. *The Good Divorce: Keeping Your Family Together When Your Marriage Falls Apart.* New York: HarperCollins, 1994.

———. *We're Still Family: What Grown Children Have to Say About Their Parents' Divorce.* New York: HarperCollins, 2004.

Ahrons, Constance R., and Roy H. Rodgers. *Divorced Families: A Multidisciplinary Developmental View.* New York: Norton, 1987.

Ahrons, Constance R., and L. Wallisch. "Parenting in the Binuclear Family: Relationships Between Biological and Stepparents." In *Remarriage and Stepparenting: Current Research and Theory,* edited by Kay Pasley and Marilyn Ihinger-Tallman. New York: Guilford, 1987.

Alexander, Richard. *Darwin and Human Affairs.* Seattle: University of Washington Press, 1979.

Anderson, Kermyt G. "Relatedness and Investment in Children in South Africa." *Human Nature* 16, no. 1 (2005): 3–25.

Anderson, Kermyt G., Hilliard Kaplan, David Lam, and Jane Lancaster. "Paternal Care by Genetic Fathers and Stepfathers. II: Reports by Xhosa High School Students." *Evolution and Human Behavior* 20, no. 6 (November 1999): 433–51.

Anderson, Kermyt G., Hilliard Kaplan, and Jane Lancaster. "Men's Financial Expenditures on Genetic Children and Stepchildren from Current and Former Relationships." Population Studies Center Research Report No. 01-484, Ann Arbor, MI, 2001.

Ayers, Lauren. *Teenage Girls: A Parent's Survival Manual.* New York: Crossroad, 1996.

Baxter, Leslie A., Dawn O. Braithwaite, and John H. Nicholson. "Turning Points in the Development of Blended Families." *Journal of Personal and Social Relationships* 16 (1999): 291–314.

Beer, W. R., ed. *Relative Strangers: Studies of the Stepfamily Processes.* Totowa, NJ: Rowman and Littlefield, 1992.

Bell-Scott, Patricia, ed. *Double Stitch: Black Women Write About Mothers and Daughters.* New York: Harper Perennial, 1991.

Berger, Roni. *Stepfamilies: A Multidimensional Perspective.* New York: Haworth, 1998.

Berke, Melvyn A., and Joanne B. Grant. *Games Divorced People Play.* Englewood Cliffs, NJ: Prentice Hall, 1981.

Bernstein, Anne C. "Between You and Me: Untangling Conflict in Stepfamilies." SAA's Counseling Corner, Stepfamily Association of America, spring 1993, http://www.stepfamilies.info/education/Articles/counseling/conflict.php.

———. "Remarriage: Redesigning Couplehood." In *Couples on the Fault Line: New Directions for Therapists,* edited by Peggy Papp. New York: Guilford, 2000.

———. "Revisioning, Restructuring, and Reconciliation: Clinical Practice with Complex Post-Divorce Families." *Family Process* 46, no. 1 (March 2007): 67–78.

————. *Yours, Mine, and Ours: How Families Change When Remarried Parents Have a Child Together.* New York: Norton, 1991.

Bettelheim, Bruno. *The Uses of Enchantment: The Meaning and Importance of Fairy Tales.* New York: Vintage, 1989.

Bjornsen, Sally. *The Single Girl's Guide to Marrying a Man, His Kids, and His Ex-Wife: Becoming a Stepmother with Humor and Grace.* New York: New American Library, 2005.

Blankenhorn, David. *Fatherless America: Confronting Our Most Urgent Social Problem.* New York: Basic Books, 1994.

Bledsoe, Caroline. "'No Success Without Struggle': Social Mobility and Hardship for Foster Children in Sierra Leone." *Man* 25, no. 1 (1990): 70–88.

————. "The 'Trickle-Down' Model Within Households: Foster Children and the Phenomenon of Scrounging." In *Health Transition: Methods and Measures,* edited by J. Cleland and A. G. Hill. Canberra: Australian National University, 1991.

Booth, Alan, and Judith F. Dunn, eds. *Stepfamilies: Who Benefits? Who Does Not?* Hillsdale, NJ: Erlbaum, 1994.

Booth, Alan, and John N. Edwards. "Starting Over: Why Remarriages Are More Unstable." *Journal of Family Issues* 13, no. 2 (1992): 179–94.

Bove, Riley B., Claudia R. Valeggia, and Peter T. Ellison. "Girl Helpers and Time Allocation of Nursing Women Among the Toba of Argentina." *Human Nature* 1, nos. 3/4 (2002): 457–72.

Brand, E., and W. Glenn Clingempeel. "Interdependence of Marital and Stepparent-Stepchild Relationships and Children's Psychological Adjustment." *Family Relations* 36 (1987): 140–45.

Bray, James H., and John Kelly. *Stepfamilies: Love, Marriage, and Parenting in the First Decade.* New York: Random House/Broadway Books, 1998.

Brown, Lyn Mikel, and Carol Gilligan. *Meeting at the Crossroads: Women's Psychology and Girls' Development.* Cambridge: Harvard University Press, 1992.

Bryan, S. H., Lawrence Ganong, Marilyn Coleman, and Linda R. Bryan. "Counselors' Perceptions of Stepparents and

Stepchildren." *Journal of Counseling Psychology* 32, no. 2 (April 1985): 279–82.

Buckle, Leslie, Gordon G. Gallup Jr., and Zachary A. Rodd. "Marriage as a Reproductive Contract: Patterns of Marriage, Divorce, and Remarriage." *Ethology and Sociobiology* 17 (1996): 363–77.

Bumpass, Larry L., R. Kelly Raley, and James A. Sweet. "The Changing Character of Stepfamilies: Implications of Cohabitation and Nonmarital Childbearing." *Demography* 32 (1995): 425–36.

Burgess, Ernest W., and Harvey Locke. *The Family: From Institution to Companionship.* New York: American Book, 1960.

Burgoyne, Jacqueline Lesley, and David Clark. *Making a Go of It: A Study of Stepfamilies in Sheffield.* London: Routledge, 1984.

Burns, Cherie. *Stepmotherhood: How to Survive Without Feeling Frustrated, Left Out, or Wicked.* New York: Random House, 2001.

Cherlin, Andrew J. "The Deinstitutionalization of American Marriage." *Journal of Marriage and the Family* 66 (November 2004): 848–61.

———. *Marriage, Divorce, Remarriage.* Cambridge: Harvard University Press, 1981.

———. *Public and Private Families.* Boston: McGraw-Hill, 1999.

———. "Remarriage as an Incomplete Institution." *American Journal of Sociology* 84, no. 3 (November 1978): 634–50.

Cherlin, Andrew J., and Frank Furstenberg Jr. "Stepfamilies in the United States: A Reconsideration." *Annual Review of Sociology* 20 (1994): 359–81.

Chillman, C. S. "Remarriage and Stepfamilies: Research Results and Implications." In *Contemporary Families and Alternative Lifestyles: Handbook on Research and Theory,* edited by Eleanor D. Macklin and Roger H. Rubin. Beverly Hills, CA: Sage, 1983.

Chodorow, Nancy. *The Reproduction of Mothering: Psychoanalysis and the Sociology of Gender.* Berkeley: University of California Press, 1978.

Church, Elizabeth A. "The Poisoned Apple: Stepmothers' Experience of Envy and Jealousy." *Journal of Feminist Family Therapy* 11 (1999): 1–18.

————. *Understanding Stepmothers: Women Share Their Struggles, Successes, and Insights.* Toronto: HarperCollins, 2004.

————. "Who Are the People in Your Family? Stepmothers' Diverse Notions of Kinship." *Journal of Divorce and Remarriage* 31, nos. 1/2 (1999): 83–105.

Cissna, Kenneth, Dennis Cox, and Arthur Bochner. "Relationships Within the Stepfamily." In *The Psychosocial Interior of the Family*, edited by G. Handel and G. Whitchurch. New York: Aldine, 1994.

Claxton-Oldfield, Stephen. "Deconstructing the Myth of the Wicked Stepparent." *Marriage and Family Review* 30 (2000): 51–58.

Coleman, Marilyn, and Lawrence Ganong. "Remarriage and Family Research in the 80s: New Interest in an Old Family Form." *Journal of Marriage and the Family* 52 (1990): 925–40.

————. "Stepfamilies from the Stepfamily's Perspective." *Marriage and Family Review* 26, nos. 1/2 (1997): 107–21.

————. "Stepparent: A Pejorative Term?" *Psychological Reports* 52 (1997): 919–22.

Coleman, Marilyn, Lawrence Ganong, and M. Fine. "Reinvestigating Remarriage: Another Decade of Progress." *Journal of Marriage and the Family* 62 (2000): 1288–1307.

Coleman, Marilyn, and S. E. Weaver. "A Mothering but Not a Mother Role: A Grounded Theory of the Nonresidential Stepmother Role." *Journal of Personal and Social Relationships* 22 (2005): 477–97.

Collins, Patricia Hill. "The Meaning of Motherhood in Black Culture and Black Mother-Daughter Relationships." In *Double Stitch: Black Women Write About Mothers and Daughters*, edited by Patricia Bell-Scott. New York: Harper Perennial, 1991.

Comanor, William S., ed. *The Law and Economics of Child Support Payments.* Northampton, MA: Edward Elgar, 2004.

Coontz, Stephanie. *Marriage, a History: From Obedience to Intimacy, or How Love Conquered Marriage.* New York: Viking, 2005.

————. "The Origins of Modern Divorce." *Family Process* 46, no. 1 (February 2007): 7–16.

————. *The Way We Really Are: Coming to Terms with America's Changing Families*. New York: Basic Books, 1997.

Cooper, Candy. "Step Shock." In *My Father Married Your Mother: Writers Talk About Stepparents, Stepchildren, and Everyone in Between*, edited by Anne Burt. New York: Norton, 2006.

Corrie, Sarah. "Working Therapeutically with Adult Stepchildren: Identifying the Needs of a Neglected Client Group." *Journal of Divorce and Remarriage* 37, nos. 1/2 (2002): 135–50.

Cott, Nancy. *Public Vows: A History of Marriage and the Nation*. Cambridge: Harvard University Press, 2000.

Crohn, Helen. "Five Styles of Positive Stepmothering from the Perspective of Young Adult Stepdaughters." *Journal of Divorce and Remarriage* 46, nos. 1/2 (2006): 119–34.

Cronin, Helena. *The Ant and the Peacock: Altruism and Natural Selection from Darwin to Today*. Cambridge: Cambridge University Press, 1991.

Crosbie-Burnett, Margaret. "The Interface Between Stepparent Families and Schools: Research, Theory, Policy, and Practice." In *Remarriage and Stepparenting: Current Research and Theory*, edited by Kay Pasley and Marilyn Ihinger-Tallman. New York: Guilford, 1987.

Crosbie-Burnett, Margaret, and J. Giles-Sims. "Adolescent Adjustment and Step-parenting Styles." *Family Relations* 43 (1994): 394–99.

Crosbie-Burnett, Margaret, and E. A. Lewis. "Use of African-American Family Structures and Functioning to Address the Challenges of European-American Post-Divorce Families." *Family Relations* 42 (1993): 243–48.

Dahl, Ann Sale, K. Cowgill, and R. Asmundsson. "Life in Remarriage Families." *Social Work* 32 (1987): 40–45.

Dainton, Marianne. "Myths and Misconceptions of the Stepmother Identity." *Family Relations* 42 (1992): 93–98.

Daly, Martin, and Margo Wilson. *Homicide*. New Brunswick, NJ: Transaction, 1988.

―――. "Is the Cinderella Effect Controversial?" In *Foundations of Evolutionary Psychology*, edited by Charles Crawford and Dennis Krebs. New York: Psychology Press, 2008.

―――. *The Truth About Cinderella: A Darwinian View of Parental Love.* New Haven, CT: Yale University Press, 1998.

Deater-Deckard, Kirby, Kevin Pickering, Judith Dunn, and Jean Golding. "Family Structure and Depressive Symptoms in Men Preceding and Following the Birth of a Child." *American Journal of Psychiatry* 155 (June 1998): 818–23.

Debold, Elizabeth, Marie C. Wilson, and Idelisse Malave. *Mother Daughter Revolution: From Good Girls to Great Women.* New York: Addison-Wesley, 1992.

Deetz, James, and Patricia Deetz. *The Times of Their Lives: Life, Love, and Death in Plymouth Colony.* New York: Random House, 2000.

Demos, John. *A Little Commonwealth: Family Life in Plymouth Colony.* New York: Oxford University Press, 1999.

Draper, Patricia, and Anne Buchanan. "'If You Have a Child You Have a Life': Demographic and Cultural Perspectives on Fathering in Old Age in !Kung Society." In *Father-Child Relations: Cultural and Biosocial Contexts,* edited by Barry S. Hewlett. New York: Aldine, 1992.

Draper, Patricia, and Henry Harpending. "Parental Investment and the Child's Environment." In *Parenting Across the Lifespan: Biosocial Dimensions,* edited by Jane B. Lancaster, Jeanne Altman, Alice S. Rossi, and Lonnie R. Sherrod. New York: Aldine, 1987.

Duberman, Lucile. *The Reconstituted Family: A Study of Remarried Couples and Their Children.* Chicago: Nelson Hall, 1975.

―――. "Step-Kin Relations." *Journal of Marriage and the Family* 35 (1973): 283–92.

Ebata, Aaron, Anne C. Petersen, and J. Conger. "The Development of Psychopathology in Adolescence." In *Risk and Protective Factors in the Development of Psychopathology,* edited by J. Rolf. New York: Cambridge University Press, 1990.

Einstein, Elizabeth, and Linda Albert. "The Instant Love Expectation: Downhill Slide to Trouble." In *Strengthening Your Stepfamily*. Circle Pines, MN: American Guidance Association Press, 1986.

Emlen, Stephen T. "The Evolution of Cooperative Breeding in Birds and Mammals." In *Behavioural Ecology: An Evolutionary Approach*, edited by John R. Krebs and Nick B. Davies. London: Blackwell, 1984.

Erera-Weatherley, Pauline I. "On Becoming a Stepparent: Factors Associated with the Adoption of Alternative Stepparenting Styles." *Journal of Divorce and Remarriage* 25, nos. 3/4 (1996): 155–74.

Falke, Stephanie, and Jeffry Larson. "Premarital Predictions of Remarital Quality." *Contemporary Family Therapy* 29, nos. 1/2 (June 2007): 9–23.

Ferri, Elsa. *Stepchildren: A National Study*. Windsor, Eng.: Routledge, 1984.

Fine, Mark A., and Andrew I. Schwebel. "Stepparent Stress." *Journal of Divorce and Remarriage* 17 (1992): 1–15.

Fine, Mark A., P. Voydanoff, and B. W. Donnelly. "Relations Between Parental Control and Warmth and Child Well-Being in Stepfamilies." *Journal of Family Psychology* 7 (1993): 222–32.

Flinn, Mark V. "Step and Genetic Parent/Offspring Relationships in a Caribbean Village." *Ethology and Sociobiology* 9, no. 6 (1988): 335–69.

Foucault, Michel. "Truth and Power." In *Power/Knowledge: Selected Interviews and Other Writings, 1972–1977*, edited by C. Gordon. New York: Pantheon, 1980.

Furstenberg, Frank, and C. Nord. "Parenting Apart: Patterns of Childrearing After Marital Disruption." *Journal of Marriage and the Family* 47 (1985): 893–904.

Gabe, Grace, and Jean Lipman-Blumen. *Step Wars: Overcoming the Perils and Making Peace in Adult Stepfamilies*. New York: St. Martin's, 2004.

Gamache, Susan. "Stepfamily Life and Then Some." *Family Connections*, Summer 1999, pp. 1–5.

Ganong, Lawrence, and Marilyn Coleman. "Adolescent Stepchild and Stepparent Relationships." In *Stepparenting: Issues in Theory, Research, and Practice,* edited by Kay Pasley and Marilyn Ihinger-Tallman. Westport, CT: Greenwood, 1995.

———. "Stepchildren's Perceptions of Their Parents." *Journal of Genetic Psychology* 148 (1986): 5–17.

Ganong, Lawrence, Marilyn Coleman, M. Fine, and P. Martin. "Stepparents' Affinity-Seeking and Affinity-Maintaining Strategies with Stepchildren." *Journal of Family Issues* 20 (1999): 299–327.

Gilbert, Sandra, and Susan Gubar. *The Madwoman in the Attic: The Woman Writer and the Nineteenth-Century Literary Imagination.* New Haven, CT: Yale University Press, 2000.

Glass, Shirley. "Infidelity." *Clinical Update* (American Association of Family and Marital Therapy) 2, no. 1 (2000): 1–8.

Glick, P. C. "Remarried Families, Stepfamilies, and Stepchildren: A Brief Demographic Profile." *Family Relations* 38 (1989): 24–38.

Glick, P. C., and S. L. Lin. "Remarriage After Divorce: Recent Changes and Demographic Variation." *Social Perspectives* 30 (1987): 99–109.

Goffman, Erving. *Stigma: Notes on the Management of Spoiled Identity.* New York: Simon & Schuster, 1963.

Gottleib, R. M. "Refusing the Cure: Sophocles' Philoctetes and the Clinical Problems of Self-Injurious Spite, Shame, and Forgiveness." *International Journal of Psychoanalysis* 85, no. 3 (2004): 669–89.

Gottman, John. *Ten Lessons to Transform Your Marriage.* New York: Three Rivers, 2007.

———. "A Theory of Marital Dissolution and Stability." *Journal of Family Psychology* 7, no. 1 (1993): 57–75.

———. *Why Marriages Succeed or Fail and How You Can Make Yours Last.* New York: Fireside, 1994.

Gottman, John, and Nan Silver. *The Seven Principles for Making Marriage Work.* New York: Norton, 1999.

Gross, Jane. "A Long-Distance Tether to Home." *New York Times,* November 5, 1999.

Haebich, Anna. "Murdering Stepmothers: The Trial and Execution of Martha Rendell." *Journal of Australian Studies* (December 1, 1998): 1–16.

Hagen, Edward, Raymond B. Hames, Nathan M. Craig, Matthew T. Lauer, and Michael E. Price. "Parental Investment and Child Health in a Yanomamo Village Suffering Short-Term Food Stress." *Journal of Biosocial Sciences* 33 (2001): 503–28.

Hamilton, William. *The Narrow Roads of Gene Land: Collected Papers of William Hamilton.* Vol. 1: *The Evolution of Social Behavior.* New York: Oxford University Press, 1998.

Hays, Sharon. *The Cultural Contradictions of Motherhood.* New Haven, CT: Yale University Press, 1996.

Hetherington, E. Mavis. Personal conversation, quoted by Dr. Ron L. Deal. "The Stepcouple Divorce Rate May Be Higher Than We Thought." Successful Stepfamilies, http://www.successful-stepfamilies.com/view/176.

Hetherington, E. Mavis, and W. Glenn Clingempeel. "Coping with Marital Transitions: A Family Systems Perspective." *Monographs of the Society for Research in Childhood Development* 57 (1992).

Hetherington, E. Mavis, and John Kelly. *For Better or for Worse: Divorce Reconsidered.* New York: Norton, 2002.

Hetherington, E. Mavis, and M. Stanley-Hagan. "The Effects of Divorce on Fathers and Their Children." In *The Role of the Father in Child Development,* edited by Michael E. Lamb. New York: Wiley, 1997.

Hewlett, Barry. "Demography and Childcare in Preindustrial Societies." *Journal of Anthropological Research* 47, no. 1 (Spring 1991): 1–37.

Hively, Will. "Family Man." *Discover,* October 1997, http://discovermagazine. com/1997/oct/familyman1237/?searchitem=stephen%20emlen.

Hobart, Charles. "Conflict in Remarriages." *Journal of Divorce and Remarriage* 15 (1991): 69–86.

———. "Experiences of Remarried Families." *Journal of Divorce* 13 (1989): 121–44.

———. "The Family System in Remarriage: An Exploratory Study." *Journal of Marriage and the Family* 50 (1988): 649–61.

Hrdy, Sarah Blaffer. "Comes the Child Before the Man: How Cooperative Breeding and Prolonged Post-Weaning Dependency Shaped Human Potential." In *Hunter-Gatherer Childhoods*, edited by Barry S. Hewlett and Michael E. Lamb. New Brunswick, NJ: Transaction, 2005.

———. "Fitness Tradeoffs in the History and Evolution of Delegated Mothering with Special Reference to Wet-Nursing, Abandonment, and Infanticide." *Ethology and Sociobiology* 13 (1992): 409–42.

———. *Mother Nature: Maternal Instincts and How They Shape the Human Species.* New York: Random House/Ballantine, 1999.

———. "On Why It Takes a Village: Cooperative Breeders, Infant Needs, and the Future." *Tanner Lectures on Human Values,* vol. 23, pp. 57–110. Salt Lake City: University of Utah Press, 2002.

———. "The Past, Present, and Future of the Human Family." Tanner Series Lecture on Human Values, University of Utah, Salt Lake City, February 27 and 28, 2001.

Ivey, Paula K. "Cooperative Reproduction in Ituri Forest Hunter-Gatherers: Who Cares for Efe Infants?" *Current Anthropology* 41, no. 5 (December 2000): 856–66.

Jacobson, David. "Financial Management in Stepfamily Households." *Journal of Divorce and Remarriage* 19 (2001): 221–38.

Jankowiak, William, and Monique Diderich. "Sibling Solidarity in a Polygamous Community in the USA: Unpacking Inclusive Fitness." *Evolution and Human Behavior* 2, nos. 1/2 (March 2000): 125–39.

Johnson, Sue. *Hold Me Tight: Conversations for a Lifetime of Love.* New York: Little, Brown, 2008.

Jones, Anne C. "Transforming the Story: Narrative Applications to a Stepmother Support Group." *Families in Society* 85 (January 2004): 129–39.

Jordan, Judith. "The Relational Self: A Model of Women's Development." In *Daughtering and Mothering*, edited by J. Van Mens-Verhulst, K. Schreus, and L. Woertman. London: Routledge, 1993.

Jordan, Judith, Alexandra Kaplan, Jean Baker Miller, Irene Stiver, and Janet Surrey. *Women's Growth in Connection*. New York: Guilford, 1991.

Josephson, Steven. "Does Polygyny Reduce Fertility?" *American Journal of Human Biology* 14, no. 2 (February 2002): 222–32.

Kaplan, David, and Molly Vanduser. "Evolution and Stepfamilies: An Interview with Dr. Stephen T. Emlen." *Family Journal: Counseling and Therapy for Couples and Families* 7, no. 4 (October 1999): 408–13.

Kate, N. "The Future of Marriage." *American Demographics* 12 (June 1996): 1–6.

Keshet, Jamie Kelem. "Gender and Biological Models of Role Division in Stepmother Families." *Journal of Feminist Family Therapy* 1 (1989): 29–50.

———. *Love and Power in the Stepfamily*. New York: McGraw-Hill, 1987.

Klein, Melanie. "Envy and Gratitude." In *Envy and Gratitude and Other Works*. 1957. Reprint, New York: Delacorte, 1975.

Knox, D., and M. Zusman. "Marrying a Man with 'Baggage': Implications for Second Wives." *Journal of Divorce and Remarriage* 35 (2001): 67–80.

Kramer, Karen L. "Children's Help and the Pace of Reproduction: Cooperative Breeding in Humans." *Evolutionary Anthropology* 14, no. 6 (2005): 225–37.

———. *Maya Children: Helpers at the Farm*. Cambridge: Harvard University Press, 2005.

Lack, David. "The Significance of Clutch Size." *Ibis* 89 (1947): 302–52.

Lancaster, Jane, and Hilliard Kaplan. "Parenting Other Men's Children: Costs, Benefits, and Consequences." In *Adaptation and Human Behavior: An Anthropological Perspective*, edited by

Lee Cronk, Napoleon Chagnon, and William Irons. New York: Aldine, 2000.

Laythe, Joseph. "The Wicked Stepmother? The Edna Mumbulo Case of 1930." *Journal of Criminal Justice and Popular Culture* 9 (2002): 33–54.

Levine, I. "The Stepparent Role from a Gender Perspective." *Marriage and Family Review* 26 (1997): 177–90.

Lorah, Peggy. "Lesbian Stepmothers: Navigating Invisibility." *Journal of LGBT Issues in Counseling* 1 (2006/2007): 59–76.

Lown, Jean M., and Elizabeth M. Dolan. "Remarried Families' Economic Behavior." *Journal of Divorce and Remarriage* 22 (1994): 103–19.

Lutz, Patricia. "The Stepfamily: An Adolescent Perspective." *Family Relations* 32 (1980): 367–75.

MacDonald, W., and A. DeMaris. "Parenting Stepchildren and Biological Children." *Journal of Family Issues* 23 (1996): 5–25.

Maglin, Nan Bauer, and Nancy Schniedewind, eds. *Women in Stepfamilies: Voices of Anger and Love.* Philadelphia: Temple University Press, 1989.

Marlowe, Frank. "Showoffs or Providers? The Parenting Effort of Hadza Men." *Evolution and Human Behavior* 20 (1999): 391–404.

Mason, Mary Ann. "The Modern American Stepfamily: Problems and Possibilities." In *All Our Families: New Policies for a New Century,* edited by Mary Ann Mason, Arlene Skolnick, and Stephen D. Sugarman. New York: Oxford University Press, 1998.

McLanahan, Sarah, and Gary Sandefur. *Growing Up with a Single Parent: What Hurts, What Helps.* Cambridge: Harvard University Press, 1994.

Meyers, L. "Relationship Conflicts Stress Men More Than Women." *Monitor on Psychology* 37 (2006): 14.

Miller, Michael Vincent. *Intimate Terrorism: The Crisis of Love in an Age of Disillusion.* New York: Norton, 1996.

Mintz, Stephen. *Huck's Raft: A History of American Childhood.* Cambridge, MA: Belknap Press, 2006.

Mock, Douglas W., and Geoffrey Parker. *The Evolution of Sibling Rivalry.* Oxford: Oxford University Press, 1997.

Morrison, Kati, and Airdrie Thompson-Guppy. "Cinderella's Stepmother Syndrome." *Canadian Journal of Psychiatry* 30 (1985): 521–29.

Mulder, Monique Borgerhoff, and Maryanna Milton. "Factors Affecting Infant Care in the Kipsigis." *Journal of Anthropological Research* 41, no. 3 (1985): 255–60.

Nevis, Sonia. "Diagnosis: The Struggle for a Meaningful Paradigm." In *Gestalt Therapy: Perspectives and Applications,* edited by Edwin C. Nevis (New York: Routledge, 1997).

Nielsen, Linda. "College Daughters' Relationships with Their Fathers: A 15-Year Study." *College Student Journal* 41 (March 2007): 1–10.

———. "Stepmothers: Why So Much Stress? A Review of the Research." *Journal of Divorce and Remarriage* 30, nos. 1/2 (1999): 115–48.

Nolen-Hoeksema, Susan. *Women Who Think Too Much: How to Break Free of Over-thinking and Reclaim Your Life.* New York: Henry Holt, 2003.

Norton, A. J., and L. F. Miller. *Marriage, Divorce, and Remarriage in the 1990s.* U.S. Census Bureau, Current Population Reports, Series P23-180, 1992.

Notermans, Catrien. "Fosterage in Cameroon: A Different Social Construction of Motherhood." In *Cross-Cultural Approaches to Adoption,* edited by Fiona Bowie. London: Routledge, 2004.

Orchard, Ann L., and Kenneth B. Solberg. "Expectations of the Stepmother's Role." *Journal of Divorce and Remarriage* 31, nos. 1/2 (1991): 107–23.

Packer, Craig. "Reciprocal Altruism in *Papio Anubis.*" *Nature* 265 (February 1977): 441–43.

Papernow, Patricia. *Becoming a Stepfamily: Patterns of Development in Remarried Families.* Cleveland: Analytic Press, 1993.

———. "'Blended' Family Relationships: Helping People Who Live in Stepfamilies." *Family Therapy Magazine,* May–June 2006, pp. 34–42.

————. "Meeting the Challenge of Stepfamily Architecture." Handout.

————. "The Stepfamily Cycle: An Experiential Model of Stepfamily Development." *Family Relations* 33 (1984): 355–63.

————. "Stepfamily Role Development: From Outsider to Intimate." In *Relative Strangers: Studies of the Stepfamily Processes,* edited by William R. Beer. Totowa, NJ: Rowman and Littlefield, 1992.

Parish, Thomas S., and Bruno M. Kappes. "Impact of Father Loss on the Family." *Social Behavior and Personality* 8 (1980): 107–12.

Parker-Pope, Tara. "Marital Spats, Taken to Heart." *New York Times,* October 2, 2007.

Pasley, Kay, and Marilyn Ihinger-Tallman. "Divorce and Remarriage in the American Family: A Historical Review." In *Remarriage and Stepparenting: Current Research and Theory,* edited by Kay Pasley and Marilyn Ihinger-Tallman. New York: Guilford, 1987.

————. *Remarriage.* Beverly Hills, CA: Sage, 1987.

————, eds. *Remarriage and Stepparenting: Current Research and Theory.* New York: Guilford, 1987.

————, eds. *Stepparenting: Issues in Theory, Research, and Practice.* Westport, CT: Praeger, 1995.

Penor-Ceglian, Cindi, and Scott Gardner. "Attachment Style and the Wicked Stepmother Spiral." *Journal of Divorce and Remarriage* 34 (2000): 111–26.

Peterson, Mary. "With Evelyn." In *Mercy Flights.* Columbia: University of Missouri Press, 1985.

Pill, C. J. "Stepfamilies: Redefining the Family." *Family Relations* 39 (1990): 186–93.

Power, Harry. "Mountain Bluebirds: Experimental Evidence Against Altruism." *Science* 189 (1975): 142–43.

Powers, T. K. "Dating Couples' Attachment Style and Patterns of Cortisol Reactivity and Recovery in Response to Relationship Conflict." *Journal of Personality and Social Psychology* 90, no. 4 (April 2006): 613–28.

Preece, Melady. "Exploring the StepGap: How Parents' Ways of Coping with Daily Family Stressors Impact Stepparent-Stepchild Relationship Quality in Stepfamilies." University of British Columbia Publications, 1996, http://www .psych.ubc/ ca/~mpreece.compdoc.pdf.

Prilick, P. K. *The Art of Stepmothering*. Waco, TX: WRS Publishing, 1994.

Quick, Donna S., Patrick C. McKenry, and Barbara M. Newman. "Stepmothers and Their Adolescent Stepchildren." In *Stepparenting: Issues in Theory, Research, and Practice*, edited by Kay Pasley and Marilyn Ihinger-Tallman. Westport, CT: Praeger, 1995.

Robins, Lee, and Michael Rutter. *Straight and Devious Pathways from Childhood to Adulthood*. New York: Cambridge University Press, 1990.

Rohwer, Sievert. "Selection for Adoption Versus Infanticide by Replacement 'Mates' in Birds." *Current Ornithology* 3 (1986): 353–93.

Rohwer, Sievert, J. Herron, and M. Daly. "Stepparental Behavior as Mating Effort in Birds and Other Animals." *Evolution and Human Behavior* 20 (1999): 367–90.

Rosenbloom, Stephanie. "My Father, American Inventor." *New York Times*, August 16, 2007.

Rutter, Virginia. "Lessons from Stepfamilies." *Psychology Today*, May 1, 1994, pp. 1–10.

Salwen, Laura V. "The Myth of the Wicked Stepmother." *Women and Therapy* 10 (1990): 117–25.

Sauer, Laurence E., and Mark A. Fine. "Parent-Child Relationships in Stepparent Families." *Journal of Family Psychology* 1 (1998): 434–51.

Schmeeckle, Maria. "Gender Dynamics in Stepfamilies: Adult Stepchildren's Views." *Journal of Marriage and the Family* 69 (2007): 174–89.

Schrodt, Paul. "Sex Differences in Stepchildren's Reports of Stepfamily Functioning." *Communication Reports* 21, no. 1 (January 2008): 46–58.

Seyfarth, Robert M., and Dorothy L. Cheney. "Grooming, Alliances, and Reciprocal Altruism in Vervet Monkeys." *Nature* 308 (April 1984): 541–43.

Shostak, Marjorie. *Nisa: The Life and Words of a !Kung Woman.* Cambridge: Harvard University Press, 1981.

Solomon, Andrew. *The Noonday Demon: An Atlas of Depression.* New York: Scribner, 2001.

———. "On Having a Stepmother Who Loves Opera." In *My Father Married Your Mother: Writers Talk About Stepparents, Stepchildren, and Everyone in Between,* edited by Anne Burt. New York: Norton, 2006.

StepTogether.org. "Disengaging," http://www.steptogether.org/disengaging.html.

Stewart, Susan D. *Brave New Stepfamilies: Diverse Paths Toward Stepfamily Living.* London: Sage, 2007.

———. "How the Birth of a Child Affects Involvement with Stepchildren." *Journal of Marriage and the Family* 67, no. 2 (May 2005): 461–78.

Strassman, Beverly I. "Polygyny, Family Structure, and Child Mortality: A Prospective Study Among the Dogon of Mali." In *Adaptation and Human Behavior: An Anthropological Perspective,* edited by Lee Cronk, Napoleon Chagnon, and William Irons. New York: Aldine, 2000.

Strayer, Janet. "Trapped in the Mirror: Psychosocial Reflections on Mid-Life and the Queen in *Snow White.*" *Human Development* 39 (1996): 155–72.

Tatar, Maria M., ed. *The Annotated Brothers Grimm.* New York: Norton, 2004.

Trivers, Robert. "The Evolution of Reciprocal Altruism." *Quarterly Review of Biology* 46, no. 4 (1971): 35–57.

———. "Parental Investment and Sexual Selection." In *Sexual Selection and the Descent of Man, 1871–1971,* edited by B. Campbell. Chicago: Aldine, 1972.

———. "Parent-Offspring Conflict." *American Zoologist* 14 (1974): 249–64.

Turke, Paul W. "Helpers at the Nest: Childcare Networks on Ifaluk." In *Human Reproductive Behavior: A Darwinian Perspective,* edited by Laure Betzig, Monique Borgerhoff Mulder, and Paul Turke. Cambridge: Cambridge University Press, 1988.

Turner, Sarah. "My Wife-in-Law and Me: Reflections on a Joint-Custody Stepparenting Relationship." In *Women in Stepfamilies: Voices of Anger and Love,* edited by Nan Bauer Maglin and Nancy Schniedewind. Philadelphia: Temple University Press, 1989.

University of Florida. Institute of Food and Agricultural Sciences. "Stepping Stones for Stepfamilies — Lesson 3: Building Step Relationships," http://edis.ifas.ufl.edu/FY034.

Verhoef, Heidi. "'A Child Has Many Mothers': Views of Child Fostering in Northwestern Cameroon." *Childhood* 12 (2005): 369–90.

Verner, Elizabeth. "Marital Satisfaction in Remarriage." *Journal of Marriage and the Family* 51 (1989): 713–25.

Vinick, Barbara, and Susan Lanspery. "Cinderella's Sequel: Stepmothers' Long-Term Relationships with Adult Stepchildren." *Journal of Comparative Family Studies* 31 (June 2000): 377–84.

Visher, Emily B., and John S. Visher. *Stepfamilies: Myths and Realities.* Secaucus, NJ: Citadel, 1979.

Visher, Emily, John Visher, and Kay Pasley. "Remarriage Families and Stepparenting." In *Normal Family Processes: Growing Diversity and Complexity,* edited by Froma Walsh. New York: Guilford, 2003.

Wald, Esther. *The Remarried Family: Challenge and Promise.* New York: Family Services Association of America, 1981.

Waldman, Ayelet. *Love and Other Impossible Pursuits.* New York: Anchor, 2007.

Waldren, Terry. "Cohesion and Adaptability in Post-Divorce Remarried and First Married Families: Relationships with Family Stress and Coping Styles." *Journal of Divorce and Remarriage* 14, no. 1 (1990): 13–28.

Walters, Marianne, Betty Carter, Peggy Papp, and Olga Silverstein. *The Invisible Web: Gender Patterns in Family Relationships*. New York: Guilford, 1991.

Waterman, Barbara. *The Birth of an Adoptive, Foster or Stepmother: Beyond Biological Mothering Attachments*. London: Jessica Kingsley, 2004.

Watson, Patricia. *Ancient Stepmothers: Myth, Misogyny, and Reality*. Leiden: Brill Academic Publishers, 1997.

Weitzman, Lenore. *The Divorce Revolution: The Unexpected Social and Economic Consequences for Women and Children in America*. New York: Simon & Schuster, 1987.

West-Eberhard, Mary Jane. "Foundress Associations in Polistine Wasps: Dominance Hierarchies and the Evolution of Social Behavior." *Science* 157 (1967): 1584–85.

White, Lynn. "Stepfamilies over the Life Course." In *Stepfamilies: Who Benefits? Who Does Not?* edited by Alan Booth and Judith F. Dunn. Hillsdale, NJ: Erlbaum, 1994.

White, Lynn, D. Brinkerhoff, and A. Booth. "The Effect of Marital Disruption on Child's Attachment to Parents." *Journal of Family Issues* 6 (1985): 5–22.

Whitsett, D., and H. Land. "The Development of a Role Strain Index for Stepparents." *Families in Society* 73 (January 1992): 14–22.

Wilsey, Sean. *Oh the Glory of It All*. New York: Penguin, 2005.

Wilson, E. O. *Sociobiology: The New Synthesis*. Cambridge, MA: Belknap Press, 1975.

Zhang, Zhenmei, and Mark D. Hayward. "Childlessness and the Psychological Well-Being of Older Persons." *Journal of Gerontology* 56 (February 2001): 311–20.

Made in the USA
Middletown, DE
23 February 2017